Trustees and Their Professional Advisors

Trustees and Their Professional Advisors

Edited by Eugene B. Burroughs

International Foundation of Employee Benefit Plans

The opinions expressed in this book are those of the authors. The International Foundation of Employee Benefit Plans disclaims responsibility for views expressed and statements made in books published by the Foundation.

Copies of this book can be obtained from:
    Publications Department
    International Foundation of Employee Benefit Plans
    18700 West Bluemound Road
    P.O. Box 69
    Brookfield, Wisconsin 53008-0069
    (414) 786-6710, ext. 8243

Payment must accompany order.
Call (888) 33-IFEBP for price information.

Published in 1996 by the International Foundation of Employee Benefit Plans, Inc.
©1996 International Foundation of Employee Benefit Plans, Inc.
All rights reserved.
Library of Congress Catalog Card Number: 96-76848
ISBN 0-89154-502-6
Printed in the United States of America

Dedication

This book is dedicated to . . .

the **TRUSTEES** of the employee benefit plans who in most instances serve without pay and face the potential of becoming personally liable for their fund-related activities,

and to their **PROFESSIONAL ADVISORS** who place the interests of the trustees, participants and beneficiaries above their own.

Because of their collective commitment, many millions of deserving recipients will enjoy the rewards of the benefit payments promised.

Table of Contents

Acknowledgments ix

About the Editor xi

Preface xiii

Introduction **Prudent Methods for Evaluating, Selecting and Monitoring Professional Advisors** 1

Chapter 1 **Legal Counsel** 21

Chapter 2 **Actuarial Services** 41

Chapter 3 **Benefit Consulting** 53

Chapter 4 **Health Care Service Providers** 65

Chapter 5 **Administration Services** 87

Chapter 6 **Investment Consulting** 105

Chapter 7 **Investment Management** 125

Chapter 8 **Custody** 151

Chapter 9 **Accountants and Auditors** 175

Chapter 10 **Arbitration** 187

Index 203

Acknowledgments

It was the Executive Committee of the International Foundation (IF) under the leadership of President and Chairman of the Board, John P. Carsten that recognized the need and authorized the publishing of this book. I am particularly gratified that they permitted me to serve in the role as the editor.

This book is not the work of one person. Many individuals, most of whom are actively involved in the educational programs of the IF, have contributed to its contents. The chapters in this book have been authored by experienced and resourceful professionals who are advisors in the various disciplines to the trustees of employee benefit plans.

Contributing chapters were: Gerard M. Arnone, Mark E. Brossman, Robert J. Cardinal, Marc Gertner, Morton I. Lorge, Terrence S. Moloznik, Paul J. Ondrasik Jr., Sherman G. Sass, James H. Scott, Thomas E. Seay, Andrew D. Sherman, John Van Belle, Donald A. Walters and Ralph M. Weinberg.

The contributing professional advisors have been joined by equally resourceful trustees who, in addition to their primary careers, serve as trustees on the boards of employee benefit plans.

Contributing the introductions to the chapters were Irving W. Cheskin, Michael Haffner, Jack T. Hayes, Henry S. Hunt, Terry Lynch, Bruce S. Raynor, Herbert R. Ricklin, Chris Silvera, James T. Stamas and John A. Viniello.

Mary Jo Brzezinski of the IF copy edited and prepared the book for publication. A resourceful supporter of all my professional activities, my wife, Betty, assisted and encouraged me in this "another project."

This indeed has been a "collective effort." I am grateful to all who have contributed. As with any participation in an IF activity, we are the richer for it!

About the Editor

EUGENE B. BURROUGHS is senior advisor to The Prudential Asset Management Company, Inc., headquartered in Newark, New Jersey. He is involved in education and research activities that are focused on the needs of the trustees and participants of Taft-Hartley funds. For 21 years he was director of investments, International Brotherhood of Teamsters, serving as the in-house investment coordinator for two large pension plans.

Mr. Burroughs is a chartered financial analyst, investment advisor representative in various states, registered securities representative and a licensed agent for life and health insurance, and has been the recipient of three presidential appointments to serve on the Advisory Committee of the Pension Benefit Guaranty Corporation.

He is a past president of the Washington Society of Investment Analysts, a former member of the board of directors of the Financial Analysts Federation and was chair of its 1985 annual conference. He received the 1991 *Pension World* Employee Benefits Man of the Year Award.

Mr. Burroughs authored the books, *Investment Success for the Employee Benefit Plan Fiduciary* and *Investment Policy Guidebook for Trustees*, Third Edition, published by the International Foundation. As further indication of his commitment to the goals of the Foundation's education program, his participation roster lists more than 400 "service credits" as author, speaker, moderator, membership booster, Advisory Director and committee chair and member. Mr. Burroughs presently serves as an Advisory Director on the IF Board of Directors.

Preface

It would not be surprising to hear a newly appointed trustee upon sitting down at the conference table at his first trust fund meeting ask, "Who are all these people, what do they do for us, and, do we really need them?" To answer just such a question, I have recruited respected professionals from the various disciplines who have been advisors to trustees for many years to describe the services they provide.

As more trustees become better informed about the various services, they will maximize the potential for the service providers to contribute to the overall successful administration of the trust funds.

When organizing the book I could have chosen to introduce the various professional disciplines in alphabetical order. In recognition that in any collective endeavor there is a natural evolutionary flow, I chose instead to introduce the services in the order that trustees address fund affairs. Beginning with legal counsel and ending with arbitration, I have organized the book in the order that a newly elected board of trustees would retain professional assistance at the beginning of their fund administration activities. The trustees would seek legal counsel, actuarial advice, administration services and may also choose to hire a benefit consultant. As assets accumulate, requiring attention, the board would seek advice from an investment consultant, hire an investment manager or managers and engage a custodian bank. Accountants and auditors would enable them to properly account for their stewardship activities, and, as time passed, they may find themselves in need of arbitration services.

Recently appointed, or elected trustees should find this order helpful; it recognizes the importance of the retained professionals working together as a "team." Experienced trustees will most probably use the book on a "rifle shot" basis: referring to selective chapters as they monitor and reevaluate periodically their various professional advisors and the services they provide.

When undertaking a search for an advisor, trustees should find the listing of questions for inclusion in a Request for Proposal at the end of most chapters especially helpful.

In addition to recruiting the professionals to write the chapters, experienced trustees were invited to provide brief introductions to the chapters. Only veteran trustees can provide the needed *perspective* essential for newer trustees to fully appreciate the contribution the professionals can bring to the table, and to identify the most salient characteristics to look for when retaining professional advisors.

The reader should be aware that although each contributor has expressed his own opinion as to the lines of demarcation between the trustees and the professional service providers, and among the professional advisors themselves, the divisions of responsibilities vary from trust fund to trust fund. The important point is that *all* the bases need to be covered by competent individuals. This is where "teamwork" is important; all members of the team endeavoring to ensure "completion" in assuring a successful stewardship of the plan.

Introduction

Prudent Methods for Evaluating, Selecting and Monitoring Professional Advisors

by Paul J. Ondrasik Jr.
and Donald A. Walters

INTRODUCTION

WHETHER YOU SERVE AS THE TRUSTEE OF A PENSION fund, a health and welfare fund or some other multiemployer fund, you have assumed a tremendous responsibility. The Employee Retirement Income Security Act (ERISA) imposes on you the legal duty to administer the fund and its benefit plan with the care, skill, prudence and diligence that someone familiar with such matters would exercise. Moreover, this "prudent man" standard, well-known at common law, has evolved into a "prudent expert" rule under ERISA. Thus, if you are unfortunate enough to have your decisions and actions challenged in court, it is likely that the standard of performance against which you will be judged will not be simply that of other trustees; it will be what the professionals—experts in their field—would have done under the same circumstances.

As a result, your service as a trustee is often

a thankless task. Most, if not all, trustees have full-time jobs with other responsibilities. Serving as a trustee is secondary; it is incidental to what you do for a living. Thus, without regard to how hard you work or how bright you might be, it is very difficult, most likely impossible, for you to perform every aspect of your trustee responsibilities at the same level of expertise that a professional would direct to the area of his or her professional concern. Fortunately, the law did not, in this instance, make the kind of "mistake" it often makes. It allows you, as trustees, to retain professionals to assist you in discharging your responsibilities.

This chapter is intended to briefly review your relationship with these professional advisors, both from a legal and practical perspective. At the outset, it provides you with an overview of the general legal standards that govern this area, with particular focus on the fiduciary issues that arise in connection with the selection and monitoring of these professionals.

It then identifies the common members of your professional advisor team and offers you a brief description of the types of services you can expect each member to provide. We hope it will suggest some practical aids and guides—in many cases procedures—that will assist you in discharging your duties when you retain and use professional advisors and, at the same time, will assist you in obtaining the maximum benefit from their services.

The Governing Law—ERISA

The governing law in this area is the Employee Retirement Income Security Act of 1974, which is universally referred to by its acronym, ERISA. The responsibility for ERISA's administration and enforcement lies largely with the Department of Labor (the DOL or the Department).

It's no secret that plan advisors are playing an ever increasing role in plan administration and management today. ERISA, of course, permits you to use plan advisors and, in many cases, encourages their use. In fact, the evolution of ERISA's prudence standard into a prudent expert test has made the use of professional advisors in certain areas a necessity to fulfill your duties and avoid liability at the same time. This is particularly true when you are involved in important plan decisions in areas where you lack expertise or in which you face a potential conflict of interest.

At the same time, the use of professional advisors is not without pitfalls of its own. The DOL is paying greater attention to service arrangements, given the volume of plan dollars that are spent on such matters. For example, the DOL is interested in knowing whether the services you are buying are appropriate as well as whether the fees paid for those services are reasonable. If they are not, you can face liability.[1]

The Department is also paying greater attention to selection and monitoring issues. Why? In some cases, these issues give the Department a basis for "upstreaming liability," to hold you as trustees responsible for your advisors' actions. If you as trustees failed to discharge your own responsibilities—if you have acted inappropriately—in selecting or monitoring those advisors, you face potential liability for their actions.[2]

Obviously, you are not looking for this type of exposure when you enter into a service arrangement. Professional advisors should be a source of assistance and comfort to you in the discharge of your own fiduciary responsibilities. They should *not* be a source of potential liability. As a result, it is important that you have a basic understanding of your own legal duties and responsibilities in this area. With this in mind, we turn now to an overview of the governing legal standards.

Basic Fiduciary Standards

Any discussion of these issues must begin with a review of your basic ERISA fiduciary responsibilities. While often overlooked in this context, these rules are fully applicable in your relationship with your professional advisors. Your responsibilities here flow from your status as the "named fiduciary" for your plan. In the Taft-Hartley setting, the role of named fiduciary is played by you, the board of trustees. It is an extremely important role because, as named fiduciary, you have ultimate responsibility for the control and management of the operation and administration of your plan (ERISA Section 402(a)). In short, you are the Harry S. Truman of plan fiduciaries—the "buck stops with you."

In performing this key role, you are fully subject to ERISA's fiduciary rules. These include the basic fiduciary duties set out in Section 404 of ERISA—which are covered elsewhere in this volume—your duty to act "solely in the interest of," and thus with "undivided loyalty" to the plan's participants and beneficiaries; your prudence obligation; and your duty to adhere to the plan documents unless they are inconsistent with ERISA.

You also have a duty to avoid prohibited transactions under ERISA Section 406. This includes the duty to avoid plan transactions with "parties in interest," i.e., parties with specified relationships to the plan that could give rise to a conflict of interest (ERISA Section 3(14)) in the absence of an exemption from these rules. It also includes the duty to avoid self-dealing on your own part when you are engaged in plan-related transactions.

ERISA exposes you to significant personal liability and penalties in the event you violate these duties. For example, if you breach your fiduciary responsibilities and, as a result, the plan suffers a loss, you can be held personally liable to make good that loss (ERISA Section 409). Likewise, if you profit personally from your breach of duty, you can be required to disgorge those profits to the plan. Id.[3] You are also subject to the "equitable powers" of the court and, in an appropriate case, could be removed from your position as a trustee. Id. Moreover, under ERISA's co-fiduciary provisions, you can, in certain circumstances, find yourself responsible for the fiduciary breaches of your fellow fiduciaries (ERISA Section 405(a)). In sum, you could be damaged—and damaged significantly—both in your pocket and your reputation if you fail to discharge your responsibilities in the manner that ERISA commands.

The Effect of Using Professional Advisors

Fortunately, ERISA does not require you to do everything yourself. In fact, the act specifically contemplates that you will use others, including professional advisors, to assist you in discharging your responsibilities to the plan. In this regard, ERISA specifically provides that the plan can authorize you to retain advisors at plan expense (ERISA Section 402(c)(2)). It also makes clear that you can delegate, i.e., turn over, investment management responsibilities to an *investment manager* within the meaning of the act (ERISA Section 402(c)(3)). The key here, however, is your plan document. Do your plan documents—trust agreement and/or plan—authorize you to retain these professionals and pay them from plan assets? You must have that authority in your documents. Thus, to protect yourself in the first instance, it is extremely important that you familiarize yourself with the documents governing your plan.

If you have this authority, what happens, from a legal perspective, when you use professional advisors? What impact does it have on your own responsibilities under ERISA? The answer really depends on what you are trying to accomplish when you look to a third party advisor. On the one hand, you may be attempting to delegate—to turn over—one of your fiduciary responsibilities to the advisor. Alternatively, you simply may be seeking advice and guidance from the advisor in connection with a plan decision you will make on your own. In the former situation, the delegation situation, you are actually transferring your fiduciary responsibility to the third party. In the advice situation, the nondelegation situation, you are not. You are retaining full fiduciary responsibility for the decision yourself and that is an important point you should always remember. Each of these situations is addressed in more detail below.

Delegation

ERISA permits you, as fiduciaries, to allocate fiduciary duties among yourselves or to delegate those responsibilities to a third party, provided that certain requirements are satisfied (ERISA Section 405(c)). If you make that allocation or delegation in accordance with those rules, you, as a fiduciary, generally will have no responsibility—and thus no liability—for the performance of the duty in question. In effect, you have transferred that duty to the third party.

The rules governing allocation and delegation of fiduciary responsibility are set out in ERISA Section 405(c). Under these rules, the first and foremost requirement is that your plan documents *must* set forth a procedure that authorizes and enables you to allocate or delegate fiduciary responsibilities. Thus, once again, your plan documents are the key; an express procedure in your plan is the essential prerequisite to any allocation or delegation of fiduciary responsibility (ERISA Section 405(c)(1)).

The remaining requirements focus on your own conduct in initially making the allocation and delegation, and thereafter in permitting that allocation or delegation to continue. To make an effective allocation or delegation of fiduciary duties, ERISA requires that you act in accordance with your own fiduciary responsibilities in establishing and implementing the procedure and in making the allocation or delegation. In other words, you must act prudently and otherwise in accord with your own ERISA duties in selecting the party who will perform the fiduciary acts in question.

In addition, you must adhere to your own fiduciary duties in allowing the allocation or delegation to continue. Thus, you must monitor prudently the party's activities and performance in order to determine whether the party should be allowed to continue performing the responsibilities involved (ERISA Section 405(c)(2)).

Several additional requirements must be satisfied when you are attempting to delegate investment management responsibilities to an investment manager. Those additional requirements are as follows:

- ▶ The plan documents must specifically permit you to delegate investment management responsibilities to an *investment manager* within the meaning of ERISA (ERISA Section 402(c)(3)).
- ▶ The party to whom you delegate that investment discretion must meet ERISA's definition of an *investment manager*. That means the party must be a registered investment advisor under the Investment Advisers Act of 1940, a bank or an insurance company qualified to engage in such business under the laws of more than one state (ERISA Section 3(38)).
- ▶ That party must acknowledge in writing its fiduciary status to your plan. Id.

What happens if you meet these requirements and thereby make an effective delegation of fiduciary responsibility to the third party? In that case, you generally will have no liability for the third party's acts or omissions in carrying out that delegated duty, unless: (a) you violated your own ERISA fiduciary responsibilities in making the selection or continuing it, or (b) you find yourself subject to liability under ERISA's co-fiduciary responsibility rules. Accordingly, to avoid potential liability in this area, you should review your plan documents to ensure that you have the authority, i.e., the power, to make a delegation. In addition, you should have procedures in place to ensure that you properly discharge your fiduciary responsibilities both in selecting and monitoring the professional.

Advice

Let's look now at the second situation—the nondelegation situation—where you are simply looking to your professional advisors for advice. This is the most typical way you will use your professional advisors outside the investment management context. Here, there is *no* transfer of fiduciary responsibility to your advisor. You remain fully responsible for the performance of the fiduciary duties in question. Moreover, reliance on professional advice is *not* a defense in the event of a fiduciary challenge![4]

This, however, does not mean that you should not look to your professional advisors for advice and guidance. Their input obviously can be quite helpful in assisting you to make an appropriate decision. Moreover, even though such advice is not an absolute defense in the event of a fiduciary challenge, the fact that you have consulted with your advisors and obtained professional advice can be very strong evidence of proper fiduciary behavior.

In fact, in many cases it can be conclusive evidence that you have discharged your responsibilities in accordance with ERISA's fiduciary rules. This is particularly true if you are acting in an area in which you lack experience or expertise or if you find yourself in a potential conflict-of-interest situation. In these situations, it is very important to seek out professional advice so no one can suggest later that you acted without consideration of factors that would be important to experienced parties faced with the same decision or without an understanding of what your fiduciary duties were under the circumstances.[5] However, for it to be effective evidence, your reliance on that advice—your use of that advice—must be reasonable; it cannot be blind. Thus, you should question your advisors to make sure the advice they are giving you makes sense and that you understand what they are telling you. And, if it's an important decision, have those advisors put their advice in writing.

The Selection and Monitoring Process

As indicated above, the effective use of professional advisors, in large part, turns on the satisfaction of your own fiduciary obligations in selecting them and then reviewing their performance. How do you fulfill your own duties in these areas? The key here is paying close attention to your basic prudence obligation as a trustee. This, of course, should be no surprise. Generally, when you enter into a relationship with an advisor, you can expect to spend significant plan dollars on their services. If you are spending plan dollars, you ought to look at that decision as an investment decision and treat it with the same importance. As a result, you should have in place an effective procedure, both for selecting your professionals and then for monitoring their performance.

Why is the implementation of such a procedure important? The adoption of and adherence to procedures has become a key component of your prudence obligation, as interpreted by both the courts and the DOL. In many respects, that prudence obligation has evolved into a "procedural prudence" standard that focuses not so much on results but on the quality and thoroughness of your decision making process.[6] Having and following a procedure demonstrates that you did not approach your decision in a haphazard fashion but in a reasonable, responsible and thoughtful way. Moreover, it helps ensure that you do, in fact, consider and evaluate the factors that are important to the decision you are making on behalf of the plan and then make a reasoned decision, based on all the appropriate information.

Selection Procedures

Unfortunately, ERISA itself offers little concrete guidance on just what should be included in these procedures. As a result, there are no hard and fast rules here; what is appropriate really turns on the facts and circumstances of each situation. However, it would appear that any prudent selection process would have a number of basic elements. They are as follows:

- *Preparation of specifications for the position you are seeking to fill:* What are your requirements? What services do you expect the professional to provide? What basic qualifications do you expect the professional to have?
- *Identification of appropriate candidates for that position:* You have a wealth of information generally available to help you identify candidates. For example, you can consult with other funds in your area or your other professional advisors to obtain recommendations. In an appropriate case, you might consider employing the services of a professional search firm. If you are looking for an investment manager and have already employed an investment consultant, that consultant might perform an initial search for and screen of potential candidates.
- *Solicitation of bids and proposals from the candidates:* Those proposals should set forth the candidates' qualifications, the manner in which they propose to provide the service, their proposed fees and references.
- *Conduct interviews with the candidates.*
- *Compare fees and never forget to check references.*
- *Make a reasoned decision based on the information you have obtained and document that decision.*

Monitoring Procedures

The monitoring process is equally undefined under ERISA. Indeed, the

DOL has issued a regulation that offers very little guidance on the subject other than to state that "at reasonable intervals" performance should be "reviewed . . . in such manner as may be reasonably expected to ensure that [the party's] performance has been in compliance with the terms of the plan and statutory standards, and satisfies the needs of the plan." 29 CFR §2509.75-8 (FR-17). However, even here the Department's regulation does suggest some basic elements of a monitoring process.

- *Conduct reviews at regularly scheduled intervals:* Establishing a schedule helps ensure that performance, in fact, is reviewed.
- *Establish standards against which the performance of the professionals is judged.*

In short, once you employ professionals, don't forget about them. The existence of a procedure prevents this from occurring.

DOL Guidance in the Investment Management Area

While ERISA itself offers little guidance concerning the selection and monitoring process, the DOL has suggested, in more concrete terms, what it believes appropriate selection and monitoring procedures should include in the investment management context.

This guidance was not issued in the form of regulations. Rather, it can be derived from the terms of consent judgments entered into by the Department in settling litigation involving investment matters arising in the multiemployer plan context.[7] Those consent judgments set forth detailed requirements that the Department expected the trustees of the plans in question to follow in selecting and monitoring the performance of investment professionals for those funds.

Before proceeding to the factors set forth in those consent judgments, a number of general observations are in order. First, these consent judgments emphasize the importance of establishing formal procedures in the investment context.

Second, the detailed and sophisticated types of information these consent judgments would have the plan's fiduciaries review both underscore how ERISA's prudence standard has evolved into a prudent expert test and indicate that the investment area is one that particularly lends itself to the use of professional advisors, such as investment consultants and performance monitoring firms, to assist trustees in performing their selection and monitoring duties. Many trustees simply do not possess the investment experience or expertise to make meaningful use of this information without professional assistance. The fact that the investment arena is also the source of greatest potential liability to plan fiduciaries in view of the magnitude of plan dollars at stake also supports this conclusion.

Finally, it should be noted that the terms of these consent judgments are not legal requirements that all trustees must follow; and, indeed, the procedures they set forth may not be appropriate or realistic for all funds. Nonetheless, they do provide trustees with an appropriate "checklist" against which to compare their own selection and monitoring procedures. Obviously, the closer trustees conform their procedures to those set forth in these consent judgments, the less likely that the DOL or some other plaintiff could mount a successful fiduciary challenge against them.

With that background, let's look at what those consent judgments reveal, first with respect to the selection of investment managers. In this area, they indicate that the key feature of the selection process is the collection and evaluation of relevant information concerning the potential investment manager and its capabilities and practices in the investment area. In this regard, they indicate that the information to be collected and evaluated should include the following:

- ▶ Whether the candidate qualifies as an investment manager pursuant to ERISA Section 3(38)
- ▶ The business structure and affiliations of the candidate
- ▶ The financial condition and capitalization of the candidate
- ▶ A description of the investment style proposed by the candidate
- ▶ A description of the investment process to be followed by the candidate
- ▶ The identity, experience and qualifications of the professionals who will be handling the plan's portfolio
- ▶ Whether any relevant litigation or enforcement actions have been initiated within a reasonably relevant time against the candidate, the candidate's officers or directors, or the candidate's investment professionals who have responsibility for the plan's portfolio
- ▶ A description of the experience and performance record, over an appropriate time period, of the candidate and its investment professionals, including experience managing other tax-exempt and employee benefit plan assets
- ▶ Whether the candidate has and would propose to utilize the services of an affiliated broker/dealer and, if so, the types of transactions for which such affiliates would be used and the financial arrangement with the broker/dealer
- ▶ The procedures to be employed by the candidate to comply with ERISA's prohibited transaction restrictions, including whether the candidate is a qualified professional asset manager
- ▶ Whether the candidate has the bonding required by ERISA
- ▶ Whether the candidate has fiduciary liability or other insurance that would protect the interests of the plan in the event of a breach of fiduciary duty

Prudent Methods

- The proposed fee structure
- The identity of client references
- The total amount of assets under the control of the candidate
- The candidate's policy with respect to the voting of proxies
- Any other appropriate and relevant information.

The consent judgments expect that this information will be evaluated by the trustees and that interviews will be conducted with the candidates under serious consideration. As noted earlier, given the sophistication of much of this information, many trustees—if they follow this course—would find the use of an investment consultant quite helpful.

Finally, the consent judgments would require that the information reviewed be verified with reliable independent sources. Indeed, they go so far as to require that inquiries be made both to the DOL and the Securities and Exchange Commission as to whether enforcement actions have been initiated against the candidate, the candidate's officers and directors or the candidate's investment professionals who will have responsibility for the plan's portfolio.

The monitoring procedures set forth in these consent judgments are equally detailed and require the review and evaluation of similarly sophisticated investment information. In this regard, they indicate that the investment manager monitoring process should include the following:

- A review, at least quarterly, of the portfolio of the investment manager for compliance with its investment guidelines
- A review, at least quarterly, of the basis on which assets under the investment manager's control are valued
- A computation, on a quarterly basis, of the rate of return for the investment manager on an overall basis, and by asset class, and, where investments are in more than one industry sector, by sector
- A comparison, at least quarterly, of the investment results of the investment manager with appropriate indices or benchmarks
- A review, at least annually, of the investment manager's practices regarding brokerage and trading, including those regarding:
  — Brokerage costs
  — Use of soft dollars
  — Quality of securities execution
  — Portfolio turnover.
- A verification, at least quarterly, of the investment manager's fee computation
- A review, at least annually, of the investment manager's proxy voting policies and performance
- A meeting with the investment manager, at least annually, to review the manager's investment performance and any significant changes

in corporate or capital structure, investment style, brokerage affiliation or practices, investment process and professional staff
- ▶ The development, and a review at least annually, of procedures for communicating information regarding the plan's investments and the investment manager among the plan's trustees, the plan's staff and the plan's service providers (including but not limited to the plan's attorneys, actuaries and custodial trustees)
- ▶ A review, at least annually, of the plan's cash management and short-term investment procedures and performances, as well as the overall performance of the plan's custodial trustee(s).

In addition, a mechanism should be established that allows the investment manager's services to be terminated as soon as prudently possible if the investment manager's performance is determined to be unsatisfactory or if it is determined that the investment manager has violated its investment guidelines. This should be addressed in your contract with the investment manager.

Any detailed analysis of the various components of the selection and monitoring procedures set forth in these consent judgments is well beyond the scope of this chapter. However, the approach taken by the DOL illustrates that the legal environment in which you operate as a trustee is increasingly complex and regulated.

We now turn to your professional advisors themselves and some practical considerations that may assist you in using their services to meet both your needs and those of your fund's participants and beneficiaries.

Professional Advisors—Some Practical Considerations

In dealing with your professional advisors, it is important to keep one fact in mind—there is no substitute for good judgment and common sense on your own part. Obviously, the advice of your fund's professional advisors, based upon their expertise and experience with similar funds, can be very helpful. However, as trustees, your knowledge of your own industry and local conditions is tremendously important. Therefore, seek the guidance of professional advisors but apply their input to your own knowledge of the issues involved. As noted earlier, do not follow their recommendations blindly. Remember that no matter how qualified your advisors might be, it is *your* fund and *you* bear the ultimate fiduciary responsibility for its successful operation.

The Typical Advisory Team

Just who are these professional advisors and what do they do? As you would expect, some larger funds might from time to time employ a professional advisor whose area of expertise is in a singular area in which that specific fund might have a unique interest. Therefore the disciplines or areas of expertise that a board of trustees might conceivably utilize from time to time could vary significantly. However, in this introductory chapter we will consider only those advisors who are commonly used by the majority of funds. The members of the common advisory "team" are as follows.

Administrator

The administrator is hired by the trustees to handle the day-to-day administration of the fund. The administrator is typically responsible for receiving and recording employer contributions, keeping the records of employees' work in covered employment, maintaining eligibility rosters, verifying eligibility for benefits or paying benefits and, in general, maintaining the fund's records.

There are two types of administration from which trustees can choose—third party administration (often referred to as *contract administration*) or self-administration. A third party administrator (or TPA) is a company that serves the fund on a contract basis. It generally serves as the administrator for one or more funds that are often unrelated and represent different unions and/or employer associations. In the case of a self-administered fund, the trustees hire the administrator (and his or her staff, if any) as employees of the fund.

Which is better? That question has no absolute answer. Some believe that because it serves more than one fund, a TPA may be somewhat more objective (i.e., since it is not beholden to any one fund or board of trustees) and that it may be in a position to bring greater resources to the task. Others believe in self-administration on the theory that it fosters a personal relationship between a plan and plan participants that makes the plan more responsive to participant needs. The truth is that both have their advantages and both can provide very effective administration. Often, the issue will turn on which approach presents the most cost-effective avenue for the day-to-day operations of your fund.

Robert Cardinal discusses the role of the administrator in detail in Chapter 5.

Fund Auditor

ERISA requires a multiemployer fund to be audited annually (ERISA Section 103(a)). In addition, funds conduct audits of contributing employers, generally pursuant to an audit policy that requires all participating employers to be audited within a stated time frame, to determine the accuracy of their contribution reports and that all monies due have, in fact, been contributed. This work is performed by the fund auditor, who is typically a CPA retained by the fund. Tom Seay further explains the duties of accountants and auditors in Chapter 9.

Fund Counsel

Fund counsel is the attorney retained by the trustees to represent them and the fund and provide legal advice. Often a single law firm is retained to perform this function. However, some funds have a policy of retaining two counsels, generally referred to as co-fund counsel. In this latter approach, one counsel is selected by the employer trustees and the other is selected by the union trustees.

The use of the co-counsel approach—though common—has been debated from time to time under ERISA. However, it is clear that it is not illegal per se; and many funds have been effectively represented under these arrangements. Nonetheless, in using this approach, trustees should keep in mind the same fiduciary admonition that governs all their activities—the duty to act solely in the interest of the plan's participants and beneficiaries. This duty of "undivided loyalty," which requires a trustee to leave his employer or union hat outside of the trustees meeting, suggests the following rules of thumb in approaching co-fund counsel arrangements:

- ▶ Make sure, that once appointed, each counsel represents the full board of trustees, not simply the side that appointed it.
- ▶ Divide responsibilities between counsel to avoid duplication of work and fees to the extent possible.

Questions are also raised about the type of attorney who should be retained, particularly in single fund counsel situations. Should it be a management-side lawyer, the union's lawyer or an attorney who has no relationship with either side of the collective bargaining table? As a threshold matter, anyone you retain should be very knowledgeable in ERISA and related law. Beyond that, there is again no clear answer. There are management attorneys who do an excellent job as fund counsel. Similarly, there are union attorneys who have proven to be excellent fund counsel. And, of course, there are "neutral" fund counsel who provide their clients with excellent representation. The key here is to retain an attorney who will represent objectively the fund and *all* trustees and who has the qualifications necessary to provide effective and competent representation.

Finally, in selecting your attorney—as is true in selecting any professional advisor—have each firm you are seriously considering make a personal presentation to the board of trustees. Make it clear that you expect the person making the presentation to be the attorney who will work with the trustees. Get a clear understanding, followed up in writing, of the fee arrangements under which services will be provided. Satisfy yourself that the attorney knows the field and will work well with and represent all trustees. For a complete discussion of legal counsel, see Marc Gertner's Chapter 1.

Investment Manager

As previously noted, the term *investment manager* is a term of art under ERISA. It refers to the party to whom the trustees may successfully delegate their fiduciary responsibility for the investment of fund assets. By definition, it can only be an insurance company qualified to do business in more than one state, a bank or a person or company registered as an investment advisor under the Investment Advisers Act of 1940.

Some of the more significant selection criteria have been discussed previously. However, it is important to remember that the selection of an investment manager often works "hand-in-glove" with your fund's asset allocation policy. While some funds (generally smaller funds) use a single "balanced" investment manager for all the plan's assets, others use different investment managers for the different asset classes reflected in the fund's investment portfolio. If you are looking for a "specialized" manager, make sure the candidate has the requisite investment expertise, i.e., don't seek equity managers, when it's a fixed income manager that you need. James Scott and John Van Belle contributed Chapter 7 on investment management.

Consultant and Actuary

While the consultant and actuary are discussed here together, quite often these services will not be performed by a single person or firm because the disciplines are quite different; and the functions are separate and distinct. The consultant typically advises the trustees on all matters that are not within the expertise of other plan advisors, including matters of plan design, and generally provides the trustees with advice and guidance on how other boards of trustees may have addressed similar issues confronting the fund. Quite often, the consultant also will play an important role in selecting other fund professionals, such as identifying appropriate candidates and assisting in establishing specifications for the position in question.

As a result, the consultant should be very experienced in all aspects of the development, implementation and ongoing operation of a benefit fund. In addition, the consultant (or actuary) for a multiemployer fund should have a strong background in multiemployer funds of all kinds. There is a significant difference between multiemployer funds and single employer benefit plans, and significant single employer experience may have little meaning when working with a multiemployer fund.

The actuary is a sophisticated mathematician who works primarily, but not exclusively, in the pension fund arena. His or her principal function is to advise the trustees as to the level of benefits that a fund can provide, based on the fund's contribution rate and asset base. In addition, in the pension plan context, the actuary performs the actuarial valuation of the plan's assets and liabilities, and the associated calculations required in the withdrawal liability area.

As noted at the outset, the consultant and actuarial functions sometimes are performed by a single firm. However, many actuaries simply do the actuarial work and leave consulting to the benefits consultant. Again, which is better? Both approaches can be done very well. Donald Walters contributed Chapter 3 on benefit consulting and Ralph Weinberg provided Chapter 2 on actuarial services.

Investment Consultant

The investment consultant is the most recent addition to the basic team of professional advisors for multiemployer funds. Given the significance and sophistication of the investment management function and the potential for liability in this context, more and more multiemployer pension funds have retained investment consultants in recent years. The investment consultant's responsibilities revolve around the selection and monitoring of investment managers and their performance, and the determination of the fund's investment policy, including asset allocation. Terrence Moloznik covers investment consulting in Chapter 6.

The foregoing is only a brief introduction to a plan's typical professional advisors and their basic responsibilities. Each of these disciplines will be discussed in much greater depth in the chapters that follow. In addition, there are chapters on health care service providers by Sherman Sass and Andrew Sherman, a chapter by Gerard Arnone on custody, and a chapter on arbitration by Mark Brossman and Mort Lorge.

Typical Areas of Concern

Duplication

From time to time, concern is expressed about the possible duplication of professional services, and certainly trustees do not want to be in the position of paying two advisors to do the same work. However, such duplication is rarely a problem, given the different disciplines of your professionals and so long as they understand their respective roles. Nor is it "unhealthy" to have two or more professionals look at the same issue, even though some overlap may occur. In reviewing that issue, each of your professionals will be operating from the perspective of his or her own quite different discipline and expertise. This helps ensure that all appropriate considerations will be put before the trustees in making a decision. In fact, in some instances, the absence of this joint overview could be a cause for concern.

Finding Competent Professionals

As noted earlier, you have a wealth of information available to you to assist in identifying competent professional advisors for your fund. Thus, finding appropriate candidates is not complicated and should rarely be a problem. For example, ask others in the field whom they would recommend. Ask local trustees of other funds. Ask the international union or national association. Ask your other professional advisors. Moreover, you are not geographically restricted in searching for advisors. Except for your administrator, there is no real advantage to dealing with a local professional. Indeed, it is not unusual for a fund to have one or more professional advisors who are located 1,000 miles or more away.

Compensating the Professional

How much should you pay your professional? As you undoubtedly have guessed, there is no easy answer to this question. However, there is a logical approach to determining whether the fees you are paying are in a reasonable range:

- ▶ Ask other trustees what they are paying. However, be very sure that the services their professionals are providing are similar to those your professionals provide. (For example, don't try to compare the annual fees paid to your attorney if he has been in litigation for the fund with the annual fees paid another fund's attorney who was not involved with litigation.) Also check on how many trustee or committee meetings that fund may have and the duration of those meetings.
- ▶ If your professionals serve on a fee-for-service basis, be sure you know the hourly rate of anyone working on your account. Also, ask for an accounting of the hours for which you are charged, with a breakdown showing both the services performed and the hourly rate charged.
- ▶ If your professionals serve on a fixed fee, have them give you the estimated number of hours as well as the hourly rates that were used in their determination of a fixed fee. Then, annually obtain a report of the number of hours actually devoted to your fund.
- ▶ Ask your other professional advisors whether the fees are reasonable in terms of their experience with other professional advisors of the same discipline.
- ▶ If you are still uneasy, put the services out for competitive bid.

In considering fees, there is one admonition to keep in mind—buy quality over price. Getting a low fee can be the worst deal you ever made if the professional is not qualified. Obviously, you don't want to pay a fee that is way out of line with the bids of other professionals. However, you have every right to pay a reasonable fee for well-qualified advisors; you are not compelled to take the lowest bidder. This, of course, does not mean that the lowest bidder will never be as well or better qualified than other bidders. They may well be. But this admonition serves as a reminder that you have tremendous responsibility—as well as significant potential liability—in administering your fund, and that you have the right to the assistance of qualified professional advisors in performing those duties.

Finally, when looking at compensation, you should avoid arrangements under which a professional is compensated on the basis of a percentage of claims paid or of fund income. In years past, such fee schedules were commonly used by consultants and administrators. However, they are rarely used today since compensation soon becomes a reflection of inflation or the growth of the fund rather than a reflection of the reasonable value of the services performed. Moreover, in situations where the professional is determining whether a benefit claim should be paid and his compensation is tied to that determination, he faces an inappropriate conflict of interest—he, in effect, is controlling the amount of his own compensation at the fund's expense. Indeed, the only area in which percentage-based fee arrangements are common today is in the investment management area. Investment managers typically are compensated on the basis of a percentage (or fraction of a percent) of the assets under their management.

Monitoring the Professional

Perhaps the last area of concern when working with professional advisors is how do you know if they are doing a good job for you?

The investment manager generally presents the easiest case. An investment performance measurement study, typically performed by the investment consultant, gives you a clear picture of how the manager is performing. Generally, that study will tell you how well the manager has performed compared to other investment managers. However, even here, numbers may be deceiving—at least in the short term—since they may reflect the conditions of the market more than the quality of your manager's performance.

Unfortunately, it is far more difficult to evaluate the performance of your other advisors; and neither the courts nor the DOL have provided guidance in this area. Thus, for the greater part, it is up to you to determine whether they are doing either a good or a poor job for you. However, you can help yourself somewhat by making sure that you have a contract with each of your professionals, except for the fund counsel and the fund auditor, with whom you should have a letter of understanding. This document, among other things, should spell out the responsibilities of the provider and give you some basis on which to review their performance. Are all services being performed? Do you wish to add other services?

Prudent Methods

Another approach that is seldom used but that can be surprisingly effective is to have your professionals meet separately with the trustees and evaluate their own performance and how it can be improved. You can also ask your advisors to evaluate each other, but this isn't likely to reveal much unless one provider is really performing very poorly. Finally, in some cases, you may wish to seek a second opinion concerning advice provided by your professional.

The bottom line both in evaluating professional advisors and in conducting yourself as a trustee and fiduciary is that it is really up to you. You can get input on everything that you are considering and from a lot of sources. However, you then have to evaluate that information and decide how it can be used. At this point your most important tool is your own common sense and good judgment. While there are times when trustees have worked diligently only to learn to their dismay that something was very wrong, such occasions are few and far between. In the great majority of situations, common sense will tell a trustee when a professional is not doing his or her job; and, if trustees have no confidence in an advisor, he or she should be replaced without regard to the kind of job he or she is doing.

Remember, it's your fund!

Endnotes

1. See, e.g., *Dole v. Formica*, 14 Empl. Ben. Cas. (BNA) 1397 (N.D.Ohio 1991); *McLaughlin v. Tomasso*, 9 Empl. Ben. Cas. (BNA) 2438 (E.D.N.Y. 1988).

2. See, *Martin v. Harline*, 15 Empl. Ben. Cas. (BNA) 1138 (D.Utah 1992); see also Letter from Olena Berg, assistant secretary for Pension Welfare Benefits, U.S. Dept. of Labor to Comptroller of Currency (Mar. 21, 1996).

3. In addition, if the Department recovers these amounts for the plan, either through litigation or a settlement, you face an additional civil penalty equal to 20% of the recovery amount. ERISA Section 502(l).

4. See *Donovan v. Tricario*, 5 Empl. Ben. Cas. (BNA) 2057 (S.D.Fla. 1984).

5. See *Katsaros v. Cody*, 568 F. Supp. 360 (E.D.N.Y. 1983), *aff'd as modified*, 744 F. Supp. 270 (2d Cir.), *cert. denied*, 409 U.S. 1072 (1984); *Donovan v. Bierwirth*, 680 F.2d 263 (2d Cir. 1982).

6. See, e.g., *Fink v. National Savings Trust Co.*, 772 F.2d 951 (D.C.Cir. 1985); *Katsaros v. Cody, supra*; see also 29 CFR §2550.404a-1(b)(1).

7. See Consent Judgments in *Arizona State Carpenters Pension Trust Fund v. Miller*, No. Civ. 89-0693 (D. Ariz., 11/1/94); and *In re Masters, Mates & Pilots Pension Plan and IRAP Litigation*, Lead File No. 85 Civ. 9545 (VLB) (S.D. N.Y., 12/15/92).

About the Authors

Paul J. Ondrasik Jr.
Partner
Steptoe & Johnson LLP
Washington, D.C.

Mr. Ondrasik practices primarily in the employee benefits field, with particular emphasis on ERISA litigation and fiduciary responsibility. He currently serves as counsel to a number of Taft-Hartley and other employee benefit plans and has represented plans, employer plan sponsors and service providers to the benefit plan field on a wide variety of matters. Mr. Ondrasik is a member of the Government Liaison Committee of the International Foundation and formerly served as an Advisory Director and as a member of the Attorneys and the Benefits Liaison Committees. He has been a frequent speaker at International Foundation educational programs since 1982.

Donald A. Walters
President
Benefits Corporation of America
Trumbull, Connecticut

Mr. Walters has more than 30 years of experience in employee benefit plans and has served as consultant to corporate, public sector and multiemployer clients. Mr. Walters has been active nationally as a speaker and has written a number of benefits-related articles. He is an Advisory Director of the International Foundation and previously served on the Investment Management and Actuaries/Consultants Committees. He has been a speaker at Foundation meetings since 1970.

Chapter 1

Legal Counsel

by Marc Gertner

Trustee's Perspective

by Henry S. Hunt

The advent of ERISA in 1974 and the following few years caused all trustees, especially those of us who were involved in collectively bargained, multiemployer, jointly trusteed plans, to experience a measure of discomfort, confusion and, in some cases, panic. It wasn't the fiduciary responsibilities mandated by ERISA that caused the concern; many of us had years of experience as either labor or management trustees and were well aware of the obligations imposed on us. What caused our trepidation was the unknown. We were sailing into uncharted waters without a compass; and, for laymen, trying to keep ahead of ERISA's shifting development would have been both foolish and imprudent.

I can't imagine a trust fund, either a pension fund or a health benefit fund, not utilizing the services of legal counsel, especially when trustees are dealing, at times, with thousands of participants and perhaps millions of dollars. The same danger exists, however, for trustees of much smaller funds when there may be only a few hundred participants. In fact, by comparison, the smaller funds may be at greater risk. In the case of a large pension fund where the full board of trustees meets quarterly and committees of the board meet monthly, I believe it is important that legal counsel is in attendance at executive, eligibility, employer accounts and full board of trustees meetings to offer guidance—advice as well as trust and plan document interpretations. It may not be necessary to have legal counsel at every monthly health fund meeting of the trustees, but I believe it is essential for counsel to review the minutes of each meeting, including pension committee meetings.

Legal counsel is indispensable in matters when the trustees are involved in a dispute with an investment manager and where the Labor Department may become involved. I can't imagine a board of trustees without legal counsel dealing with the Family and Medical Leave Act, Americans with Disabilities Act, not to mention the various regulations involving pension and health fund contributions on behalf of nonbargaining unit employees.

For years the trustees of one of the funds of which I am also a trustee—a pension fund—wrestled with the goal of permitting contributions by employers on behalf of construction superintendents, expediters, officers, etc., who at one time were journeymen and participants of the fund and whose employers wished to make contributions on their behalf. Then suddenly we received a gift from heaven. Well, not really heaven; it was from the Labor Department, which promulgated regulations permitting such contributions under certain circumstances and conditions. Our legal counsel—two very competent and professional specialists—developed a participation agreement with its parameters; and, on June 1, 1992, the trustees put the NBU Agreement into effect. (In July of that year the International Foundation, at its Construction Industry Institute in Lake Tahoe, had a session devoted to nonbargaining unit participation agreements. As I recall, it was the first International Foundation session on the subject.) Before the trustees were finished congratulating the attorneys and themselves, we received another gift. The original NBU was too cumbersome. A much simpler solution by the Labor Department was the principle of "Alumni." So back to the drawing board went our attorneys. The point of all this is that if not for legal counsel we would still be wrestling with the original problem.

Some disciplines in the legal profession are much maligned and, in some cases, justifiably so. In my experience, however, attorneys who specialize in labor relations and employee benefits are undoubtedly the least tainted.

In a nutshell, without legal counsel you're on a steep hill with a slippery surface. You're also taking small steps toward a distant goal.

INTRODUCTION

Lawyers are a frequent object of jokes, although some yarn spinners protest that their stories are not jokes but true stories. After 30 years of service as counsel to boards of trustees of collectively bargained, jointly trusteed, multi-employer employee benefit plans, a good joke (particularly a lawyer joke) is frequently a welcome relief after a two and one-half hour trustee meeting.

In this day and age of intensive scrutiny, rigid enforcement, economic uncertainty, and multiple and often conflicting interests to be served, a good sense of humor is a prerequisite to serving (and surviving) as a named fiduciary of a Taft-Hartley plan. In a more serious, albeit perhaps jaundiced, view, competent legal counsel is the best security blanket a trustee can have (even better than trustee fiduciary liability insurance), since there is no deductible and no recourse premium. A serious, dedicated board of labor and management representatives with competent and professional legal counsel can overcome the numerous and significant obstacles besetting trustees of Taft-Hartley plans in the late 1990s.

What Is the Role of Fund Counsel?

In a well-organized and prudently operated employee benefit plan, the role of legal counsel is virtually without limit. Many commentators on Taft-Hartley plans have analogized them, particularly companion employee pension benefit and employee welfare benefit plans with common plan cosponsors, to small insurance companies. That is, the plans receive monthly income (employer contributions rather than premiums, but a regular stream of income nonetheless) from which they pay hospital, medical, surgical, dental, optical, major medical, disability income and death benefit claims and/or make periodic retirement income payments, with lump-sum payout options in some cases, to older, retired persons. In this context, fund counsel is the equivalent of vice president and general counsel of an insurance company.

Each day a new series of problems may face fund counsel. Initially and periodically thereafter, counsel must draft the legal documents establishing and providing for the implementation of the plan(s). The law involving communications by and between the plan and its participants and their beneficiaries has gotten extremely complex, with the plans held to high standards, frequently judged and adjudged with the benefit of 20/20 hindsight.[1] The communications must be done not only completely, correctly and legally proper, but often in words and phrases that can be understood by the average plan participant[2]—a subjective, amorphous and often changing standard at best.

The trustees' counsel must be prepared to respond to any and every issue that may arise for the trustees and their other service providers.

Collections are an area of responsibility of the trustees generally delegated in great measure to fund counsel. The test of the common law of trusts was that a fiduciary had a legal responsibility to collect all monies due and owing to the trust fund. This has been generally carried over under the ERISA prudent man rule. Initially, it is a prohibited transaction for the trustees to extend credit to a party in interest, i.e., allow a contributing employer to be late in contributing the total amount due and owing to the plan under the collective bargaining agreement.[3] To state the proposition is to demonstrate its impossibility of performance, but this is only the starting point of counsel's duties in the area of collection.

A frequent area of work for fund counsel is the interpretation of the otherwise clear and unambiguous terms of the plan document to a member's specific set of facts. Is a bone marrow transplant a generally accepted procedure for treatment of a leukemic dependent child and thus covered for the $100,000 cost, subject to deductibles and copayments; or is it experimental in nature and thus not covered at all? Is a member who is getting old and tired, who is unable to keep up with the younger and perhaps better trained journeymen plumbers or truck drivers or ironworkers or printers, caused in part by 30 years of heavy smoking and drinking, totally and permanently disabled from working in the trade for which he is trained and experienced? Which of the two Mrs. John Does is the lawful spouse of recently retired member John Doe and entitled to his surviving spouse benefits?

Twenty years ago, a $25 million pension plan was a BIG plan. Today, Taft-Hartley plans with assets in the billions of dollars are not uncommon.[4] Twenty years ago, a $50,000 health claim was a major topic of trustee discussion. Today, that threshold is likely to be $250,000. A major trustee involvement today is in the area of the investment of plan assets. This involves a full gamut of trustee activities: prudently selecting an investment manager, drafting an investment policy statement, monitoring the investment manager's performance, voting proxies or monitoring proxy voting, monitoring brokerage costs and best execution, making fiduciary decisions on securities lending and/or use of derivatives, and/or developing a policy on global investing, and/or rethinking the guidelines on asset allocation, etc.

Many journeymen plumbers and pipefitters and their counterpart mechanical contractors, many meat cutters and their counterpart grocery store operators, many printers and publishers are uncomfortable making fiduciary decisions involving tens of millions of dollars in these areas, even though counsel says they have a duty to do so, at least without a measure of leadership, direction and comfort from fund counsel in assisting the trustees in recognizing, considering and acting on investment issues in a prudent and lawful manner. This is, of course, in addition to the comfort provided to the trustees by having a knowledgeable investment manager actually managing the assets of the plan.

Legal compliance is an ongoing trustee responsibility but with the initial responsibility on fund counsel. Like love, it has become a "many splendored thing," with compliance and enforcement being with the Department of Labor, Internal Revenue Service, Pension Benefit Guaranty Corporation, Equal Employment Opportunity Commission, Securities and Exchange Commission, Health Care Financing Administration and Social Security Administration, to name but a few review, regulatory and enforcement bodies.

Again, the role of fund counsel is without limit, varying only with the times. A competent legal counsel marking the boundaries of safe harbor within the sea of legislation, litigation, regulation and administration is the trustees' security blanket. With competent legal counsel, a board of trustees of a collectively bargained, jointly trusteed, multiemployer employee benefit plan subject to ERISA can proceed without undue concern for legal or monetary liability.

Authority to Hire Fund Counsel

If there were any doubts before September 2, 1974, that the laymen trustees and named fiduciaries of employee benefit plans needed a team of well-trained, knowledgeable and energetic service providers to guide and aid them in the operation and administration of their plans, even a quick perusal of the Employee Retirement Income Security Act of 1974 (ERISA) made it clear beyond doubt that such a team of advisors was mandatory, a *sine qua non* to a named fiduciary fulfilling his or her fiduciary duties under the act.

The drafters of ERISA were cognizant of this fact and expressly provided in Section 402(c)(2):

(c) Any employee benefit plan may provide—

* * *

(2) that a named fiduciary, or a fiduciary designated by a named fiduciary pursuant to a plan procedure described in Section 405(c)(1), may employ one or more persons to render advice with regard to any responsibility such fiduciary has under the plan; . . .

This is in addition to the express authority in named fiduciaries to appoint an investment manager.[5] Thus, there is a legislative permission to engage one or more advisors to aid the trustees/named fiduciaries.

Of equal importance is the authorization found in all well-drafted trust agreements to engage the advisors necessary and desirable to enable the plan trustees to carry out the operation and administration of the plan. The significance of this plan document authorization is the provisions in ERISA Section 404(a)(1)(D) which limit the scope of the fiduciaries' conduct to operate and administer the plan "in accordance with the documents and instruments governing the plan. . . ."

Although the issue has rarely been raised by the Department of Labor or the Internal Revenue Service in an enforcement proceeding, because it is "always" provided for in the plan documents and is expressly allowed by Section 402(c) of ERISA, strong support for the legal authority to engage all necessary advisors can be gleaned from the words and interpretation of the ERISA prudent man rule, Section 404(a)(1)(B), which provides:

(a) (1) Subject to Sections 403(c) and (d), 4042, and 4044, a fiduciary shall discharge his duties with respect to a plan solely in the interest of the participants and beneficiaries and—

* * *

(B) with the care, skill, prudence, and diligence under the circumstances then prevailing that a prudent man acting in a like capacity and familiar with such matters would use in the conduct of an enterprise of a like character and with like aims.

In fact, the overwhelming majority of named fiduciaries of employee welfare benefit plans and employee pension benefit plans have engaged and regularly utilize professional advisors, including legal counsel. Therefore, if you seek to employ "the care, skill, prudence, and diligence" that prudent plan fiduciaries familiar with the operation and administration of employee benefit plans subject to ERISA "use in the conduct of an enterprise of like character and with like aims," you too must engage fund counsel, as they have.

Conversely, because of the application of the ERISA prudent man rule, it would, in all probability, be a per se breach of fiduciary duty for trustees to attempt to administer a Taft-Hartley employee benefit plan in the 1990s without legal counsel. In a 1993 case, an analogous issue was whether it was a per se breach of fiduciary duty for the trustees of a regional multiemployer health and welfare plan to engage as sole legal counsel a very recent law graduate who had never done any legal work for a Taft-Hartley health and welfare plan but who was eager to learn and charged a very low hourly rate. Trustees' counsel settled early to avoid having to defend that proposition.[6]

Clearly, there is no ERISA mandate that plan named fiduciaries hire any professional advisors. Clearly, it would be imprudent if all plans hired a full team of advisors. A small welfare plan probably does not need an enrolled actuary. A small joint apprenticeship and training plan probably does not need an investment manager or an actuary or a conventional consultant. All plans operating under ERISA, the Internal Revenue Code, the Americans with Disabilities Act, the Securities Acts, and local laws in some substantive and procedural areas in the myriad of areas discussed above must have legal counsel.

Whom Should You Hire?

The general answer to that question is very easy, so easy that you do not even need a lawyer to answer it. Hire the most well-trained, knowledgeable, experienced, competent ERISA counsel you can find. Even when accepted without reservation, the implementation of this response is neither easy nor always clear.

If the reader should question the validity of this general response, it is suggested that the reader read again and ponder the role of fund counsel as explained previously. If the reader should question the validity of this general response, it is suggested that the reader read and reread the court decisions and/or consent decrees in *Coal Operators, Donovan v. Mazzola, Davidson v. Cook, Masters, Mates and Pilots*, and the Arizona building trades investment litigation. If the reader should question the validity of the general response, it is suggested that the reader be reminded that in the past five years the Department of Labor has conducted more than 15,000 civil investigations, filed several hundred civil lawsuits, collected $481.6 million in monetary restitution arising from breach of fiduciary duty situations, and obtained in conjunction with the Justice Department 268 criminal indictments and 90 convictions or guilty pleas.[7] Clearly, the best, the most experienced, the most competent fund counsel available is in the best interests not only of the plan and its participants and beneficiaries, but also in the best interests of the trustees and their financial solvency.

Although your trust agreement and ERISA both contain authorizations for the trustees to engage legal counsel, neither provides any definite guidelines on how to find and select them. Some general guidelines are found in the enumeration of general fiduciary duties, ERISA Section 404(a). Thus, fund counsel must be hired:

(a) to act solely in the interest of the plan participants and their beneficiaries of your plan;
(b) to assist the fiduciaries of your plan in maximizing benefits, with only reasonable and necessary expenses;
(c) while you and your fellow trustees acting as ERISA prudent persons;
(d) in accordance with the plan documents of your plan.

Perhaps the most difficult of these concepts for the trustees to accept is that although they, as the plan trustees, engage legal counsel, meet with fund counsel on a regular basis at their meetings, seek and receive fund counsel's opinions, approve fund counsel's invoices for professional services, and engage in privileged communications with fund counsel, the ultimate clients are not the trustees but the plan participants and their beneficiaries. The role of fund counsel is analogous to that of corporate legal counsel, where the attorney (or, more often, a firm of attorneys) is engaged by the board of directors but really represents the shareholders. The attorney-client privilege is vested in the participants and shareholders, not the trustees and/or directors.

In the very early years of Taft-Hartley employee benefit plans, the 1950s and 1960s,[8] most fund attorneys were the attorneys used by the local union in its collective bargaining that gave rise to the plan or to its continued existence. As the law of employee benefits became more complex, employer association counsel became more involved. In the 1990s, there is a discernible movement toward the development of a legal specialization in the representation of employee benefit plans subject to ERISA.

Historically (but hopefully not in the future), the major obstacle in the selection and engagement of fund counsel has been the irrelevant and nonprofessional attributes of an attorney under consideration. Historically, one side of the table would argue for attorneys of liberal persuasion who tended to vote a straight Democratic ticket and supported shutting down construction projects with replacement labor, with deliveries to the jobsite by replacement truckers; while the other side argued equally vocally for conservatives who were devoted to the GOP, favored right-to-work laws, open shops and who used the "ABC" as a hypothetical entity. Frequently, trustees insisted that their collective bargaining counsel be fund counsel, without a moment's consideration of:

(a) the general fiduciary duties test for counsel, or

(b) the protection that competent counsel provides to the trustees.

Although nothing in ERISA expressly bars use of the local union's counsel or the association's counsel, or both, a close reading of ERISA Section 406(a) and (b) shows a grave potential for conflict. The provisions of Section 406(b), the fiduciary prohibited transaction prohibitions, are particularly insightful and stringent:

(b) A fiduciary with respect to a plan shall not—

(1) deal with the assets of the plan in his own interest or for his own account,

(2) in his individual or in any other capacity act in any transaction involving the plan on behalf of a party (or represent a party) whose interests are adverse to the interests of the plan or the interests of its participants or beneficiaries, or

(3) receive any consideration for his own personal account from any party dealing with such plan in connection with a transaction involving the assets of the plan.

There are no statutory exemptions to Section 406(b), and no administrative exemptions can be granted.

There is a paucity of authority on the specific subject of whether the local union's attorney or the association's attorney may serve as fund counsel.

Walter Slater, former Area Regional Administrator of Pension and Welfare Benefit Administration in California, acting as an impartial umpire under Section 302(c) of the Labor-Management Relations Act of 1947 (LMRA), found a legal conflict to exist. In a 1982 deadlock arbitration, *In Re Allied Food and Commercial Workers Health and Welfare Fund and Employer Trustees and Union Trustees* (June 5, 1985, Arb. Lloyd L. Byars), the arbitrator ruled a potential conflict of interest does exist when the local union's labor counsel serves as fund counsel. Therefore, when the employer trustees moved for the removal of fund counsel because they were uncomfortable as fiduciaries in taking legal advice from the union's attorney, even though the union trustees deadlocked the motion, the arbitrator ruled that counsel had to be removed.

This is consistent, by analogy, with a line of cases trying to establish the relative roles of plan trustees versus collective bargaining parties in the operation and administration of the plan.

The language of ERISA Section 404(a), to wit:

(a)(1) Subject to Sections 403(c) and (d), 4042, and 4044, a fiduciary shall discharge his duties with respect to a plan solely in the interest of the participants and beneficiaries and—

    (A) for the exclusive purpose of:

        (i) providing benefits to participants and their beneficiaries; and

        (ii) defraying reasonable expenses of administering the plan;

    (B) with the care, skill, prudence, and diligence under the circumstances then prevailing that a prudent man acting in a like capacity and familiar with such matters would use in the conduct of an enterprise of a like character and with like aims;

    (C) by diversifying the investments of the plan so as to minimize the risk of large losses, unless under the circumstances it is clearly prudent not to do so; and

    (D) in accordance with the documents and instruments governing the plan insofar as such documents and instruments are consistent with the provisions of this title and title IV.

(2) In the case of an eligible individual account plan (as defined in Section 407(d)(3)), the diversification requirement of paragraph (1)(C) and the prudence requirement (only to the extent that it requires diversification) of paragraph (1)(B) is not violated by acquisition or holding of qualifying employer real property or qualifying employer securities (as defined in Section 407(d)(4) and (5)).

leaves little doubt that trustees are supposed to act for the benefit of plan participants and their beneficiaries to the exclusion of everyone else. The U.S. Supreme Court has placed its imprimatur on this interpretation.[9]

Over the years, trustees have become very familiar and comfortable with the generally accepted methodology for hiring an administrative manager; i.e., a written request for proposals and a subcommittee of trustees and advisors to screen the responses and narrow the field to two or three finalists who are interviewed by the entire board. However, trustees seem less comfortable with this approach in interviewing for and selecting fund counsel. This format is acceptable, but there is no "one way" to do it. What is vital is that the trustees exercise prudent methodology, acting solely in the interest of the plan and its participants to engage competent legal counsel.

Most trustees know one or more ERISA counsel—from serving on plans, from attending International Foundation seminars, from reading literature of the industry. If other names are needed, other business agent trustees, other employer association executives and other advisors to the plan are excellent sources of possible candidates for counsel.

A written request for proposal is an excellent opening gamut because it enables the trustees, or their legal counsel search subcommittee, to obtain a wealth of information on a number of candidates in a relatively short period of time and with little expense to the plan.

Ultimately, a face-to-face interview with all trustees present is essential. As much as any professional relationship, the attorney-client relationship of fund counsel with the named fiduciaries of Taft-Hartley employee benefit plans requires a good working relationship—"good chemistry among the players." This can only be evaluated on a face-to-face basis. If counsel is truly knowledgeable on ERISA and the fiduciary duties of trustees of Taft-Hartley plans, he will understand the somewhat awkward situation and will make it easy for the trustees to do their job.

The result is a simply stated rule. There is no violation in having counsel to the local union or to the employer association serve as fund counsel. However, a potential area of conflict does exist. The trustees, as named fiduciaries of the plan, are obliged by law to act solely in the interest of the participants in the plan and their beneficiaries (as well as for their own financial interest), and to hire the best, most experienced, most knowledgeable, "competent" trust fund counsel available to them.

How Many Counsel Can the Trustees Hire?

This question is like the question of a child: Mommy, how many balls of string does it take to reach the sky? The answer: One, if it were long enough.

The answer to the question of how many attorneys can trustees prudently hire to represent a plan and trust is "one," or "as many more as it takes to prudently and properly represent the interests of the plan and its participants."

The question posed is often a smoke screen for the question of whether the trustees can hire co-counsel: the local union's counsel as counsel for the union trustees and the employer association's counsel as counsel for the employer trustees. For the reasons discussed and by virtue of the authorities cited above, the answer is no. However, the trustees may, and in fact should, hire enough attorneys to provide the best and most competent legal services available to them in all the various areas in which legal representation is needed. The only limitations are:

    (a) all fund counsel shall represent all of the trustees and, through the trustees, all of the plan participants and their beneficiaries;

    (b) no attorneys shall provide duplicative services; and

    (c) the charges of each individual attorney and of legal counsel in the aggregate shall be reasonable.

Employee benefit plans subject to ERISA operate under a myriad of federal and, occasionally, state laws. They are subject to regulation by several different federal agencies. A number of substantive areas of the law are involved. It is not unusual that highly superior trust fund counsel lacks expertise in collections; that collection counsel cannot respond to questions about soft dollars, Section 28(e) protection of brokerage and execution costs; that securities counsel cannot advise the board adequately about a possible real estate investment; that real estate counsel cannot prudently opine whether a proposed change in welfare plan design will violate the Americans with Disabilities Act et al., etc., ad infinitum.

As to each and every area of the law in which the trustees have to act in their named fiduciary capacity, they need and are entitled to competent legal counsel. It is unusual that any one attorney can be expert in all of these areas. Therefore, the trend in Taft-Hartley plans is to engage a law firm with multiple attorneys expert in multiple areas of the law to give the trustees the necessary and desired level of competent professional representation. If all of these areas cannot be fulfilled within one firm, multiple firms can and should be employed, but subject always to the three limitations:

    (a) all fund counsel shall represent all of the trustees and, through the trustees, all of the plan participants and their beneficiaries;

    (b) no attorneys shall provide duplicative services; and

    (c) the charges of each individual attorney and of legal counsel in the aggregate shall be reasonable.

Documentation

The Department of Labor in its enforcement of ERISA has adopted a rule that all service providers shall have a written engagement and service agreement with the plan and its trustees. This is true for legal counsel.

This is an important protection to both parties to the contract. It enables each to know exactly what is expected from counsel—what fund counsel will do and will not do; how fund counsel expects to be compensated; what other considerations there are to the relationship; when and how the relationship can be terminated, etc. The agreement must be in writing and should be reviewed by both parties at least annually, and amended as necessary.

Compensation

One of the more difficult aspects of the relationship between the trustees and fund counsel is the area of compensation. The prevailing method of compensation is a fee-for-service arrangement. For example, it takes counsel four and one-half hours to prepare a draft of the amended and restated trust agreement, and the agreed-upon hourly rate for this type of work is $150 per hour; therefore, the bill is $675.

This arrangement, although of longstanding practice and comfortable to fund counsel, is frequently uncomfortable to the trustees. First, members who just negotiated a new collective bargaining agreement with a new wage rate at $X per hour are uncomfortable with legal counsel who charge two, four, six or eight times as much per hour. It is very difficult, if not impossible, for a person who is a loyal and competent employee working conscientiously at his or her trade or craft to agree that another person is worth two, four, six or eight times as much pay. Second, the trustees as buyers are buying the proverbial pig in the poke. When you buy a suit of clothing or a new automobile, when you take your family out to Sunday brunch or buy two tickets to a baseball game, you know upfront and in advance what it costs. Only with fund counsel is the cost of a service unknown. Finally, in many plans the employers must bid their services to get work; if they err in the bid, they absorb the loss.

The change has been slower in Taft-Hartley plans than in other areas of the world of business, but more and more professional service providers are being forced to state upfront a price for fixed and determinable types of professional services.

In prior years, a common form of compensation of fund counsel was a retainer. In a true retainer, the client (i.e., the trustees) pays a fixed amount for which counsel provides all needed legal services for a finite time period. Although there are no reported cases, this arrangement is undoubtedly illegal, imprudent and improper.

In a true retainer arrangement, three things can happen:
1. The lawyer's quote and fee are in excess of the reasonable value of the services actually rendered.
2. The lawyer's quote and fee are less than the reasonable value of the services actually rendered.
3. The quote and the reasonable value of the services are exactly the same.

In the first case, you have a per se violation of ERISA Sections 404(a), 404(a)(1)(A) and 404(a)(1)(B). You engage legal counsel to keep you out of breach of fiduciary responsibility. For your attorney to cause you to violate your fiduciary duties is unconscionable.

In the second case, you have an unhappy professional service provider. This is not a good position for a client (or a patient) to be in. As no merchant sells his wares below cost for very long and stays in business, no professional service provider provides long-term quality professional services at a loss for very long. Whether it is to resign the account or cut back on the quality of the services or on the quantity of the services, it is not a prudent position for plan fiduciaries to be in.

As to the final case, if the attorney (or the trustee) is that omniscient (or lucky), fund counsel should be playing the stock market, roulette or the horses and making real money.

An ongoing concern of the trustees must be compliance with ERISA Section 404(a)(1)(A), which provides:

(a)(1) Subject to Sections 403(c) and (d), 4042, and 4044, a fiduciary shall discharge his duties with respect to a plan solely in the interest of the participants and beneficiaries and—
   (A) for the exclusive purpose of:
      (i) providing benefits to participants and their beneficiaries; and
      (ii) defraying reasonable expenses of administering the plan;

This provision carries with it two elements. First, the service must be necessary and appropriate to the administration of the plan. Services of legal counsel are generally within that test.[10] Second, the price paid must be reasonable. In Department of Labor regulations under Section 408(a)(2),[11] the Department of Labor indicated that what is reasonable compensation depends on the facts and circumstances of a particular case. Reference is also made to Internal Revenue Code Section 162 and the regulations thereunder dealing with compensation that qualifies as a trade or business expense for purposes of a tax deduction. The Treasury regulations also indicate that reasonable compensation is the amount that would ordinarily be paid for like services, by like enterprises and under like circumstances. Reference is also made to reasonable compensation being that which is arrived at through a fee bargain between unrelated parties.

The preferred methodology for compensating fund counsel is to pay a pre-discussed and agreed-upon hourly rate for services, with the rate being based, *inter alia*, on counsel's experience, the difficulty of the project, what comparable counsel are charging and comparable trustees are paying, etc., times the hours spent, plus the reasonable cost of necessary expenses, payable in arrears.

The International Foundation of Employee Benefit Plans has published several studies on administrative expenses, including legal counsel compensation, as has Commerce Clearing House. These are of limited value but do provide some insight into what other like and similar plans are paying. Talking with fellow trustees of like and similar plans is an excellent source of relevant information.

The trustees have an ongoing obligation to monitor the issue of counsel's compensation and to satisfy themselves at least annually of its reasonableness.

Responsibilities of Fund Counsel

Earlier, the analogy was made that companion pension and welfare plans are analogous to a small insurance company. Carrying that analogy forward, the participants are the shareholders/policyholders, the ultimate beneficiaries of the plan's benefits. The board of trustees is comparable to the board of directors of an insurance company; they set the basic policy and direction in which the corporation is to go. It is important for the trustees to acknowledge that their role is one of policy setters and direction providers for the plan. They cannot and should not attempt to handle each and every detail of the plan themselves.

The administrative manager is the chief operating officer of the plan/insurance company. In the context of a Taft-Hartley plan, the administrative manager is the glue that keeps the plan functioning. On a day-to-day basis, taking in the money, keeping the records, paying claims and benefits, and responding to members' questions, the administrative manager is the "main man." Fund counsel is obviously analogous to general counsel of an insurance company, responsible for all aspects of legal compliance. The enrolled actuary is comparable to the company's chief underwriter, while the plan's independent certified public accountant is comparable to the insurance company's controller.

From the perspective of fund counsel, perhaps a more accurate and incisive analogy would be to a harbor pilot in a major port such as New York. Fund counsel charts the path and steers the trustees and the plan through the maze and morass of legal dangers. Instead of sunken ships and subsurface rocks, you have the Department of Labor, the Internal Revenue Service, the Securities and Exchange Commission, the Equal Employment Opportunity Commission, legislation, regulation and enforcement on a myriad of issues from collections to plan design to administration, from recordkeeping to investments, from mandatory communications to prohibited communications.

Obviously, fund counsel must be well versed in numerous aspects of the law. Fund counsel needs to be an expert not only in ERISA, but must be attuned to recognize other areas so fund counsel or counsel in charge of the other areas can be involved in the situation and resolve it before it becomes a legal problem. For this reason, it is important for fund counsel to attend all trustee meetings and committee meetings. Frequently, problems can be avoided early on, when a trustee begins to espouse a possible change in benefits, investment philosophy or administration; and, at this stage, counsel can advise the board of the legal implications of the suggestion. Minutes are important and do reflect decisions made, but legal counsel can comprehend rationale, which frequently is equally important to the actual action, only if fund counsel participates in the discussions.

Fund counsel's relationship with the trustees must be one of mutual trust and confidence based upon the highest level of personal and professional respect. It is not important for the attorney and some or all of the trustees to be good friends, to golf or hunt, dine or vacation together. Too close a relationship and too much social involvement can be an impediment to professional objectivity; a doctor will rarely if ever operate on family or an extremely close friend. What is crucial is that each and every trustee respect the honesty, integrity and competency of fund counsel, fund counsel's basic fairness and impartiality, his independence and his expertise.

As the trustees can hire legal counsel to represent them and, through them, the plan and its participants and their beneficiaries, so too the trustees can fire counsel. Counsel must have a written engagement agreement,[12] and it must provide a date or procedure for termination. But, it is important that fund counsel be secure in fund counsel's professional relationship with the trustees; there is no danger of being terminated as long as he continues to possess and exercise competency, integrity and impartiality. As long as fund counsel renders the highest quality of professional services on a timely basis for a reasonable fee, there should be no danger to continuing as fund counsel.

Too often trustees want to tell counsel the result they want from his research or threaten that if counsel does not say or do what they want, he will be fired. Clearly, counsel works for the plan and its participants via the trustees, but it must be on a highly professional level.

An annual executive session conference between the board and fund counsel is very helpful to make sure that no misunderstandings have occurred, to reinforce the mutuality of respect and confidence. Some disagreements are to be expected, and some friction will occur in the best of relationships. The parent does not exist who did not at some time want to shake or paddle his or her child. But, you do not throw them out because of a disagreement.

To accomplish the desired balance between client and attorney, between trustees and counsel, it is essential that each fully understands and appreciates the roles and responsibilities of the other. An attorney who is mindless of a business agent's sworn and heartfelt duty to fully and faithfully represent the interests of the members deserves to be reviewed for termination. An attorney who is mindless of an employer trustee's obligation to fellow employers to keep plan expenses down and thereby avoid further employer costs, which can create an uncompetitive economic situation for all union employers, should never have been hired and, if hired, should never have been allowed to continue as fund counsel. But, the business agent and/or the employer representative cannot dictate to fund counsel how counsel should research problems or what conclusions to reach—or else the trustees will not be discharging their general fiduciary duties under ERISA Section 404(a).

Conclusion

The relationship between the trustees of a collectively bargained, jointly trusteed, multiemployer employee benefit plan subject to ERISA is an ongoing, alive and oft changing one. Hence, a conclusion is not in order in a discussion of the relationship; it would be passé before it was in print.

It is suggested that the Honorable Chief Justice Benjamin Cardozo of the Court of Appeals of the State of New York, writing over 65 years ago (46 years before the enactment of ERISA), set forth the standard of conduct of Taft-Hartley trustees. In his opinion in *Meinhard v. Salmon*, 164 N.E. 454 (NY Ct. App. 1928), Justice Cardozo wrote:

> Many forms of conduct permissible in a work-a-day world for those acting at arm's length are forbidden to those with fiduciary ties. A trustee is held to something stricter than the morals of the marketplace. Not honesty also, but the punctilio of an honor the most sensitive, is then the standard. As to this, there has developed a tradition that is unbending and inveterate. Uncompromising rigidity has been the attitude of courts of equity when petitioned to undermine the rule of undivided loyalty by the disintegrating erosion of particular expectations. Only thus has a level of conduct for fiduciaries been kept as a higher level than that trodden by the crowd.

This is, in my opinion, the most eloquent enunciation of the code of fiduciary conduct that most Taft-Hartley trustees seek to attain and maintain. To do so in the last decade of the twentieth century, in the milieu of ERISA, the Internal Revenue Code, the several Securities and Exchange Acts, Americans with Disabilities Act, Family and Medical Leave Act, GATT provisions, United Services Employment and Reemployment Rights Act, qualified domestic relations orders and qualified medical child support orders, requires competent legal counsel with knowledge, expertise, integrity and impartiality beyond that manifested by the crowd. Hopefully, the foregoing can help named fiduciaries who bear a most onerous task fulfill their fiduciary obligation with the punctilio of honor of the most sensitive.

Suggested Checklist for Request for Proposal (RFP)

1. If your firm is engaged to serve as fund counsel, please list all attorneys who would expect to render legal services on behalf of the plan and its board of trustees, and the area of specialization of each. Please attach a brief vita on each.

2. Are all of the attorneys listed pursuant to the prior question rated by Martindale & Hubbell? If so, provide the Martindale & Hubbell rating for each.

3. Does your firm represent any employer associations? If so, please list the full name, address and telephone number of each, together with the name of the executive director of each such association.

4. Does your firm represent any labor unions? If so, please list the full name, address and telephone number of each, together with the name of the business manager of each union.

5. Does your firm represent the boards of trustees of any Taft-Hartley employee benefit plans subject to ERISA? If so, please list the full name, address and telephone number of the chairman and secretary of each board listed.

6. As to the attorney from your firm who will be responsible for the plan if your firm is engaged as fund counsel, please list the major speaking and writing accomplishments dealing with the representation of such clients.

7. What is the policy of your firm as to continuing legal education for its attorneys?

8. Please describe in detail the billing rates, practices and policies of your firm that would apply if your firm were engaged to serve as fund counsel.

9. Have any Taft-Hartley employee benefit plans represented by your firm been engaged in litigation during the past three years, other than collection proceedings brought on behalf of the plan? If so, without disclosing any information that is not a matter of public record, please describe the nature and cause of the proceedings, the travel of the litigation and the outcome, if completed.

10. Please describe the materials in your firm's law library dealing with employee benefit plans, including books, subscriptions, magazines, services, periodicals, etc.

11. If your firm were engaged as fund counsel and thereafter your firm was asked to commence collection proceedings against a local corporation for which your firm was also currently rendering legal services, what steps and procedures would you employ as to the plan?

Endnotes

1. See, for example, Owen M. Rumelt, "Legal Aspects of Plan Communications," 36 *Employee Benefit Issues—The Multiemployer Perspective* (1994); Rory Judd Albert, "The 'Legal' Side of Employee Benefit Communication," Ibid. (1994); Timothy J. Parsons, "Update on Legal Aspects of Communication," 35 *Employee Benefit Issues—The Multiemployer Perspective* (1993).

2. The Department of Labor, following the lead of Congress, has made this test, "written in a manner calculated to be understood by the average plan participant," the test for writings under Title I, Subtitle B, Part 1, Reporting and Disclosure. See, for example, ERISA Section 102(a), Plan Description and Summary Plan Description, and the regulations thereunder.

3. Since a delinquent contribution by an employer participating in a multiemployer Taft-Hartley plan would be a per se prohibited transaction, the DOL promulgated Class Prohibited Transaction 76-1 (3/25/76), *FR* 76-8766). Under Subsection A, if the trustees have established and implemented a regular, systematic and diligent plan, program and procedure of delinquency control, the delinquency of a contributing employer shall not constitute a prohibited transaction.

4. It has been estimated by Employee Benefit Research Institute that the assets of the private and public pension industry exceed $5 trillion.

5. ERISA Section 402(b)(3) provides that any employee benefit plan may provide that a person who is a named fiduciary may appoint an investment manager(s) to manage the assets of a plan. Section 403(a)(2) provides that if a provision exists in the plan document, then the named fiduciary(ies) may appoint an investment manager(s).

6. *Wilde et al. v. Walbrun et al.; Bell et al. v. Orrell et al.* (U.S.D.C.N.D.Ind. 1993).

7. Data supplied by Charles Lerner, director of enforcement, Pension and Welfare Benefits Administration, U.S. Department of Labor, based upon 1994 report of secretary of labor to Congress.

8. Cynthia J. Drinkwater, "History of Taft-Hartley Plans," *Trustees Handbook*, 4th Edition, International Foundation of Employee Benefit Plans (1990).

9. In *NLRB v. Amax Coal Co.*, 453 U.S. 322, *reh. denied*, 453 U.S. 950 (1981), the Supreme Court held that the efforts of a union to coerce an employer in the appointment of a trustee to a trust fund established under Section 302(c)(5) of the LMRA did not constitute an unfair labor practice because such a trustee was not a collective bargaining representative of the employer within the meaning of Section 8(b)(1)(B) of the National Labor Relations Act.

> The language and legislative history of §302(c)(5) and ERISA therefore demonstrate that an employee benefit fund trustee is a fiduciary whose duty to the trust beneficiaries must overcome any loyalty to the interest of the party that appointed him. 453 U.S. at 334.

Amax is in accord with prior Supreme Court decisions concerning congressional intent with respect to the use of LMRA Section 302 trust funds. *Arroyo v. United States*, 359 U.S. 419 (1959); *Walsh v. Schlect*, 429 U.S. 401, 410-411 (1977) (congressional purpose in enacting LMRA Section 302 was to combat corruption, extortion and possible abuse of power by union officers); *Hurn v. Retirement Fund Trust*, 113 LRRM 2054, 2058 (9th Cir. 1983) (cites *Amax* for its use of language and legislative history of ERISA and LMRA Section 302(c)(5) in defining trustees' duties). *Amax* is entirely consistent with prior cases which show that trustees on the one hand and collective bargaining parties on the other have different responsibilities and loyalties.

In *National Union of Hospital and Health Care Employees, Division of RWDSU, AFL-CIO, etc., and Sinai Hospital of Baltimore, Inc.*, 248 NLRB No. 86, 103 LRRM 1459 (1980), the NLRB held that:

> ... although Section 302 <u>trustees may be expected to champion the interests of their respective principals, they must do so in a manner which is consistent with their fiduciary obligations</u> rather than utilizing their alleged fiduciary capacity as a pretext to circumvent bargaining obligations under the Act. 103 LRRM at 1462 [citation omitted; emphasis added].

In *Sheet Metal Workers, Local No. 493 et al.*, 234 NRLB No. 162, 97 LRRM 1476 (1978), *aff'd sub. nom., Central Florida Sheet Metal Contractors Association v. NLRB*, 664 F.2d 489 (5th Cir. 1981), *reh. denied*, 673 F.2d 1324 (5th Cir. 1982), the NLRB ruled that trustees of a fringe benefit fund must act independently; that is, without loyalty to the side that appointed them.

> [W]e conclude that the SASMI [national Stabilization Agreement for Sheet Metal Industry] trustees are not collective-bargaining representatives within the meaning of Section 8(b)(1)(B) of the Act. . . . As the discussion above makes abundantly clear, . . . <u>the trustees of a joint trust fund like SASMI are required to act solely in the interests of the beneficiaries of the trust fund. The fiduciary obligations imposed on the trustees are of overriding importance</u>, and, <u>although they should, of course, carefully consider all recommendations submitted by the parties who have appointed them, the trustees are bound to exercise their independent judgment when making decisions</u> with respect to the administration of the trust fund.

97 LRRM at 1486 [emphasis added]. See also, David W. Silverman, "Federal Labor Policy—Another View of Trustees' Responsibilities," 36 Employee Benefit Issues—The Multiemployer Perspective, International Foundation of Employee Benefit Plans (1994); James I. Singer, "A Practical Look at ERISA Fiduciary Responsibilities," Ibid., Section II, pp. 498-499.

10. DOL Regulations §2550.408b; *Donovan v. Bierwirth*, 680 F.2d 263 (2d Cir. 1982); *Katsaros v. Cody*, 568 F.Sup. 360 (E.D.N.Y. 1983), *aff'd as modified*, 744 F.2d 270 (2d Cir.), *cert. denied*, 469 U.S. 1072 (1984).

11. DOL Regulations §2550.408c-2.

12. A policy established by the Pension and Welfare Benefits Administration in its enforcement of ERISA by voluntary compliance, and now generally accepted and followed without question.

About the Authors

Henry S. Hunt
Executive Vice President
Allied Construction
 Employers Association
Brookfield, Wisconsin

Mr. Hunt has served as a management trustee on a number of health and pension funds since 1957. He was President of the International Foundation in 1985 and currently serves on its Past Presidents Council. Mr. Hunt has been a speaker and moderator for Foundation educational programs since 1967 and has served on various Foundation committees over the years.

Marc Gertner
Senior Partner
Shumaker, Loop & Kendrick
Toledo, Ohio

For over 25 years, Mr. Gertner served as fund counsel to more than four dozen Taft-Hartley pension, welfare and related employee benefit plans. He has also been active in ERISA litigation, representing both trustees and plans in voluntary compliance audits and actions brought by the Department of Labor under ERISA and serving as an expert witness in ERISA proceedings.

Mr. Gertner has given over 150 presentations on employee benefits over the past 25 years to various organizations, and has participated in the writing of four professional books and has written more than 50 articles on employee benefit plans subject to ERISA. Mr. Gertner has been an active speaker, writer and committee member since 1970 and served on the Foundation's Board of Directors as an Advisory Director.

Chapter 2

Actuarial Services

by Ralph M. Weinberg

Trustee's Perspective

by Terry Lynch

The services provided by our actuarial consultant have been invaluable. Virtually every fund decision is made with his input.

As chairman of the fund, I feel his most important responsibility is to calculate the various contribution requirements for the proper funding of our pension plan. By doing this, we are able to continuously monitor the financial well-being of our fund. This procedure enables the trustees to maintain the reserves necessary to meet the financial obligations for our current retirees and for those who will be retired 20 years from now.

When the trustees decide to raise the benefit level for future and or past service, the actuary's counsel is essential. He must consider such factors as projected workload, investment performance and the contribution rate needed to support the proposed raise. When these and other factors are reviewed, he can then advise the trustees of the appropriate benefit enhancements. The trustees can then communicate with confidence to the participants that the funds are available to generate a pension increase.

Another of his important duties is to assist the administrator and trustees in drafting communications to our members. It is essential that the information communicated be put into language that can be easily understood by our membership.

At our fund, when a project has to be undertaken, the actuary is usually the professional who takes charge. This approach has always worked well for us because he is respected by all of us who are involved with the fund: the trustees and the other professionals.

I think it is very important for the management and labor trustees to work cohesively together for the benefit of the participants. On our particular board, the labor trustees work very well with our counterparts on the management side of the table. I really believe that one of the main reasons our pension fund has done so well is because all of the trustees have such great confidence and respect for our actuarial consultant.

INTRODUCTION

This chapter is about actuarial services being provided to the trustees of multi-employer and public plans. The chapter covers the following major topics:
1. Services provided
2. Actuarial service organizations
3. Duties and responsibilities of actuaries and trustees
4. Selecting an actuary
5. Fee arrangements
6. Conflicts of interest.

Services Provided

Depending on the type of plan, the actuary must provide certain required services. All other services fall into the category of "project work" and would be performed only at the request and pleasure of the board of trustees. Most funds find that there are a number of fund professionals that are capable of providing certain types of services to the plan. In this case, I find that the administrator is best suited to make the decision as to which professional should provide a particular service. That decision should be based on experience, availability and professional fees. For example, if the trustees authorize the production of a booklet describing the highlights of the plan of benefits, the administrator, the attorney and the actuary should all be capable of providing that service. In the final analysis, all three should work together, but only one should be designated for producing the initial draft.

A list of services that the actuary can provide is shown below:
- Actuarial valuation of the assets and liabilities of the plan
- Calculation of various contribution requirements for proper funding of the plan
- Asset/liability modeling and projection studies
- Calculation and certification of individual participant benefits
- Preparation of individual participant benefit statements
- Calculation of accrued benefits and vested status
- Preparation of required governmental filings
- Preparation of other required reporting and disclosure to participants
- Calculation of costs for proposed plan modifications
- Development of actuarial factors, benefit forms and procedures needed for proper administration of the plan
- Assisting fund counsel in development of plan amendments
- Preretirement planning
- Plan design services

- Investment consulting services
- EDP and general consulting
- Employee communications
- Legislative and regulatory updates
- Surveys.

Actuarial Service Organizations

What are the characteristics of the organizations that employ actuaries to provide these kinds of services? Sole practitioners may provide the types of services described earlier, but in most cases the actuary is employed by an organization large enough to be able to provide most, if not all, needed services. In either case, the plan actuary must be an enrolled actuary.[1]

There are two types of organizations that employ actuaries to provide services to plans—insurance companies, and actuarial and employee benefit consulting firms. In most cases, these organizations have a broad array of resources that are needed to provide all requested services. Smaller organizations may be able to provide only the most basic services. All organizations, regardless of size, are equipped to handle all of the work related to the conduct of an actuarial valuation of the fund's assets and liabilities and are able to provide the contribution requirements of the plan on a number of alternative bases. In addition, each actuary is trained and has the computer resources to be able to analyze the fund's cash flow needs and liquidity requirements.

The larger organizations that provide actuarial services employ professionals who have backgrounds in actuarial science, law, insurance, mathematics, investments, compensation, communications, accounting, computer science, health care, finance and economics. In almost all cases, these organizations have a research facility, the professionals of which provide up-to-date information on pending legislation, proposed and issued regulations, survey data and information on new developments. Most organizations employ actuaries with specific experience and expertise in providing actuarial and benefit consulting services to a broad range of plan sponsors, including multiemployer funds and public plans.

Duties and Responsibilities of Actuaries and Trustees

What responsibilities fall on the shoulders of the trustees? Which ones fall on the actuary? These are often difficult questions to answer and may depend on the unique characteristics of the plan, the trustees and the group of professionals that provide services. In general, the responsibility for making decisions falls on the shoulders of the trustees. However, the input they receive from fund professionals forms the basis for the decision making process. For example, suppose that the fund actuary is requested to analyze the funded status of the plan to determine whether there is sufficient margin for benefit improvements. To assist the trustees in making their decision, the actuary must complete the following:

- An actuarial valuation of the liabilities and assets of the plan
- An analysis of the proper level of reserves
- A determination of whether future events may occur, which are not anticipated by the actuarial assumptions, that may adversely impact the fund in the future.

Are trustees expected to analyze whether the actuary's analysis is correct and complete? Clearly, the answer is no. What responsibility then do the trustees really have? Are they expected to blindly accept the actuary's analysis? Again, the answer is no. The trustees must have a clear understanding of the information the actuary provides, for without such clarity, they would not be in a position to make a decision on what improvements, if any, are appropriate for adoption. Thus, there is a shared burden of communications—the actuary must provide a clear and concise summary of the findings and the trustees must understand what is being presented and the implications of the information.

Beyond providing the information in a clear and concise manner, does the actuary have the responsibility to make recommendations? Generally, no, unless the board of trustees has specifically requested the actuary to do so. Let's go back to the benefit improvement example. Unless otherwise requested, the actuary should only report to the trustees that the funded status of the plan and other pertinent factors are such that benefit improvements are or are not affordable. If the trustees have requested the actuary to cost out specific types of improvements, then, of course, the actuary is duty-bound to provide those results. However, the actuary should not volunteer a recommendation for the specific improvement that should be adopted unless requested to do so. In any case, the actual decision falls on the shoulders of the trustees. As a result, actuaries are generally not considered fiduciaries under ERISA since they are not exercising discretionary authority or control respecting the management or disposition of plan assets.

What about meeting certain reporting and disclosure requirements? Whose responsibility is it to be sure that required governmental reports are complete and filed on a timely basis? Generally, the trustees should be able to rely on the administrator, the actuary and the other fund professionals to properly handle administrative matters such as this. However, ultimately the plan sponsor is the entity responsible for proper administration of the plan. So, it would be wise to have the fund professionals report on the status of required filings at trustee meetings.

Selecting an Actuary

Let us assume that the trustees find themselves in need of a new actuary. How do they go about finding that individual? Depending on the size of the board, the establishment of a subcommittee to conduct a search may be appropriate. If the board consists of six trustees or fewer, it makes sense to have the entire board involved in the search process. In any case, the first step is to decide on the key criteria that will be used in the selection process. Among the criteria that should be considered are the following:

- Capability of the actuary/firm
- Is local service important?
- What experience does the firm have in serving like funds?
- What is the reputation of the firm?
- What services does the actuary need to provide to the plan?
- Is the firm large enough to provide services needed by the plan? Does the firm have the resources?
- Fees.

Once the criteria have been established, it is time to begin the search. The search process for public plans may be governed by legal requirements. The first decision the subcommittee needs to make is how formal a process is appropriate. Each fund is different, but I suggest that in all cases a request for proposal (RFP) be prepared for distribution to individuals or firms selected by the board or subcommittee. The RFP process is important to determine which firms should be invited to make an oral presentation to the trustees. So, how do you find the names of those individuals or organizations to whom the RFP should be sent? The answer depends, in part, on the criteria for selection, examples of which are listed above. Here are some suggestions for developing a list of potential bidders:

1. Discuss your needs with other funds in your area. Find out who the actuary is and whether that firm or individual meets the criteria you have established.
2. Check with the nearest local Society of Actuaries or American Academy of Actuaries office for a list of firms in your area.
3. Check with your trade association, government finance association or international union for the names of firms or individuals who serve like funds in other areas of the country.
4. Get the names of the largest actuarial and benefits consulting firms in your area from the local business publication.

By going through this process, you should be able to develop a list of six to ten potential candidates to whom the RFP can be sent. The subcommittee, perhaps with the assistance of its fund professionals, next needs to develop the RFP. I suggest that the RFP be relatively brief, hitting the key elements that allow the actuary to describe the firm, the services that can be provided, the resources the firm has available to provide those services and information on professional fees.

Remember—the RFP process should only assist the trustees in selecting a group of finalists who will make oral presentations to the full board. If the RFP is too long and detailed, it will miss the mark because trustees may not take the time to read each response cover to cover and may then miss one or more key elements of the response that should cause a candidate to be included or excluded from the group of finalists. More importantly, the final decision should be made primarily on the basis of the oral presentation, not on the RFP.

Let's assume that you plan on sending the RFP to ten organizations. I suggest that you adhere to the following guidelines as the RFP process unfolds:

- ▶ Include the most recent actuarial report and audit report as attachments to the RFP. Also include the most recent booklet describing the terms of the plan.
- ▶ Provide a brief summary of your type of plan in the introductory material, including how your plan is administered, how many trustees serve on the board, how frequently you meet, etc.
- ▶ Spell out what services you need the actuary to provide and ask the firm what other services they could provide beyond those requested.
- ▶ Ask the actuary to provide a general description of the firm and its resources, biographies of the service team including their experience in serving like funds and information on how they prefer to bill for their services. They also should be requested to provide an estimate of their fees for providing the requested services.
- ▶ Advise the actuary that all questions or requests for additional information be directed to a specified individual, generally the plan administrator or fund counsel. I further suggest that they be advised that contact with any member of the board of trustees will cause the firm to be dropped from the list of candidates.
- ▶ Provide the answers to all questions and any additional information to *all* candidates.

This is a process that should work for almost all funds, regardless of size or complexity. However, if the subcommittee decides that the unique characteristics of your plan require face-to-face communications with candidates, then a bidders conference should be considered. Under this approach, all prospective bidders would be invited to attend a meeting shortly after receipt of the RFP. The purpose of the meeting would be for the subcommittee to describe whatever additional information it wishes to provide to the candidates that was not appropriate for inclusion in the RFP. The conference would also allow all candidates to ask questions and for all candidates to hear the same answers at the same time.

The deadline for submitting the proposal to the administrator should be the close of business hours on a selected date. It should be made clear in the RFP that failure to provide the proposal by the due date will disqualify the candidate from consideration and that guideline should be adhered to without exception.

Once the proposal has been received, all members of the subcommittee, or the full board as the case may be, should carefully review each proposal. Any unanswered questions should be noted. Then, the candidate list should be pared down to a short list, and each organization on the short list should be invited to make a formal presentation on a selected date. Each board of trustees needs to decide upfront whether the short list will be determined solely by the subcommittee or whether input will be sought from the full board.

On the day of the formal presentations, each organization should be allowed between 30-45 minutes for their formal presentation, with an additional 15 minutes for questions. The formal candidate interviews are the most important part of the process. In most cases, it will be difficult to differentiate one candidate from another on the short list from the information provided in the proposal. However, frequently the actuary's knowledge, experience and communications skills will come out in the formal presentation. The board of trustees should make every effort to hone in on communications skills since the success of the ongoing relationship depends heavily on the actuary's ability to communicate his or her findings and perspectives to the trustees in a clear and concise manner. To accomplish this in the formal presentations, I suggest that the subcommittee or the full board develop a short list of key questions that will challenge the actuary to come up with the best possible response without the advantage of advance preparation. For example, the trustees might consider asking one or more questions similar to the following:

1. Assume that you find an error in a benefit certification completed by the prior actuary. How would you proceed?
2. How would you deal with a situation where one or more of your fellow professionals are not completing their work on a timely basis, which is going to cause you to miss a deadline you have promised?
3. If there are excess reserves, should those be spent on benefit improvements or used to reduce future contributions?

After the formal presentations have ended, the board should attempt to reach consensus on a new actuary at that meeting, if at all possible. If time does not permit a complete discussion of each of the candidates, each trustee should rank order the candidates and make notes with respect to the reasons for the ordering of each candidate. I recommend that the trustees attempt to make a decision as soon as possible. The actuary selected should be notified by telephone, and all candidates should be notified in writing of the board's decision.

Fee Arrangements

So you've selected an actuary and now it is time to finalize the agreement on professional fees. In many cases this will have been resolved during oral interviews. There are numerous types of fee arrangements that can be agreed upon including:

1. A *fixed fee* arrangement (sometimes called a retainer arrangement), where the actuary agrees to provide all or a specified list of services for a predetermined fixed fee.
2. A *fee-for-service* arrangement, where the actuary bills for services on the basis of an hourly rate for each individual on the team who is providing services to the trustees.
3. A *fee-for-service with a maximum* arrangement, where the actuary also bills for services based on hourly rates for each individual on the team providing services, but where the total charges for the year cannot exceed a predetermined maximum fee. Like the fixed fee arrangement, this type of arrangement requires that the parties agree on a specified list of services that will be included in determining when the maximum fee is reached.

Which of these arrangements makes the most sense depends on a number of factors. However, I believe that the fee-for-service arrangement is the fairest for both sides, since in all cases the actuary will be paid for all services rendered and the trustees will pay only for services they receive. These two points are not true under any other arrangement. However, it is important for the trustees to seek fee estimates for any major projects the board wishes the actuary to complete under any arrangement, but particularly under the fee-for-service arrangement.

Conflicts of Interest

All actuaries are governed by the Code of Professional Conduct.[2] This code provides the following:

An actuary shall not perform professional services involving an actual or potential conflict of interest unless:
  (a) the actuary's ability to act fairly is unimpaired; and
  (b) there has been disclosure of the conflict to all known direct users whose interests would be affected by the conflict; and
  (c) all such known direct users have expressly agreed to the performance of the services by the actuary.

A *direct user* of an actuary's services is a principal (i.e., present or prospective client or employer) having the opportunity to select the actuary and able to communicate directly with the actuary about qualifications, work and recommendations.

If the actuary is aware of any significant conflict between the interests of the direct user and the interests of another party relative to the actuary's work, the actuary should advise the direct user of the conflict. The actuary should also include appropriate qualifications or disclosures in any related actuarial communication.

Also, enrolled actuaries are governed by certain standards of performance pursuant to regulations issued by the Joint Board for Enrollment of Actuaries.

In addition, I believe the actuary has a responsibility to disclose a perceived conflict, even if the actuary does not believe there is an actual or potential conflict. For example, assume the actuary is providing actuarial and consulting services to a financial institution and that financial institution is engaged by the trustees to invest all or a portion of the fund's assets. This situation does not create either an actual or a potential conflict. However, the trustees may perceive this as a conflict of interest, in which case the actuary should disclose and discuss this with the board of trustees.

In and of itself, providing services to both a participating employer and a fund is not a conflict. However, depending on the specific types of services offered, there may be a potential conflict. For example, assume that the actuary for a multiemployer fund is asked to support its methods and assumptions in a withdrawal liability arbitration involving a participating employer for which his or her firm provides actuarial and consulting services. Further assume that the service team for the participating employer is located in another office than the one in which the actuary serving the fund resides. Whether or not the other office is going to participate in any fashion in the arbitration, this situation requires disclosure of an actual or potential conflict.

It is important to understand that once disclosed, it is not required that a second actuary be brought into the situation. As noted in subparagraphs (a) and (c) of the Code of Professional Conduct, the actuary is permitted to provide services to both parties if his or her ability to act is unimpaired and if both parties agree to having the actuary perform any necessary services.

Suggested Checklist for Request for Proposal (RFP)

1. What are the names, addresses and telephone numbers of three client (fund type) references?

2. What is the name, address and telephone number of a fund client you have lost within the last five years?

3. Was your valuation system built and maintained in-house or did you purchase (or lease) a vendor's system? Describe in detail the hardware used by your firm.

4. How do you ensure quality?

5. What approach does your firm use to stay abreast of (1) the latest technology and (2) legal and legislative developments?

6. What distinguishes your firm from your competitors? Why should we select your firm?

7. Who would be attending meetings and who is the number two person we would use if number one was unavailable? (Need to ask to distinguish the actuary/consultant from the marketing people.)

8. How long does it take your firm to complete the actuarial valuation?

9. What additional services does your firm provide?

10. What is your long-term modeling and forecasting capability?

11. In terms of expected annual revenues, how important is this engagement compared to your list of current clients (e.g., largest, fifth largest, about average, etc.)?

12. Would you anticipate the need for additional staffing if you were selected?

Endnotes

1. Enrolled actuaries are approved by a federal agency based on examinations and/or relevant experience. They must complete 36 hours of continuing education requirements over a three-year enrollment cycle to maintain their designation, in accordance with regulations issued by the Joint Board for Enrollment of Actuaries.

2. Issued by the American Academy of Actuaries. Most recent effective date is January 1, 1994.

About the Authors

Terry Lynch
Labor Trustee
International Association
 of Heat and Frost Insulators
 and Asbestos Workers Local 17
Chicago, Illinois

Mr. Lynch is a third generation asbestos worker and graduate of Northern Illinois University. He serves his union of over 800 active and 500 retired members. His varied leadership roles for the International Association of Heat and Frost Insulators and Asbestos Workers Local 17 include secretary-treasurer for the union and chairman of the board of trustees for the health and welfare, pension, and annuity funds. The retirement fund of Local 17 has combined assets of over $135 million.

Ralph M. Weinberg
Consulting Actuary
Milliman & Robertson, Inc.
Chicago, Illinois

Mr. Weinberg is primarily responsible for managing the pension consulting activities for Milliman & Robertson, Inc. in Chicago. He has over 25 years of experience in the design, funding, communication and administration of both qualified and nonqualified retirement plans, working with corporate, multiemployer and public plan sponsors. Mr. Weinberg is an enrolled actuary under ERISA and a member of the American Academy of Actuaries. He served as an Advisory Director on the Board of Directors of the International Foundation of Employee Benefit Plans and was a member of various other committees. Mr. Weinberg currently serves on the Actuaries/Consultants Committee. He frequently speaks and writes articles on employee benefit topics.

Chapter 3

Benefit Consulting

by Donald A. Walters

Trustee's Perspective

by Herbert R. Ricklin

The ultimate responsibility for decision making for Taft-Hartley jointly trusteed health and pension plans rests with the board of trustees. The trustees are responsible for deciding benefit levels, plan expenditures, investments and generally how the fund will operate and be administered. The labor trustees, who are officials of the union, and trustees from contributing employers may meet as a board only four to eight times a year. Their day-to-day responsibilities are running a labor union or a functioning business. How are they then to make accurate decisions on these complicated benefit matters?

As in all critical business decisions, facts must form the basis of determinations. The decisions of the board of trustees affect the lives of the participants, families and beneficiaries. To obtain the necessary knowledge and facts, the trustees must rely on experts, for if they do not, they are doing a disservice to the people they represent. To establish a benefit plan, to understand the costs now and the implications for the future, takes experience and expertise.

In fact, the courts have ruled that when plan fiduciaries (trustees) are not well informed on aspects of employee benefit criteria, it is incumbent upon them to seek the advice of experts. Often that means the employment of a benefit consultant to present to the board the facts, figures and processes that are necessary. Sometimes part of this advice may come from an administrator, attorney or actuary.

I find the greatest utilization of a benefit consultant is in the health benefit area. Here it is necessary not only to understand the cost of each medical, surgical and hospital benefit, but also the alternatives. It is usually necessary to rely on an outside source for this information. Obviously, the consultant should be totally nonpolitical. He or she should be dedicated to the best interest of the fund by assisting the trustees. Derived from the experience and exposure to other similar Taft-Hartley funds, the opinions of the consultants should also be welcomed by the trustees.

In the pension world, a consultant may calculate and provide cost criteria and information on rules and regulations concerning the eligibility and application of a plan. Some actuaries take on the dual role as consultant. The board of directors may also turn to the consultant to provide them with recommendations of the other professionals and to assist through the proposal and selection process. This could include the services of an accountant, attorney, actuary, investment consultant and health benefit provider companies.

The consultant's role is not limited to a fact finder. He or she should also be an educator. The consultant will work closely with the other professionals to bring about a smoothly operating fund. He or she should continually be bringing forth recommendations to improve administration and operation. The benefit consultant searches for sensible opportunities to decrease the operating costs so that participants receive the maximum benefit from contributions.

The following chapter will give the reader an overview of the consultant's role.

BENEFIT CONSULTING

Of all the professional advisors who serve the trustees of multiemployer funds, perhaps the most difficult to define in terms of the services provided is the consultant. This is largely true because there is no singular aspect of concern with which he or she deals. In fact, there is no listing of the specific responsibilities with which the consultant is charged. In a general sense it could be said that the consultant's concerns are all of those things that are not the specific concern of another professional advisor. However, the truth of the matter is that the consultant's responsibilities will vary significantly from one fund to another.

To some degree this is reflective of the experience and style of the consultant. To a greater extent it is reflective of how the trustees choose to use their professional advisors.

In addition to the variance in responsibilities cited above, the nature and objectives of pension funds, as opposed to health and welfare funds, present different issues and concerns that the consultant must address.

Consulting Services

Perhaps a better approach to evaluating the role of the consultant is to first take the broad brush approach of looking at those issues that a consultant might be involved with for various funds over the course of a year. Some of these, in random order, are discussed below.

Pension Fund Issues

- ▶ Plan design
  - —Eligibility rules
  - —Benefit service
  - —Vesting service
  - —Suspension of benefits/reemployment
  - —Benefits
  - —Levels and alternatives
  - —Spousal rights.

  Note: Design issues, parameters and alternatives are a byproduct of and constrained by the actuarial valuation.
- ▶ Prepare a written analysis of the comparative advantages of continuing as a defined benefit pension fund versus those of converting to a cash balance plan or a defined contribution plan.
- ▶ Develop cost estimates for benefit improvements, including accelerated entitlement.

- ▶ Develop bid specifications (RFPs) for submission to designated investment consulting firms and/or investment managers.
- ▶ Prepare a written comparative analysis of proposals received.
- ▶ Present the actuarial valuation to the trustees.

  Note: This is not true of all consultants, and the question of who presents the actuarial valuation to the trustees is usually a reflection of the policy of the actuarial consulting firm. In some firms the actuary rarely meets with the trustees to discuss his or her valuation. In other firms he or she alone would make such presentations. However, inasmuch as the valuation is prepared by the actuary regardless of who presents it, we refer you to Chapter 2, which discusses the role of the actuary.
- ▶ Assist the trustees in the selection of other professional advisors including preparing bid specs (RFPs) and conducting searches for trustees.
- ▶ Provide input on and drafts of trustee policy and position statements.
- ▶ Provide input on or drafts of summary plan description (SPD).
- ▶ Continually advise trustees of trends, judicial and legislative developments that might impact the trustees and/or the fund.
- ▶ Conduct ERISA compliance audits.
- ▶ Continually apprise trustees of industry trends and developments, products, services and innovations and their appropriateness.
- ▶ Assist trustees and administrator in development of member communication pieces.
- ▶ Assist in the preparation of administrative forms and procedures.
- ▶ Along with fund (legal) counsel, advise trustees on issues involving fiduciary responsibility.

It should be noted that while the foregoing listing of services was developed in contemplation of a defined benefit plan, it differs little from those services that would be provided for a defined contribution or annuity plan and even less from those services that would be provided for a cash balance plan. In both cases the difference is largely actuarial. However, once an annuity fund has been established, investment decisions made and administrative procedures established, the consulting services required on an ongoing basis are fewer than for other pension funds.

Health and Welfare Funds

- ▶ Design or revise eligibility rules.
- ▶ Design or revise benefits to meet trustee objectives consistent with fund economics.
- ▶ Develop cost estimates of benefit improvements or additions.

- ▶ Negotiate renewals with benefit providers and/or recommend obtaining competitive bids.
- ▶ Prepare bid specifications (RFPs) for submission to designated companies or individuals.
- ▶ Prepare a written comparative analysis of the competitive bids received.
- ▶ Prepare and review with trustees a written annual report of the total operation of the fund, including a line analysis of:
  - —Fund income versus expense
  - —Eligible employees versus employees for whom a contribution was made in the fund
  - —Hours worked in covered employment
  - —Administrative costs and their reasonableness
  - —Benefit costs
  - —Total costs
  - —Operating gain or loss
  - —Reserves—the nature and amount
  - —A projection of the coming year's probable experience and resultant operating gain or loss
  - —Conclusions and recommendations.
- ▶ Analyze and/or design cost-containment schemes.
- ▶ Analyze alternative health care delivery systems, PPOs, POS plans, HMOs, stand-alone prescription drug programs and formulary options, stand-alone dental programs and managed care programs.
- ▶ Continually advise trustees of new innovations, products and services and their appropriateness.
- ▶ Continually advise trustees of trends, judicial and legislative developments that might impact the trustees and/or the fund.
- ▶ Assist the trustees in the selection of professional advisors, including preparing bid specs (RFPs) and conducting the searches for the trustees.
- ▶ Provide input and drafts of trustee policy and position statements.
- ▶ Provide input for or drafts of SPDs.
- ▶ Conduct ERISA compliance audits.
- ▶ Advise trustees of insurance coverages that are mandated or are otherwise in the best interest of the fund and the trustees; prepare bid specs and analyze proposals received.
- ▶ Along with fund (legal) counsel, advise trustees on issues involving fiduciary responsibility.
- ▶ Assist trustees and administrator in development of member communication pieces.
- ▶ With respect to self-administered funds, assist in the preparation of administrative forms and procedures.

▶ Develop three-year economic projections and required employee contributions for bargaining parties (i.e., union and employers).

Again, it is important to recognize that the responsibilities of a given consultant, and thus the services he or she renders, might well vary significantly from one fund to another. This is very likely a reflection of the fact that one board of trustees chooses to get the consultant's input and advice on a broader range of issues than does the other board. It does not, however, mean that one board is right and the other wrong. Both could well be acting prudently based upon the facts and circumstances peculiar to their individual funds.

With respect to those trustees whose basic inclination is to maximize the use of their consultant, this predilection must necessarily be tempered by the depth and breadth of experience of the individual consultant. From time to time trustees may elect to retain a consultant with lesser experience when there is qualified staff support; and, in some cases, this works well. In other cases it simply hasn't worked; either the final input was inadequate or the cost was too high.

One service that can be tremendously important that has not been mentioned is coordinator of professional services. Some trustees find it very helpful to have one professional advisor coordinate not only all professional services but also, in essence, the total administrative operation of the fund. In this role the contemplation is that the coordinator will be sure the professional advisors work as a cohesive unit in the best interest of the fund, the covered participants and the trustees. A major focus is to see that all necessary or desirable work is done timely and cost effectively with a minimum of duplication of effort. Those trustees who take this approach feel it simplifies their job, provides them with added protection as fiduciaries and serves to hold costs at a reasonable level.

These trustees will more often assign this responsibility to the consultant. However, some will have fund counsel take on this responsibility while others will designate the administrator to fill this role. In any event, it should be noted that the majority of boards of trustees do not have any professional advisor serve in this capacity.

Consulting Firms

Recognizing that it only costs a few dollars to have cards printed that proclaim a person to be a consultant, how can you be sure you have a good one?

You never really know how good, or bad, a consultant is until you have him or her serve you for a period of time. Nonetheless, you have to at least make every reasonable effort to assure yourself that a consulting candidate is qualified before hiring him or her. So what do you do? What do you look for? How can you be sure?

Some people are very concerned with how long the company has been in business, but this is of very questionable importance. In theory the fellow who just bought his calling cards and set up his company last week might have been a consultant to hundreds of funds over a period of 20 or more years while working for other people. On the other hand, a given company might be economically strong and have been in business for 30 or more years while only entering the multiemployer benefit funds field within the last year.

The better gauge clearly is that of the experience of the individual consultant with whom you would be working. How long has he or she been in the multiemployer benefits field and in what capacity? What specific funds has he or she served as a consultant? (Get names and telephone numbers of trustees you can call relative to the quality of services he or she has been providing.) Can your other professional advisors provide input on his or her qualifications? The chances are that you can get all the background information you need in order to make an informed decision and with a minimum amount of time invested.

Is there an advantage or disadvantage to retaining a consultant who also serves as an administrator? There is no one clear answer to this question but, on the surface, it would appear there is a degree of conflict of interest. As a consultant, the individual will from time to time address issues concerning eligibility rules and possible changes as well as new or improved benefits and their effective dates. In some instances there will be one approach that will best handle the problem and at the same time be in much the best interest of the fund participants.

However, it might be contrary to the computer program or system the administrator uses for this and other funds. Thus, the administrator, as a consultant, might not even discuss it with the trustees or, if it is raised as a possibility, might arbitrarily shoot it down. Additionally, the volume of reading required to simply stay on top of legislation, proposed legislation, new regulations, court decisions, etc., etc., is such that few people have the time to perform both roles effectively.

In summary, though there are a few people who apparently do both jobs very well, as a general rule it is not in the best interest of the fund or the trustees to have the same person or firm serve in both capacities.

Duplication of Services

From time to time we hear expressions of great concern over the duplication of effort among professionals. Largely it is a trustee's concern lest the fund is being needlessly overcharged. On a few, rare occasions the complaint is voiced by one professional advisor about another.

Where the concern is that of one or more trustees, it should be discussed openly with the professionals. Very likely, a single discussion is all that will be needed to put everything in balance.

If one professional has a problem with another, he or she should lay it on the line with the "offender" and try to work it out. The last thing that a professional should do, unless it is critical to the successful running of the fund, is to worry the trustees with hurt feelings. Of course, if it is hurting the fund's performance, it must be reported to the trustees.

While we have raised this subject, we would hasten to assure the reader that only rarely does this constitute a problem. The reality is that some overlap is desirable. If the attorney does not have a sense of plan design, administration, etc.; if the consultant has no sense of the laws and the day-to-day operation of the fund and if the administrator is not concerned with plan design issues and legal constraints, the fund is in real trouble.

Selection of a Consultant

If your fund wants to change its consultant, how do you go about getting a good replacement?

Perhaps the first thing you and your fellow trustees should decide is how you want to use your consultant. If you want a technician who can address a limited range of specific issues at your direction, you probably don't need someone very heavy. If, however, it is your intent that he or she continually look to the total operation of the fund and all of its components from the dual standpoints of what is in the best interests of the fund and its participants, you need someone with significant multiemployer experience.

A very good source of names of consultants of all sizes and degrees of experience would be the other professional advisors you employ. Of course, you can also inquire of your international union or national management association or the people you know who serve as trustees of other funds. One thing that makes it easier is that like the other professional advisors, other than the administrator, there is no advantage to having a local consultant. Great numbers of funds have consultants who live hundreds of miles away.

One thing you might want to consider is setting aside the fancy brochures and the impressive biographies and simply talking with prospective consultants about how they would handle certain situations. Drop tough questions on them to see how they think on their feet. Do their responses make sense? Do they show a knowledge of multiemployer benefits?

Remember, it is not the people in the office but the consultant who will be with you in your meetings. It is that person who will either do the bulk of your work or explain a problem or concern to an associate well enough that the associate will do a good job. There continues to be a lot of truth in the old axiom "What you see is what you get."

Remember, in most states there are no licensing requirements for consultants. They are not regulated in any sense; even going to the big name firms is no real assurance. With the tremendous number of mergers and acquisitions in the benefits consulting industry over the past ten years, there can be significant variation from one office to another and variations of experience and qualifications in the same office. This is not knocking large firms; many are quite good overall. It is simply suggesting that whether you consider a large or a small firm, focus on the individual whose job it will be to work with and help you.

Finally, though the question had been raised for many years when ERISA was still a note on a memo pad on a senator's desk, there still is no one clear answer to how much you should pay a consultant. The only thing you can reasonably do is to ask questions about hourly rates of competing firms and individuals and seek a fixed fee of each firm for exactly the same, written list of services you want them to provide. However, there is nothing in the law that compels you to take the lowest bidder if the better qualified person's fee is reasonable.

Suggested Checklist for Request for Proposal (RFP)

1. Please provide a brief history of your company, its corporate structure, its ownership, its experience in employee benefits in general and its experience in multiemployer health and welfare funds or multiemployer pension funds specifically.

2. If you are selected as the fund's consultant, who would have primary consulting responsibility and who would interface with the trustees?

3. Please provide a biography or otherwise indicate the experience in employee benefits in general and multiemployer health and welfare or multiemployer pension funds specifically of that person or persons named in response to question 2.

4. Does your company have a relationship, either direct or indirect, with the trustees, the union, the employer association, any participating employer or any service provider to the fund? If so, please explain.

5. Are there any relationships that could be interpreted as your now being a party in interest with respect to the fund?

6. Do you serve in any capacity other than consultants or consultants and actuaries to any employee benefit plan or fund? If so, please define the other services provided (i.e., administrator, fund counsel, etc.) and identify the clients to whom these services are provided.

7. For how many multiemployer health and welfare or multiemployer pension funds does your company serve as consultant? For how many funds does the person (or persons) indicated in response to question 2 serve as consultant?

8. Please provide three multiemployer fund references with the following information:

    ▶ Name, size of fund

    ▶ Name, address and telephone number of a union trustee and of an employer trustee.

9. In providing consulting services, do you work on a fee-for-service basis?

10. Will you accept commissions as an offset in whole or in part against your fee?

11. Do you or would you accept expense reimbursements or any other form of monies from any service provider with respect to any insurance purchased by the fund?

12. Do you or would you provide the trustees with an annual statement of commissions, expense reimbursement or other form of compensation, either direct or indirect, which you receive with respect to insurance or other services purchased by the fund?

About the Authors

Herbert R. Ricklin
President
Ricklin-Echikson Associates Inc.
Millburn, New Jersey

Mr. Ricklin is president of a nationwide human resource consulting firm and has more than 30 years of experience in the human resources and labor relations fields. He is a professional trustee and independent fiduciary to Taft-Hartley benefit plans and the sole management trustee and acting chairman to the District 65 Pension and Education Plans. Mr. Ricklin is co-chairman of OCAW Local 8-86 Merck Employees Trust. He serves on the Board of Directors of the International Foundation as a Voting Director and is currently a member of the Trustees Committee. Mr. Ricklin has served on many other committees, and has been a speaker and author for the International Foundation and other employee benefit associations.

Donald A. Walters
President
Benefits Corporation of America
Trumbull, Connecticut

Mr. Walters has more than 30 years of experience in employee benefit plans, and has served as consultant to corporate, public sector and multi-employer clients. He has been active nationally as a speaker and has written a number of benefits-related articles. Mr. Walters is an Advisory Director of the International Foundation and previously served on the Investment Management and Actuaries/Consultants Committees. He has been a speaker at Foundation meetings since 1970.

Chapter 4

Health Care Service Providers

by Sherman G. Sass
and Andrew D. Sherman

Trustee's Perspective

by James T. Stamas

Over the years, I have served as a trustee for a local hotel workers fund in the Boston area and as a national trustee of the Hotel and Restaurant Industry International Union Health and Welfare Plan (HEREIU). In both of these roles, I have been all too aware of the need for knowledge of the issues swirling around health insurance plans. That trustees must rely on outside experts and providers to assist them in understanding how industry trends, legislative initiatives and health care economics can affect their funds and, in turn, their participants, is a given. In particular, trustees must get unbiased, high-quality professional assistance on a wide range of issues concerning the health care plans they oversee.

Because the health care market is becoming increasingly sophisticated and so many options exist in terms of benefits coverage, trustees must be able to rely on professionals who are clearly experts in their industry. Further, they must be comfortable that the advice they are receiving is unbiased. The best advisors have no economic or other ties to any particular medical care provider or insurance carrier. This will ensure that they receive objectively measured reports about the potential options that exist for covering their members.

Trustees need to know that their advisors are monitoring health care service providers continually. This in-

cludes a need for receiving regular reports and information about the specific providers dealing with their funds as well as for in-depth monitoring of the health care industry in general.

Trustees must also be kept informed about the trends and developments in the overall marketplace. They must be told about new ideas for the cost-effective provision of services. They must understand how these services can be delivered at the highest quality levels.

Trustees must be sure that they can rely on their professional advisors to regularly survey the marketplace. These advisors must also have the ability to provide detailed, sophisticated requests for proposals (RFPs) for health care coverage and to make recommendations as to when it is appropriate to seek competitive proposals. Then these advisors must be able to carry through the entire RFP process at the highest levels. This includes analyzing the bids, understanding the abilities and limitations of the bidders as well as the needs of the fund.

This chapter is all about that discipline. I am pleased to be able to introduce it because working with health care service providers has been an integral part of my experience as a trustee. My advice: Find a trustworthy, highly ethical consulting firm that has no audiences to please other than you, the trustees. Then use that consultant to provide you with all the assistance (and more) just mentioned.

I have worked closely with the authors of this chapter on all the issues covered. They have presented the challenges facing trustees in a clear and easily understandable manner. I encourage you to read this chapter with your fund in mind.

PREFACE

THE DRIVING FORCE BEHIND MUCH OF THE DYNAMISM IN THE HEALTH CARE INDUSTRY is the perception of the providers of health care services of what it is that will make them more attractive to the buyers—usually the group purchasers of services. Momentum is being fueled by the expectation that group health plan sponsors will continue to exert pressure for lower prices, better management of costs, higher quality and increased satisfaction of the consumers. The dramatic changes in ownership, control and management of health care service providers reinforces the need for plan sponsors to reexamine the basic elements of selecting, negotiating, contracting, monitoring and evaluating the performance of providers.

In short, reexamining relationships with providers is even more important in this current competitive climate characterized by large, often multi-armed provider organizations. Knowledgeable purchasers should be able to appeal to this competitiveness to gain more favorable terms and perhaps better services. This is important for plan sponsors to keep in mind.

Some trustees of jointly managed funds are only too aware that many providers in the managed care environment have little experience with multiemployer plans. Their exposure to corporate benefits programs often means that such providers will demand compliance with the practices that were honed in the corporate market without regard to the special practices of jointly trusteed plans. Frustrations can develop quickly as these different employment and plan cultures clash. As a result, plan sponsors of multiemployer plans must work closely with their consultants, administrators and counsel as they work through the process of selecting health care providers. This chapter should assist trustees in identifying the steps that must be taken.

This chapter is intended for the serious shoppers for health care service providers. These shoppers are on a purposeful course to select one or more provider organizations and are prepared to think through what they want to achieve through the changes they are contemplating. They will study what they have to do to implement money-saving programs including what changes may be required in the design of the present plan of benefits. They will weigh the expectations from managed care procedures against the members' possible reactions to limitations on their present freedom of choice of providers and procedures.

The material in this chapter will be treated under these topics:
 1. Plan design
 2. Administrative design and interface
 3. Payment method and risk bearing

4. Possible provider organizations
5. Request for information (RFI)
6. Request for proposals (RFP)
7. Selection
8. Contract negotiation
9. Implementation
10. Ongoing monitoring and periodic review and evaluation.

The centerpiece of this ten-part course of action is the request for proposal (RFP). Preceding the preparation of the specifications that accompany the RFP, trustees will have to make preliminary decisions on why and what they want to change; in what direction they want to turn; and with what intended results. The RFP will have to reflect this planning.

The RFP will also have to contemplate the initial implementation of the new program as well as the continuing relationship with the selected provider organization, all of which will be incorporated into a written agreement. The implementation includes the communication of the changed arrangements to the members; and the RFP and, later, the agreement will spell out the reciprocal responsibilities for this important work as well as other obligations and responsibilities of the parties. This will all be addressed in this chapter.

In the following discussion, whenever the term *trustees* is used, we are also referring to their professional advisors. Clearly, throughout the entire process covered here, the trustees should be looking to their consultants who are familiar with the general and specialty provider markets; and who will be reporting to and advising the trustees as to the plan design alternatives and financial constraints that will control their choices.

Plan Design

The key features of the plan of benefits will, of course, have to be presented to prospective bidding providers. Accordingly, the trustees will have to decide whether to proceed with the *current* plan or a *modified* design. Financial constraints are often the key consideration governing the choices of plan design. The trustees manage plans that generally receive contribution income at *fixed* negotiated rates; they are confronted with *rising* costs of benefits; and they appreciate that design features of the plan are a function of these costs.

The design features that will be reviewed start with the trustees' perception of the needs of the members and then focus closely on the impact of projected costs. The amount of the deductible and the percentages of plan and member payments, and/or flat dollar copayment levels per service, are also among the features to be determined. In addition, what incentives are to be provided to members to encourage and reward utilization of network providers? What will be the maximum out-of-pocket payment per member or per family unit? These are illustrative; the list is not meant to be exhaustive. It should be clear, even from this short list, that the trustees will also have to focus on the custom of various possible provider organizations in order to anticipate whether the preferences of the trustees for the plan design coincide with the provider's parameters. So, for example, some provider organizations may only accept flat dollar copayments per service; they may not be willing to retool to permit percentage coinsurance payments.

Other high level plan design issues must be reviewed as well. For example, where and how certain coverages are provided (e.g., is dental surgery covered under the medical plan or the dental plan); member complaints and appeals; payment of claims that may be payable under workers' compensation or by other third party payers.

The trustees must be alerted to the prospect of having to reconsider one or several plan features if a bidding provider offers an otherwise attractive proposal. But, even though the initial design decisions may be labeled as tentative at this prebidding stage, it is recommended that the trustees should not leave it entirely to the bidding providers to fix the total design. In short, working from an awareness of the constraints of some provider networks, the trustees should adopt an initial and complete plan design, at the same time allowing for the possibility of having to trim some features during negotiations with providers.

Administration Design and Interface

Here, too, the trustees will want to consider what alternative possibilities are available, and whether certain of these administration systems may not be compatible with the systems in place with some providers. To start, the trustees should determine what their preferences are and how strongly they want to maintain their position in light of what they find when shopping the market. For example, if a fund office or an independent administrator now does a very good job of processing and paying claims, and handling member questions and appeals, should the members' comfort level be challenged by a network provider that takes over these tasks? If the trustees expect members' reactions to be negative, then in addition to the perception that moving to a preferred provider system for obtaining health care services is itself a significant limitation of choice of provider, the trustees may decide to work out a way to retain the traditional administration or to segment administration services, say with member relations being retained by the fund office and with claims processing and utilization review delegated to the provider organization(s).

Anticipating another related issue, in the RFP, questions could be posed about whether the provider organization would permit the fund office or independent administrator to load onto their computers the provider organization system for processing claims (assuming the provider organization has a developed and proven system for screening and flagging claims as a key component of their claims management). Alternatively, could the fund office have full, online access to the provider's systems? Or, should the fund office handle only the member contact services, as long as the provider organization agrees that the fund office would have online, viewing (read-only) access to the claims processing files for each claimant?

The interface between the fund office and the provider office must also be anticipated with respect to eligibility determination. Will the provider organization have to check each claimant's eligibility, one at a time, with the fund office? Or, will the trustees grant the provider access to computer eligibility files? Would such an arrangement necessitate refashioning the current eligibility record system so that the provider could work with the file directly? And, what about plan records for eligible dependents? Many provider organizations familiar only with corporate plans have come to take for granted that each eligible member has completed and updated, as necessary, an enrollment form showing current address as well as a list of dependents with their ages. Fund office records, especially in industries with high turnover or seasonal employment, can never be expected to be complete and up to date with this information. How will this important administration matter be accommodated with a provider organization? And, will the provider agree to be responsible for its errors that result in benefits provided to ineligible individuals?

Multiemployer plans contend with retroactive determination of eligibility (and ineligibility). But providers, especially in respect of capitated programs, often are confounded by this practice, unless they are forewarned. To the extent that the provider organization determines eligibility and benefits coverage, the RFP should anticipate the fund auditing claims payments and such audits should also encompass compliance with eligibility, plan provisions and other limitations and exclusions.

Payment Method and Risk Bearing

Most trusteed plans have already decided whether their basic health plan is to be insured, self-funded or partially self-insured, that is if either a minimum premium type arrangement or other stop-loss mechanisms have been put into effect. Now, when shopping the market anew, whether for basic or for ancillary benefits, these issues should be revisited. The trustees should be informed about the range of options available, including alternative approaches for purchasing administrative services only, payments per capita or per claim processed or as a percentage of claims paid, and how a provider network compensates its participating providers—on a fee-for-service or capitation basis. Further, especially when inviting proposals from HMOs, the trustees should consider the consequences of community rating versus experience rating. Experience rating may be prospective or retrospective; or in the case of self-funding, experience rating may be said to be reflected immediately.

If there is an interest in HMOs, the trustees should include a question in the RFP about whether an HMO will agree to experience rate physician services; and further, how the HMO will value each physician service, especially when the physicians are on salary or on a capitation payment scheme themselves. These questions could also be raised as to other experience-rated, capitated plans, such as dental benefit programs.

At this stage, the trustees should express their preference for the payment and risk methods, allowing for possible reconsideration in the event an otherwise attractive proposal comes in with a different payment/risk component.

Possible Provider Organizations

The trustees will, of course, want to develop a list of possible vendors and providers and provider networks. Funds may choose to contract with one or more single source providers. Others may choose to contract directly with a number of individual providers, such as hospitals, ancillary service providers, physician group practices or even individual practitioners, thereby developing their own network. (The issues to be planned for in that scenario are not covered here; this discussion focuses mainly on selecting provider networks.)

Generally, a longer list should be assembled to start and then a process of elimination and selection should be followed, unless the search is very focused from the beginning, in which case the trustees will work with a short list of candidate organizations who are known to offer particular services or features.

The provider organizations are marketing all the time; the trustees will have received many unsolicited proposals. But, in developing a list of possible provider organizations, the trustees will surely look to their consultants and to their administrative staff. The consultants know the key provider organizations, either through direct experience on behalf of other client plans or through the professional literature. Most administrators will be familiar with the names of vendor organizations.

The problem is less in the preparation of an extensive list of possible providers but rather in how to winnow them down to a manageable, and at the same time appropriate, list of providers to be seriously considered. Who should get the request for proposal? Only those organizations that are qualified, experienced and likely to meet the carefully honed requirements that the trustees develop? What can be done in advance of mailing out the RFP to try to ensure that only qualified bidders are solicited by the trustees? The request for information (RFI) process considered in the next section can be helpful in eliminating potentially problematic providers.

Request for Information (RFI)

There are several approaches for screening prospective bidders according to criteria established by the trustees before going to a full-scale analysis of proposals responding to the RFP. Whichever route is chosen, the first steps require the trustees to fix the minimum criteria a prospective bidder must meet.

The trustees could prepare a request for information before the RFP is developed. This RFI would spell out the minimum requirements for a prospective bidder to be qualified to receive an RFP. The RFI could be sent to the long list.

Alternatively, the trustees could go directly to the RFP stage. If this is decided upon, then the minimum criteria for consideration should be highlighted at the outset along with a declaration that no bidder will be considered unless that bidder agrees to all the minimum requirements.

Another alternative to be considered in connection with mailing the RFP to the long list, is to invite prospective bidders to a bidders' conference. At this forum, the trustees or their representative or consultant would enumerate, then reinforce, each of the minimum requirements.

It is often a difficult task to define what it takes to qualify as a bidder to be taken seriously. Not only should the trustees identify the necessary experience that the bidder must have and the attributes that the bidders must enjoy, but the trustees should attempt to anticipate the conditions that either the trustees or the vendor might demand and to which the other party would not agree. Some of the fundamental items to be considered: the number and geographic distribution of the participating providers; previous experience with multiemployer plans of similar size; whether the network requires executed contracts with all participating providers; whether such agreements contain requirements that the trustees specify including, e.g., that specialist physicians be board certified or board qualified, that all practitioners maintain minimum levels of malpractice insurance, and that they agree to comply with utilization review and quality assurance standards.

The plan of benefits, or certain provisions of the plan, should be reviewed with an eye toward which features are *inviolate*, not to be adjusted to meet the demands of a new provider organization. These provisions should be set out in the minimum requirements list. For example, earlier in this chapter we referred to the importance trustees place on retaining the current functions of the fund office. Being explicit about this as a minimum demand could save a good deal of frustration later.

Further, the provider network should be asked to state explicitly how much of each participating provider discount the vendor is obligated to pass through to the fund. (There are still some network organizations that will not commit to passing along 100% of the discount. This requirement should be determined at the outset.) The trustees will want to know whether a network organization requires its participating providers to pay a fee of any sort to the network. The expectation that negotiated discounts will attach to member coinsurance amounts should be deemed a minimum standard. Multilingual member service personnel of the vendor is another possible requirement that may be made mandatory for any prospective provider. Adequate systems capability, e.g., toll-free telephone access, sufficient data storage and processing capacity, should also be minimum criteria.

It may not be possible to anticipate all contingencies, but the expense of negotiating a full-scale agreement that falls apart in the last stages because of some avoidable obstacle makes the attempt to follow this process worthwhile.

Request for Proposals (RFP)

We have already mentioned the required attributes and the minimum standards that the trustees will identify, perhaps in advance of the RFP, in order to eliminate unqualified vendors. Before presenting a long list of sections of a well-crafted RFP, we recommend some additional, basic issues that should be thought through and then reflected in the RFP. For example: What is motivating the trustees to engage a new vendor? Lower costs per service because of discounted fees and charges from the participating providers with which the vendor has contracted? Lower total costs because of the expected utilization review and management of utilization? Assuming both objectives, the RFP should be crafted so that each of these elements is identified and questions are posed that will realistically permit comparative projections of cost and savings among the competing vendors. The trustees may also identify these possible reasons to seek a change in providers: a search for higher quality of health care services, for improved access to care and for an increase in member satisfaction.

In all cases, however, the trustees will want to judge how the bidders propose to achieve optimum quality of necessary services, mindful that competition on the basis of cost controls alone could result in less than appropriate levels of quality care. The trustees may start with concern about exposure to liability when directing patients to a network of selected providers. But their motive for inquiring about quality goes beyond this defensive posture. Prudence will also move them to seek the best for the members that their dollars can buy.

Questions will have to be included that elicit responses that will permit a close analysis of price and quality. Comparison of other significant features, such as quality assurance and access (including matching the locations of the providers with the distribution of the covered members) must be anticipated by appropriate questions in the RFP.

The trustees will also want to resolve the rules for the bidding process:

for example, requiring a declaration of intent to bid; a fixed deadline date and time for submission of bids; whether bids are to be sealed and if the opening of bids is public; how to handle questions from prospective bidders and whether responses are to be forwarded to all; treatment of incomplete or incorrect bids; and whether late bids will be rejected completely.

Preparation of the RFP should also be grounded on important provisions to be included in the contract, whether or not they are "mandatory" items. Elements of administration, communication with members, complaints and disputes resolution, reporting details, audits and monitoring clauses as well as expected methods of periodic evaluation of performance once the contract is effective should be anticipated by questions in the RFP. For example, the type and frequency of reports should be spelled out.

With this background, here are brief descriptions of the sections of a typical RFP:

- Background and descriptive information including type of plan and governance (e.g., multiemployer plan with joint board of trustees); demographics of covered group including age, service, gender, dependents and geographic distribution; historical information including whether the plan was fully or partially self-insured or self-funded; and administration particulars
- Plan design, summary of current eligibility rules and plan of benefits
- Proposed plan of benefits if different than the current plan, along with proposed design changes and, if applicable, any changes in the eligibility rules
- Prior claims experience keyed to any changes in the benefits
- Proposed, or required, interfacing of administration functions, e.g., whether eligibility determination and member services will be retained by the fund office, or if the fund office will process and settle claims, using the provider's claims software
- Separate items that correspond to these (or other) criteria for evaluating the provider organization: prior relevant experience, size and geographic distribution of network, credentialing criteria, quality assurance program, standard contract with participating providers, detailed description of managed care features, price components for vendor services, description of fee and charges arrangement with network providers, individual practitioner turnover, percent of primary care providers with closed practices, i.e., not open to any newly enrolled patients, and fee schedules for reimbursing participating providers. References should be specified
- Minimum required criteria, that is, not meeting these would preclude further consideration, for example, demonstration of financial soundness

- Minimum contractual requirements including among other items minimum reports
- Other contractual requirements: term of contract; multiyear role guarantees; specified quality and performance standards; termination, subcontracting, insurance and indemnification provisions; and assumption of certain fiduciary responsibilities
- Forms for submitting financial proposal
- Optional: opportunity to submit an alternative proposal as to plan design, administration or financial arrangements
- Other provider network issues:
  (1) Credentialing of participating providers and monitoring of compliance, including licensure, board certification, professional liability insurance, standard contract with participating providers, etc.
  (2) Performance standards and quality assurance provisions and monitoring the network's compliance
  (3) System for complaint investigation, resolution and appeal and final determination.
- Other capitation and insured plan issues:
  (1) State licensure
  (2) Rating by appropriate rating agency, if applicable.

The RFP should be anticipated by previous consideration of what is basic and primary to the trustees and, of course, these decisions should be reflected in it. The RFP should also anticipate the negotiation of the agreement and the monitoring and evaluation of the performance that will follow the selection of the provider organization and the installation and implementation of the new provider program.

Selection

The trustees will cause the bids to be analyzed and the analysis to be presented in a written report. It will save time, and possible frustration, if the first category of review and analysis covers compliance with the minimum criteria. Even with the screening that was performed earlier, either by a preliminary RFI, or other means, some bids may come through now that could be ruled out in this first review stage. Other bids may be ambiguous as to some of these minimum standards and should be included in the analysis, highlighting however those responses that require clarification and could be problematic.

When the bids come in, analysis should be designed to give appropriate weight to several cost elements: the vendor's charges for administration and managed care services and the expected level of discounted charges for the participating providers' services. The cost of such managed care and utilization review services may be appropriately higher for a vendor that contends that more effective management of utilization can more than offset the higher expenses or even higher unit service costs.

Turning to the evaluation criteria, those responses such as fees and charges that can be quantified should be tabulated, and the results should be compared in a table that shows the rank order of the bidders. If fee schedules or rates for reimbursing providers for specific services or procedures were requested, these should be ordered according to rank. The same process should be followed with any other quantifiable responses. A comparison of the combined elements of costs should be presented, and this analysis should include, as applicable, risk-assuming alternatives and/or pricing alternatives.

A more daunting task is "ordering" responses for the nonquantifiable criteria, one-by-one, in sequence. Here, rank ordering is not appropriate, generally. Rather, each response should be presented, by topic, for each bidder, such as ownership, organization, assumption of liability, etc. This should be followed by a discussion that identifies the leading contenders according to the strength of their showing in respect to all of the criteria and raising doubts and questions that remain to be resolved for particular bidders. If there is a clear winner at this stage, that conclusion should be presented. It is likely to be more complicated, however; strong showings as to some criteria may have to be balanced against weaker responses to other measures.

At this point, the trustees may decide to invite the leading contenders for face-to-face interviews. Such sessions often serve to clear up issues about which the trustees have reservations and can also include some in-person negotiation with providers who have resisted complying with some significant demand or requirement. This process could mean the trustees relax a requirement or that the provider backs off. After any such negotiations, the trustees' demands and expectations should be summarized in a written statement to the bidder, confirming the bidder's commitment. Apart from any specific issues to be clarified or negotiated, interviews may be required for some trustees who believe they can only be comfortable dealing with a provider with whom they have met.

Even after the trustees select the successful bidder, some heavy negotiations may follow. Putting it all down in a written contract that is acceptable to both parties and to their legal counsel often reveals gaps in understanding, and may reveal matters not specifically raised in the RFP and in the bid. The written notice of the trustees' selection should advise that the award is subject to negotiating the contract and arriving at a final agreement.

Contract Negotiation

Theoretically, negotiating the contract should be a straightforward, efficient process. As was explained earlier, the RFP is the centerpiece of the selection process and all significant elements of the provider organization's obligations should be elicited there. Accordingly, responses should be found to the RFP questions in the responses received.

Once it appears that the deal is negotiated, the trustees should prepare a letter of intent setting forth all the significant substantive features of the arrangement, and the provider organization should be asked to sign as accepting and agreeing. These preliminaries, before contract language is proposed, may be protracted since the substantive terms of the deal may require more clarification.

Not all items will have been anticipated in the RFP or perhaps even in the next stage of clarifying or improving the terms offered in the proposal. Some controversial matters may not appear until proposed contract language is exchanged. The extent to which there may be difficulties in determining contract language depends on the context, especially the bargaining power of the parties. It may be assumed that all large provider organizations will have developed standard forms of agreement and that they will be insistent, when challenged, that uniformity of contracts is necessary for the efficient, predictable and equitable management of their business. But, certain clauses in standard contracts may be problematic for a fund. For example, a standard clause providing a limit of 30 days for retroactive reinstatement of eligibility could not be accommodated readily by most funds that work with a more liberal test, say 90 days, to allow for delayed receipt of employer remittance reports that show hours data.

Further, as applicable, providers may contend that their agreements have been filed with state regulatory bodies and are not readily amendable. Except for certain national and large interstate health trust funds, many plans may not choose to challenge these assertions. Most plans will find negotiating to be time consuming; but negotiating most of the terms of the contract, apart from the sections that spell out "exceptions" can be completed quickly. Large plans, however, may have their own strong preference for standard contract clauses that they have developed and that they argue should remain uniform among all their service providers. It is these situations that may result in protracted contract negotiations. It may be helpful to utilize a rider or addendum to explicitly supersede problematic portions of the agreement proper.

The timing of the contract negotiations—how long it will take to get to a signed agreement—is yet another element that many plans should consider early on, in setting a target date for implementing the new provider arrangement (whether or not a change in design accompanies the new provider system). Once the selection of a new provider organization is made, the members of the plan and even the trustees may well expect that the new arrangement will be operative shortly; and there could be pressure to announce and implement the new program quickly. Can the trustees go ahead and implement the new provider arrangements before the contract is executed? The risks are apparent: The trustees may lose most of their bargaining power once the plan is put into effect.

Here is an overview of the sections of an agreement between a plan and a provider organization. After the preamble or recitals section, and a section setting out the definition of terms, it is helpful to collect in one section all the obligations and responsibilities of the provider organization, and to do the same for the responsibilities and obligations of the plan. Following is a sample list of contract items that set forth the provider organization's obligations in a comprehensive service agreement:

- ▶ Providing access to a network with the geographic distribution, sufficient size and adequate quality and diversity of providers
- ▶ Binding each participating provider through a provider agreement with the vendor
- ▶ Credentialing providers
- ▶ Monitoring compliance of the providers regarding licensure, insurance, quality of care issues, plus the consequences of finding noncompliance
- ▶ Explaining the grievance and complaint processes
- ▶ Spelling out the repricing of claims based on provider agreements
- ▶ Providing utilization management services—either directly or as coordinated with other organizations
- ▶ Requiring adherence to payment schedules, for example, no balance billing
- ▶ Setting up requirements regarding in- or out-of-network referrals
- ▶ Establishing quality assurance programs and standards
- ▶ Providing specified reports, on a set schedule
- ▶ Complying with federal and state laws
- ▶ Providing all necessary administrative services
- ▶ Providing updated directories
- ▶ Providing communications materials as well as assistance with enrollment meetings
- ▶ Listing member services functions
- ▶ Designating dedicated key personnel
- ▶ Establishing penalties for noncompliance.

On page 85, a sample table of exhibits is provided showing the form used in a comprehensive services agreement. This table provides further delineation of the obligations of the provider organization.

Following is a sample list of contract items which set forth the fund's obligations:

- ▶ Determining eligibility and verifying eligibility to participating providers

- Processing and paying claims directly to participating providers
- Paying "clean" claims within a specified period
- Compensating the provider organization for estimates and reconciliation adjustments
- Encouraging participants to utilize participating providers.

In this example, the fund processes claims and pays providers. In other arrangements (especially with integrated utilization review and utilization management services conducted by the provider organization) the processing of claims and paying of participating providers may be retained by the provider organization.

The agreement should then provide for the required types and level of insurance to be maintained by the provider organization, including general liability, professional liability, and errors and omissions insurance. This section should also provide for indemnification obligations of both parties and mutual hold-harmless language. Legal counsel should be concerned with all sections of the agreement but especially with the language of these clauses.

The plan, or its designee, should be granted the right to conduct audits of the provider's files and records to monitor performance of the stipulated obligations of the organization. Another section should address the maintenance, inspection, ownership and release of administrative and medical records as they pertain to this plan. The confidentiality of patient records in respect to both parties should be addressed. Subcontracting by the provider organization should be subject either to prior consent or prior notice, as the plan is able to negotiate.

The term of the agreement should be specified, together with provision for renewal. Termination with or without cause before the expiration of the term (within the prescribed ERISA limits), and what constitutes cause and how to cure a claimed material breach, should all be spelled out. Further, the responsibilities of the provider for the run out of claims incurred before the termination should be addressed, along with whether the administrative fees under the agreement continue in effect during the run-out period (or whether current fees include run-out services for a prescribed period). The agreement should also include sections on resolving disputes, amendments, assignment, to whom notices must be sent, etc.

Usually it is considered good form to avoid using exhibits to set forth the obligations of either party, but they can be appended to amplify or illustrate detailed procedures pursuant to the obligations that are set out in the agreement. A review of the appendix to this chapter will show that sample agreements' exhibits generally conform to this style.

Following close review by legal counsel to the trustees of the final agreement, whatever the nature of the negotiations leading up to the final form of agreement, the trustees and the provider organization will execute the agreement. Meanwhile, assuming that the parties have waited for such signing before making the new arrangements effective, preparation for the implementation of the agreement should already be underway.

Implementation

The complexity of implementing the new agreement is a direct function of whether the arrangement is an off-the-shelf program for the provider organization, and, if not, how much customization is necessary. In some cases, what is routine for the provider organization may be new and unusual for the plan as well as for the participants; and preparing for the new arrangement may involve adjusting familiar procedures (and attitudes) to accommodate and adapt. Accomplishing these changes at the fund may take much effort and time.

The installation of the new provider arrangements and/or plans of benefits should have been anticipated before the agreement was executed. Here, too, special needs should have been identified by the trustees in the RFP; and the corresponding demands should have been raised in negotiating the deal and the agreement. Cutting across the discrete steps for implementing the program summarized here are some pitfalls encountered in the early stages of installing a new managed care program. For example, if the new program is offered as an alternative to an existing one and the participants will have to make an annual election, it is often very difficult to get people to do it. Also, in capitated programs where people have to select primary care providers, they often fail to do so, and this can result in excess payment to the vendor because it will still receive payment from the client but will not have to pay out a portion of that payment to providers.

Some of the key issues and steps that have to be accomplished in implementing a new arrangement include finalizing a timetable with the provider, announcements and more detailed communication with participants and establishing a set of protocols and procedures for addressing general questions as well as specific concerns and problems that may arise.

A critical part of this process is the determination of a specific schedule with the provider for the implementation of a new provider and/or new benefit structure. This timetable must include setting up and testing the data interfaces with the fund office, completing any elements of the benefit program or provider network that may be new or different, announcing—and explaining—all changes to plan participants, arranging for a smooth and orderly transition from a prior provider (including the payment of any of the run-out claims) and finalizing the exact implementation and changeover dates.

Effective communication with participants is central to the success of the implementation process and perhaps to the success of all the changes.

Communication materials for distribution to the members have to be drafted, in clear concise presentation. A series of options will need to be considered, and decisions will have to be made about the timing of distribution, the media of presentations, use of other announcement approaches (posters at worksites, payroll stuffers, audio or videotapes, features or articles in newsletters, etc.), how and when to modify the summary plan description, and whether to schedule special membership meetings with material prepared for such sessions. The trustees should also consider other communications items, including the languages of the descriptive material and whether the announcements should be combined with other information on plan design, benefit changes or other issues.

Another important planning step is the determination of and the decisions on where to direct members' questions. The trustees should review and consider who will answer participants' initial questions to assure timeliness and consistency of responses. A next step is to set forth where members are to be directed for additional information and guidance. Certain questions such as eligibility, effective dates and benefit options could probably best be answered by the fund office. Other questions, such as those about accessing a panel of providers, or obtaining benefits might best be answered directly by the provider. A system for directing and then tracking and resolving member complaints and more difficult questions should be established upfront.

Additional issues and questions that must be addressed in an implementation process include: Are there differences in the program from the provider's conventional arrangements so that the organization has to prepare special instructions for the participating providers and for the organization's staff? Does the fund office staff require special training beyond familiarity sessions? Does either party have to hire additional, perhaps specialized, personnel to administer the new arrangement? Does either party have to purchase and install new equipment required for the integrated administration of the new program, particularly computer hardware and software, and perhaps dedicated telephone lines?

The fund should review whether provider insurance policies have to be augmented. Do provider licenses have to be perfected or state filings amended? Has each party selected a key person to coordinate the implementation and to be the principal trouble-shooter, to handle and resolve the initial bugs that may appear?

The context determines how extensive the planning and execution of each stage must be in this process of implementing the new arrangement. Awareness of the particular issues of installing and setting up a new provider program will not only assist the trustees during the RFP and contract stages, but will also permit the trustees to make reasonable estimates of realistic target dates and additional work and costs for program changes and implementation schedules.

Ongoing Monitoring and Periodic Review and Evaluation

It is a standard course of business and a key responsibility of the trustees to assure the ongoing monitoring and regular periodic evaluation of all organizations and entities providing services to the fund and its participants. A primary purpose for solid, regular monitoring and review is to assure compliance with the current contract and to determine on an ongoing basis whether the provider is meeting the expectations of the trustees and the plan participants. It is important to track the delivery of services to members, the resolution of member complaints and overall member satisfaction level and to measure this experience against set benchmarks. Further, the trustees will also need to determine if there should be changes in a contract or arrangement midterm, or what changes to implement at the end of one contract and the start of another. Projecting ahead to the end of the contract term, the trustees will be able to make the appropriate determination of whether to renew a contract, to renegotiate the terms of the contract and the delivery of services, or to undertake a new bidding process.

Regular standard reports on contract compliance, claims, utilization levels and patterns, capacity and quality should be required by contract. The completion and delivery of these reports should be tracked. These reports will enable the trustees to measure results for compliance and meeting expectations. Such reports might include updated information of the size and distribution of network providers, the delivery of services, claims processing and other waiting times (e.g., days to get an appointment), and certain measures of quality tracking and control.

Claims reports are another useful tool for contract compliance and also for evaluation of benefit programs generally, as well as plan design, cash flow and budget projections. These reports should include in-network and out-of-network utilization (by percentage of members and by dollars of benefits payments), number of referrals, and claims experience (in a format comparable to earlier periods). With the specific example of health insurance coverage, claims data should be broken down by hospital, physician, ancillary services (perhaps also ambulatory surgery and emergency room utilization) together with data and information on diagnoses, age and sex distributions. Separate detailed reports might also be requested in a number of ways, e.g., member/dependent, COBRA participants, retirees, etc.

In addition, depending upon the program, the trustees may wish to retain third parties to conduct additional review and evaluation. This could take the form of an onsite audit of the provider, various types of desk or record audits, or the use of a specialty firm to review data and claims extracts. Onsite services could include claims audits (accuracy, speed, results) or actual peer review audits of services delivered. Claims data audits could result in certain conclusions about utilization patterns, identify areas where certain types of health promotion or disease prevention/screening programs could be used or where plan design and benefit modifications might be called for.

The trustees may also want to consider organizations that issue accreditation reports, such as the National Committee for Quality Assurance (NCQA) and others. Data and utilization reports may be very helpful to trustees. Such information can be used to make comparisons with expectations, from plan to plan and over time. In recent years, the level of standardization and the ability to make accurate comparisons have been enhanced and improved. For example, the HEDIS (Health Plan Employer Data and Information Set) developed by NCQA provides standardized measures for HMOs of quality, member access and satisfaction, utilization, finance and health plan management. Other standards reporting methods are becoming more accepted as well.

Further, the provider should be expected to record member questions and complaints. The responses and resolution of these issues should also be tracked and a summary report provided to the trustees. The importance of this system is not only to assure that each problem is resolved but also to be able to detect emerging patterns that require basic changes, modifying procedures and practices to improve member satisfaction.

Regular reviews should also be undertaken with respect to ongoing administration, system interfaces, the satisfaction level of the fund office staff, the resolution of administration problems (eligibility, member access, communications) and other issues. The fund office staff should be able to contact designated people at the provider; monitor and track problems as well as their resolutions; and should be involved in this review. The fund office staff will pay a key role in making needed changes and improvements.

The evaluation of the communications with members should be reviewed and analyzed. Has the information been received and understood? What has the volume of questions been? Have certain questions been asked repeatedly? Are the utilization levels what were expected? Are there known external reasons for variations on utilization levels, say a significant change in membership levels or demographics? A result here could be to design and distribute additional or different types of employee communications.

Attempts should also be made to evaluate overall participant satisfaction levels. This might be accomplished by again reviewing the number of member complaints and the success at resolving outstanding issues. Another approach could be through surveys, either broad or focused.

The process is now completed. As the expiration of the contract approaches, the trustees, together with consultants and staff, review compliance with contracts, utilization, administration interfaces, member satisfaction, plan design, budget constraints and other items that may be relevant. After analyzing and interpreting this experience, a series of decisions follow that may include negotiations with the current provider or providers; considering benefit design modifications; soliciting information about other prospective providers that could replace or be added to the benefits program; and determining when to undertake a new bidding and RFP process.

Appendix

The sample table of exhibits shown below illustrates what could be included in a comprehensive services agreement.

Sample Provider Contract Table of Exhibits

Exhibit A   Benefits Description Document

Exhibit B   PPO Provider Directory (as of contract effective date)

Exhibit C   PPO Standard Provider Agreements

    1. Hospital Participation Agreement

    2. Physician Participation Agreement

    3. Ancillary Health Care Service Provider Agreement

Exhibit D   Physician, Hospital and Ancillary Health Care Provider Credentialing Criteria

Exhibit E   Health Plan Quality Assurance Program

Exhibit F   Claims Processing Process

Exhibit G   Audit Protocols

Exhibit H   Liability Description

Exhibit I   1. Utilization Review Document

    2. Prior Authorization and Concurrent Review Document

Exhibit J   Managed Care Mental Health Program

Exhibit K   Managed Care Retail Prescription Drug Program

Exhibit L   Management Reports

Exhibit M   Quarterly Results Report

Exhibit N   Claims Lag Report

About the Authors

James T. Stamas
President
Stamas Partners
Andover, Massachusetts

Mr. Stamas provides consulting services in organization planning, executive search and human resources on a domestic and international level. He has 30 years of management experience, which has provided him with unique experiences in organizational planning and human resources management. Mr. Stamas has served as chairman of both the Human Resources Council and Labor Relations Committee of the American Hotel and Motel Association. In 1995, he became dean of the School of Hospitality Administration at Boston University.

Sherman G. Sass
Senior Consultant
The Segal Company
Boston, Massachusetts

Mr. Sass recently retired as senior vice president and director of The Segal Company. He has extensive experience in working with providers on behalf of jointly trusteed clients. During his 40 years with Segal, he was an advisor to single employer, public employer and multiemployer retirement and group insurance plan clients. He currently works as a senior consultant for several of the company's largest clients. Mr. Sass has spoken on employee benefits at International Foundation educational meetings and for other groups and has written a number of employee benefits articles.

Andrew D. Sherman
Vice President,
 Benefits Consultant
The Segal Company
Boston, Massachusetts

Mr. Sherman provides consulting services to public and private health and pension benefit plans. He serves as a consultant to numerous corporations, universities and other nonprofit entities as well as to a number of collectively bargained health, pension and annuity funds. Mr. Sherman is an expert in innovative plan design for health and welfare funds. He has been widely quoted in the press and has written a number of articles on employee benefit issues.

Chapter 5

Administration Services

by Robert J. Cardinal, CEBS

Trustee's Perspective

by Jack T. Hayes

Readers are fortunate that Robert Cardinal is willing to share his considerable experience with trust funds as the author of the administration services chapter.

In my experience as a 25-year trustee, several areas leap out as being vital. We all like to sleep well at night, and excellence in administration provides that opportunity.

Administration is the conduit through which all parties link in providing essential services to participants.

Proper administration identifies the transactions performed along with maintaining the myriad of details required by good business practices, as well as the law.

Sound administration assures a continuity of action essential to dispense fair treatment for all. A steady hand at the tiller is the best assurance that influential forces do not detour a proper course of action.

With the plethora of administration services resources available, no trust should accept less than excellence in the areas of communications, eligibility determination, record maintenance and auditing, claim handling and appeals services.

A fund is best known for the quality of its administration services. Often this determines the way its many publics perceive it to be.

If service is dispensed thoughtfully, fairly and in an understanding way, it will be well considered. Each trust should be striving for this goal.

There ought to be no difference in viewpoint between either labor or management fund trustees that providing the most appropriate administrative services at a reasonable cost is a basic criterion for prudent trustees.

Finally, while the administration service duties of a trust can be assigned, the legal responsibility cannot. We as trustees stand together, and the buck stops with us. That is the best case for seeking excellence in this area.

INTRODUCTION

Administration services can best be thought of as your hired office staff or the trust's "back office." The trust funds that you serve, whether they be Taft-Hartley or public funds, are very complex operations. This complexity grows with each passing year and the advent of new regulations and case law that impact your trust operations. This requires an organization with expertise and experience in these particular types of administration services in order to protect the trust and the trustees.

Your trust administration office is the first line of communication with your members and their families. For health and welfare plans, the administration office is your link to the medical providers who serve your participants. This demands staff qualified and capable of accurately communicating benefit information to your participants without making improper commitments on behalf of the trust.

It would be well to clear up at the start of this chapter the confusion over the use of the word *administrator*. Unfortunately when Congress passed the ERISA legislation in 1974 they used the term *plan administrator* as the title for a named fiduciary within the act. This has caused confusion ever since. Plan administration for Taft-Hartley and some public plans had been going on for years before ERISA was conceived. Normally the *plan administrator* as denoted in the ERISA legislation is the board of trustees or the public agency sponsoring the plan. The services that we are discussing in this chapter are sometimes referred to as plan management, claim management or administration services. This is to distinguish them as ministerial duties that are performed at the direction of the trustees and not generally allowing discretion to these providers of services. As is discussed in another section, a provider of administration services may become a fiduciary by virtue of a particular action or the consequences of that action.

Contracting Arrangements

There are two ways that trust funds arrange for administration services. Trusts can either employ a staff or contract with a professional service firm called a third party administrator (TPA). These two methods are normally referred to as salaried administration and contract administration, respectively. It is possible to divide a trust's administration services between the two methods. The services should be identical between the two methods, and the choice is one for the trustees. There are advantages and disadvantages to each method, and the choice is often dictated by the size and complexity of the trust fund and the philosophy of the trustees. Both work successfully and both will be discussed here.

The use of salaried administration provides a totally dedicated staff who work only for the trust and whose first loyalty lies with the trust as their employer. The trust is free to select and utilize whatever systems and computers they desire, and many trusts feel this gives them additional flexibility. Your trust must of course be of a size to support the special skills and qualifications required. Some of the disadvantages stem from these same factors. The trust is now an employer and responsible for the rental or ownership of an office, equipment and supplies. The trust now has an employment relationship with the key staff rather than a professional contractual one; and, in the event of poor performance in some area, they may find it more difficult to make changes or corrections. In the case of a small or medium sized trust, the trustees should carefully consider how to obtain the highly qualified services occasionally required for a particularly complex medical claim or a difficult pension question. The TPA is expected to have this capability available on its staff. The small trust salaried staff may not be able to justify keeping this expertise on their staff for the rare occasions when the special knowledge is required. The trustees should assure themselves that arrangements have been made to obtain this expertise when required. Some trusts have contract or retainer arrangements with consultants or specialists to handle these situations. All trusts using salaried administration services should be certain that the plan manager attends all the necessary professional seminars and training offered by organizations such as the International Foundation of Employee Benefit Plans, and obtains professional qualifications and certifications such as CEBS or equivalent.

Those trust funds utilizing contact administration usually issue a request for proposal (RFP) to several experienced and qualified TPAs, obtain proposals and interview finalists before awarding a contract to the selected firm. This process will be discussed in greater detail later in this chapter. The contracted TPA is then responsible for providing office space, equipment, supplies and systems. The TPA is responsible for providing adequate professional and clerical staff *as well as* the backup and support staff required. The ability to accomplish this and the qualifications of the staff should be a major criteria for your selection. Many trust funds are now including performance criteria in their contracts, which if not met must be corrected or the trustees have the option to move the contract.

In summary, either method will work. Trusts utilizing salaried administration have complete control over their staff; however, they also have a longer term and legally restricted arrangement with the staff as their employers. Those trusts utilizing contract administration have less day-to-day control over the operations of their trust office, but they also have the flexibility to change administrators or any of the staff without worrying about an employment contract. This is the problem of the TPA who is the employer. Often the TPA can assign the individual to another account or job for which they may be better suited.

Administration Services

Administration services can be divided into those services that are generally required by all funds, those required by most funds, and those that are specific to a particular type of fund (e.g., health and welfare). Let us first discuss those usually required by all funds.

It is the administrator's responsibility to operate the entire process of billing and collecting contributions from employers. Normally, each month a remittance form is sent to each employer listing the members last known to be working for that employer together with the contribution rates preprinted for the appropriate fringe benefits for each member. It is the responsibility of the employer to (a) add or subtract member names to accurately reflect that particular month's activities, (b) enter the correct number of hours (or other units) for each reported member, (c) extend out the calculations with totals and (d) remit the form and a check to the trust office (usually via a bank lockbox).

The administrator then has the responsibility of reviewing and balancing each employer's submittal. For those reports with shortages or overages in the payments, either error notices or delinquency notices must be prepared and sent immediately. Each trust should have a delinquency procedure, including ground rules for the administrator as to what is a mathematical error and what is a delinquency. The administrator is responsible for monitoring and conforming to these delinquency procedures. This includes notifications to trustees and trust counsel, followup notices, notices to members if required, notice of requirement to post bonds, etc.

The administrator through its accounting department must then ensure that all funds received and all hours reported are correctly recorded and posted to the accounts for each employer, for each plan or fund, and of course for each member's account.

For almost any fund, the administrator should issue periodic financial reports to the trustees. For most funds these will be issued either monthly or quarterly. These reports should show both a balance sheet and an operating statement with comparisons to prior year and prior period reports. The administrator should point out any anomalies and call the trustees' attention to actual or potential problems. For many funds, the trust consultant and/or actuary will also comment on these reports and may present the numbers in a different manner to the trustees. Trustees should ensure that no matter how they are presented, the reports all stem from the same numbers from the administration office; or the trustees should have a clear understanding of how and why the numbers are different. An example of the latter are investment gains and losses that may be recognized differently in an actuarial report than in a financial statement and may be different in a consultant's report because the consultant may have the latest results, while the administration is obligated until the bank trustee reports the investment results.

As mentioned earlier, the administrator must also keep the trustees current on the status of all delinquent employer accounts regardless of what kind of trust is involved. Trustees also have an obligation to inform their fellow trustees and the administration office if they have any knowledge or reason to suspect that a particular employer might be having more than the normal problems with paying bills and should be followed more closely than normal.

Another responsibility common to all funds is the paying of fund expenses. The administration office should receive all bills or expense accounts. Each request for payment should be reviewed against trust standards and for correctness and reasonableness. The trustees should have a policy stating which bills the administration office can authorize payment for and which, if any, require approval by the trustees prior to payment. For example, normal retainer fees for a consultant or trust counsel might be approved by the administrator but any special fees or charges such as the annual actuarial evaluation or charges for a lawsuit might require trustee approval. Trustees should also have a published expense policy for trustees' expenses, and the administrator should review expense reports against this policy before approving them for payment.

Checks must then be cut for each expense/account combination. It is possible that a single expense will require two or more checks if it is divided between two or more trusts. Examples of these are trustee expenses to attend trust meetings or seminars when the trustees serve more than one trust fund. The authorization to sign checks should also be subject of a trust policy. Some or all may be signed by the administrator and then reported to the trustees. Others or all may have to be signed by one or more trustees. If trust policy is to require that trustees sign all or most checks, it is advisable to have the administrator authorized to sign in an emergency or authorized to sign certain time sensitive checks such as insurance premiums, government fees, etc. Unfortunately, trustees are not always conveniently available when the checks need signing. The trustees can require reports and retroactive review of these payments, but you are running a business and certain payments do have to go out in a timely manner.

Generally, all funds will require some form of reporting and disclosure to government agencies and participants. This is also a responsibility of your administrator. These reports are often prepared in conjunction with other professionals. For example, the 5500 report to DOL and IRS each year must include the actuarial evaluation for a pension fund and a copy of the audit for all ERISA funds. If 990 forms are submitted to the IRS, these are often prepared in conjunction with the auditors.

Regardless of what kind of fund you are a trustee for, you will occasionally (or often) find the need to communicate with your participants and or the employers. The coordination and often the preparation of these communications are the responsibility of your administrator. This usually includes the distribution and mailing of these communications. If the mailing is to be done by someone else such as an HMO or insurance company the administrator should be responsible to prepare the up-to-date mailing labels to be used by the mailer. No matter how this is coordinated, the trustees should require and the administrator should ensure that trustees see and approve any communication that goes out to members or employers. In addition the administrator should ensure that each trustee and union office receives a copy of the complete packet before the recipients receive theirs so they can be prepared to answer questions.

It is prudent and in fact now seems to be required by AICPA audit standards that trust funds conduct periodic payroll audits. Again, the trust fund should have a written policy regarding these audits and their frequency. It is not unusual to have them on a three- or five-year cycle (one-third or one-fifth each year) and in addition whenever any trustee or combination of trustees, depending upon your policy, requests an audit of an employer. The purpose of these audits is to ensure that the trust funds are receiving all the funds that are due and that members are receiving credit for all the hours to which they are entitled. It is the responsibility of the administrator to at least coordinate these audits. Many times the administrator also has the capability to perform the audits. If the payroll audits are performed by the administrator, the auditors will usually review the audit procedure and some of the audit files and work papers each year. Periodically, the administrator should either prepare or have prepared a report to the trustees showing the audits performed and the results as well as the expenses.

In addition to the payroll audits, each trust should have an annual audit by a qualified CPA firm and a report presented to the trustees. While the audit is covered in another chapter of this book, the administrator is responsible for preparing all the necessary data for the auditor. Often the administrator is required to send out the confirmation letters as required by the auditor. The administrator is responsible to ensure that the trust office has the necessary internal controls so the trust will have a nonqualified or "clean" audit opinion. The administrator is responsible to ensure that all transactions throughout the year are conducted and prepared in such a way as to produce the audit trails required by an auditor in order to review the trust operations.

Most trust funds will require some form of calculation and records to determine eligibility for benefits. The exception will be apprenticeship funds, joint labor-management funds, hiring hall and similar types of funds not requiring individual eligibility. The administrator is responsible for the calculation, recording, tracking and reporting of all eligibility.

In the case of health and welfare funds, eligibility for medical, dental, vision and similar benefits will usually be determined based upon the hours or dollars or other units reported for a particular month. Musicians for example sometimes use gigs and waiters or bartenders may use shifts. For convenience we will talk about hours, but it could be any unit appropriate to the trade or craft. Usually a minimum number of hours or dollars are required before an individual is eligible. In order to make the system run more smoothly, many funds use lag months where the hours or dollars reported for a particular month grant eligibility for a period one or two months in the future. For trades or crafts with normal fluctuations in available hours, trust funds often utilize hour or dollar banks. These banks, which are common in the construction trades, allow a member to accumulate hours or dollars earned that are above the minimum required for eligibility and use these at some future date when his or her hours or dollars may not meet the minimum. A maximum is usually established by the trust as to how many hours or dollars may be held in the bank. Trustees should ensure that the trust financial statements reflect the liability of the trust for the benefits that are covered both in the future by the lag month system and by the hours accumulated in the hour banks.

In the case of medical and associated benefits, it is the responsibility of the administrator to provide the proper eligibility information to all the necessary outside providers, including insurance companies, HMOs, PPOs, prescription drug plans, dental plans, vision service plans, and alcohol and drug abuse plans. If the administrator pays any or all of these claims themselves, then the eligibility information must be entered into the claim system so that member claims can be processed in a timely manner. In many cases this eligibility information is also entered into a system that is available on line in the union offices so members can verify eligibility at their union local or employer's office.

A most important responsibility of the administrator is to respond to the numerous requests from hospitals and other medical and dental providers for coverage or eligibility information. This is a most critical area because if the information is given improperly, the trust could potentially be responsible for a large claim that it would not otherwise have covered. This is especially important in the fringe areas of the plan or medical practice. The provider offices in these areas (such as plastic surgery) will almost always call and are very careful to ask the question in the manner most likely to elicit a favorable response. The trustees should ensure that the administrator's personnel protect the plan through the use of caveats stating that the information given was based upon the information given by the office, and final determination of coverage can be made only after the claim information is received. It is very useful if the administrator sends a fax of this caveat with the pertinent information at least to hospitals.

Determining the member's eligibility for pension benefits is different from health and welfare but an equally important responsibility of the administrator. Pension eligibility has many facets, all of which can be answered only after a thorough review of years of accumulated data regarding hours worked, dollars earned and contributions made. The administrator must first determine that the applicant meets basic criteria such as age and years of service. The administrator then establishes that the applicant has enough vesting credits to be fully vested in the plan or, if not, what percentage of vesting they have. Finally, the administrator applies the formulas determined by the trust document to determine the level of benefit for which the participant is eligible. This is the starting point for completing an options report for the participant, showing benefits with and without joint and survivor benefits or with partial joint and survivor benefits. Other special plan features such as "pop-up" benefits are also shown on this option form. If the spouse is younger or older than the applicant, the factors must be adjusted in accordance with the actuarially developed formulas.

Health and Welfare Plan Services

Some of the duties of the administration office that are specific to particular types of funds include those for medical and related benefits. Eligibility records now require a whole new level of complexity. Eligibility must now be maintained for each dependent. Eligibility must include the status of divorces and/or marriages for spouses. Records should also be maintained of dependent ages to monitor when dependent children reach the age when they must be full-time students in order to maintain eligibility or when they reach the age when they are no longer eligible and must be offered COBRA benefits.

For those dependent children who are in the age range specified by your plan document where they must provide proof of full-time student status, the administrator must provide special services. This age range is often 19 through 23 or 25 years of age. Usually the plan rules require that a student be enrolled in an accredited institution for at least 12 hours of study per semester or quarter. The administrator is responsible for ensuring that a current student status form from the school is on file. Otherwise all claims must be held up until a correct form is received from the school. Usually the spring status form is allowed to carry the student's eligibility through the summer until the fall term.

Some time ago, a federal budget act instituted new requirements for coverage for plan participants who otherwise might not have been allowed to remain on your trust fund's health plan. This law is referred to as COBRA. When a member **or** a dependent loses coverage from your plan under certain conditions, your plan must continue to offer them coverage in the same manner as for an active participant. You may charge them up to 102% of the full cost of an active member's coverage. These circumstances are called *qualifying events*. For a dependent, this includes loss of coverage through divorce, death of the spouse, or reaching the age of majority when a plan no longer provides coverage as discussed in the prior paragraph. Under these circumstances, coverage must be extended for up to 36 months. For a member and associated dependents, this event can be the member's loss of coverage through loss of employment or insufficient hours to qualify for coverage. This circumstance requires that coverage be offered for 18 months. Under certain circumstances involving disability, this coverage may have to be offered for up to 29 months.

This is not an attempt to recite all the intricacies of COBRA but to explain that the administration office is responsible to administer the COBRA law, monitor all the records, send out the required notifications, bill the participants if this is trust policy and collect the premiums. From all this, the administrator determines COBRA eligibility, notifies providers and pays claims. The administration office is responsible for ensuring that when COBRA eligibility expires, the individuals are notified in advance and removed from the eligibility records.

A recent requirement that your administrator must handle is the advent of qualified medical support child care orders (QMSCOs). These are similar to the qualified domestic relations orders (QDROs) discussed under the pension plan section. A court has the authority under certain circumstances, e.g., a divorce and child custody settlement, to issue a court order requiring that the plan place the child on the plan with all the rights of a normal beneficiary. This requires that the administrator place the custodial parent in their records and be certain that all notices normally sent to the members are now sent to this custodial parent on behalf of the child or children referenced in the order.

Another aspect of medical plan administration is the need to coordinate benefits with other group health plans. This is commonly referred to as coordination of benefits (COB). If a dependent has other group insurance coverage because of other employment or coverage by another divorced parent, your plan may pay in what is referred to as the secondary position. In these circumstances, the administration office must first identify that there is other coverage, then determine who pays in the primary position and, if your plan is secondary, determine what the benefits of the primary plan are for this claim. Your plan may then pay what the primary plan does not pay up to 100%

of charges or perhaps only up to 100% of what your plan would pay depending upon your plan rules. All of this is governed by a complex series of rules that are in your plan document and plan booklet. Most plans generally follow the guidelines set forth by the National Association of Insurance Commissioners (NAIC). However, because Taft-Hartley plans are governed by ERISA, they may vary from the guidelines although this is harder to administer. The important point of this chapter is to realize that it is the responsibility of your administration office to ensure that all this is done properly and legally. Periodically, the administration office should provide both the consultant and the trustees with a report that shows the cost savings to the plan as a result of applying COB rules. A great deal of the effectiveness of your COB program is dependent upon your administration office being properly trained to recognize COB opportunities and to pursue them diligently.

A similar administration duty arises when a health claim is potentially also covered by workers' compensation insurance or by other third party insurance such as automobile or homeowners insurance policies. In these cases it is again incumbent upon the administration office to have properly trained personnel who can recognize these situations. Once identified, the administration office must proceed in accordance with the rules of the particular state is which you are operating to either have the claim paid by the appropriate third party insurance or to file a lien against the settlement to reimburse the plan. In the case of automobile or homeowner claims, the plan often requires that the participant or dependent sign a prepared subrogation agreement in which the participant agrees to repay the plan upon receipt of a settlement from the other insurance. The plan then goes ahead and pays the medical bills until the liability claim is settled. The administration office has the responsibility to ensure that the court case is tracked and that settlement is forthcoming. Many times subrogation claims are not settled for two or three years; however, they are usually for significant sums.

One of the major responsibilities of the administration office for self-funded health plans is to pay the claims in accordance with plan benefits and rules. This subject could well justify its own chapter or book. However, from the trustees' viewpoint, this is your front line to enforce the plan of benefits and to serve your members and their dependents. If a member does not agree with the plan interpretation of the administration office, or feels that the trustees should make an exception in his or her case due to special circumstances, the administration office is responsible to obtain a release form and an appeal request from the member and present this appeal to the board or the appeals committee as appropriate. Otherwise the administration office processes the claim according to plan rules, issues checks to either the provider or the member and issues explanation of benefits (EOB) forms to all parties. The EOB should explain the calculations that led to the benefit payment, explain the disallowances, show the participant payment required if any and explain the reason for any adjustments. In addition, the EOB should explain the rules and the participant's right to appeal in accordance with ERISA.

Modern day cost-containment measures include the use of preferred provider organizations (PPOs) and utilization review and case management firms. This will require that your administration office maintain up-to-date lists of providers and their rate schedules in order to pay claims properly. It may be necessary to obtain precertification from the utilization organization before paying bills or before incurring charges. The administrator is also responsible for ensuring that if a diagnosis appears to be major, the case management organization is brought into the case as soon as possible. This can save the plan significant amounts of money and improve the quality of care for your participants.

It is the obligation of the administration office to maintain all claim statistics and produce reports for consultants, auditors, actuaries, insurance companies, government agencies and, of course, the trustees. This should include payments by type of service, by provider, by diagnosis, by time period, by type of plan and by class of participant. A very important report is called the *lag report*, which shows the month of service for all the payments made in any month. This report is used by consultants, auditors, etc., to estimate the value of the claims incurred but not reported (IBNR) to the administration office. The total of these claims is a liability of the trust fund and must be recorded on the balance sheet. With the advent of managed care, statistics such as average length of stay (LOS) in hospitals by diagnosis and hospital days per 1,000 participants are increasingly important.

Pension Plan Services

The eligibility records for a pension plan may share common data with the health plan; however, the pension has its own unique set of data requirements. Your administrator must be aware of these and maintain them accurately. A major difference between health and pension plan data is that pension data is often maintained for the entire career or lifetime of the individual. When a pension is calculated, a plan can find itself in a dispute over service credits or contributions going back many years. This is often true if an individual has a break in service or pre-ERISA service, and the availability of these records determines whether or not the individual can have a fair resolution of his or her appeal.

The administration office must have accurate records of each participant's date of birth and the date of birth of the spouse(s) involved. If there is a death benefit involved, the administration office should keep the signed original of the beneficiary designation in a safe and secure place. It is difficult to ask the participant what he or she intended after they are deceased and spouses and ex-spouses are fighting over the benefit.

As I briefly mentioned in the health plan section, it is very important that your administration office maintain accurate and complete records regarding qualified domestic relations orders (QDROs). These are court orders that require specific distribution of pension assets between a participant and his or her ex-spouse. There are very strict guidelines to which the order must adhere, and the administration office works very closely with trust counsel to establish QDRO procedures and in accepting individual QDROs. It is not this chapter's purpose to explain all the intricacies of QDROs, but it is appropriate to note that a QDRO cannot require a pension plan to make any distribution of assets or payment of any pension that it would not normally distribute or pay. The QDRO can direct to whom a portion of the payment is made, but it has to be paid only at a time when the plan would normally allow payment and the total amount paid is no more than would normally be paid.

Each hour or dollar reported by an employer must be credited to a participant's account. These hours must be credited whether or not the employer pays for them. ERISA is very clear on this obligation on the part of multiemployer pension plans. The enforcement of the delinquency procedures discussed earlier has great significance for pension plans since the plan must grant a benefit for all hours worked regardless of whether or not the funds were received.

Inasmuch as the pension calculations are done years later, it is necessary to find a way to constantly monitor the accuracy of the data reported and recorded. Three methods that your administration office should use are:
1. The payroll audit programs previously discussed
2. Posting of hours reported by participant, by employer each month in a manner and method that enables the participant to check the accuracy of the reported information, i.e., online reporting to the union local offices and/or copies of remittance reports
3. Periodic reporting of service and vesting credit for each participant. At least annual reporting is recommended and in fact is required if requested by a participant.

Pension plans also have special recordkeeping needs in the case of terminated participants who have left the plan. If individuals have sufficient vesting credits to qualify for vested benefits, their records must be maintained until they are entitled to benefits. At that time the administration office must conduct certain searches and procedures in an attempt to locate these individuals and pay the benefits to which they are legally entitled. For those participants who are not fully vested, the administrator must maintain records at least until the individual has been out of the plan longer than the longest break in service allowed. It may be wise to keep these records forever inasmuch as the participant could challenge the records upon which the vesting was calculated at some later date.

The administration office through its accounting department must maintain a close liaison with the various investment managers, the banks and the co-trustee in order to ensure that the latest investment results are posted to the general ledger for the pension plan and reflected in its financial statements. For a mature defined benefit pension plan, the investment results dwarf the contributions from employers. The administration office is also responsible to provide all the information required by the plan actuary for his or her annual plan valuation report. This will include the accurate records of dates of birth as previously noted.

Pension benefit calculations and payments differ based upon whether the plan is a defined contribution plan or a defined benefit plan. Some pension plans have both. Under a defined benefit plan, the participant is guaranteed a particular level of benefits if they meet the vesting requirements based upon the hours worked and/or the dollars contributed by employers. The investment risk is the responsibility of the trustees. If investment returns are high or actuarial results positive, then the trustees will occasionally increase the benefit levels either for past, current or future credits. For these plans, the pensions are normally calculated when the individual is considering retirement.

For defined benefit plans, it is not unusual for the application to be several pages long. It is the very important responsibility of the administrator to prepare this form, which must clearly show all the options available to the participant with the costs or benefits for each option. The number of options is dictated by government requirements and plan design. All plans are required to comply with federal regulations regarding joint and survivor benefits protecting the spouse. If joint and survivor benefits are waived, the spouse must also sign this portion of the form. The law requires that this signature be notarized or witnessed by a plan representative. This could be a plan trustee or a designated administration office person. The law grants the spouse the right to a survivor benefit of at least 50% of the member's benefits unless specifically waived by the spouse. The actuary will have already calculated how much the member's pension will be reduced if this or any other joint and survivor benefit is chosen. The spouse may choose to waive this right in exchange for the higher pension when the member is alive.

In addition, the pension may offer options such as "pop-up" rights. These clauses return a member's benefits to full value in the event that the spouse predeceases the retiree. Again, the actuary will have already calculated tables for the administrator's use that will show the amount of reduction in the member's pension if the pop-up option is elected.

The administration staff will often sit down with the pension applicant and spouse and explain all the options and their implications. Trustees and administration office staff should take care, however, not to advise the participant on which option to elect. After the form is completed, the pension must be presented at a meeting of the board of trustees for approval. The administration office is responsible to prepare the pensions for approval for each trust meeting and to have the information necessary to respond to trustees' questions.

Applications for early retirement and applications for pensions based upon disabilities require significant additional work for the administration office. Frequently, the administration office will be required to arrange for a plan-selected physician to examine the applicant in the case of a disability application and then present the report to the board of trustees. Sometimes the retirement will be granted for a conditional period, which the administrator will then monitor. Upon reaching the end of this period, the disability pension may have to be re-reviewed or the participant must present evidence of a continuing disability.

In defined contribution pension plans the employers contribute a negotiated amount per period (hour, week, month, etc.) with no guarantee of a set retirement benefit. The participants may also be allowed to contribute pre-tax money to this plan. The participants take all the risks and rewards of the investments. While there may be vesting schedules similar to defined benefit plans for the employer contributions, the participants' contributions, if allowed, are immediately 100% vested to the participant. Some plans may allow participants to have options as to the level of risk for their individual balances, usually selecting or dividing the balances between at least three different options with varying levels of risk. Other plans do not allow the participant to select. Instead, the trustees select an investment manager to manage all the balances in a conservative manner.

These defined contribution plans require different procedures when an individual terminates or retires. The participants may have the option of withdrawing their cash balances. If this is allowed, the administrator must obtain the necessary information from the participants to determine the method of payment and whether or not it is to rolled over to another tax-exempt plan or whether the administrator must withhold taxes on behalf of the plan. This requirement for tax deduction by the administrator is critical inasmuch as the plan is responsible for the taxes whether or not they are withheld. If a participant leaves a balance with the trust, then the administrator is responsible for maintaining the account balance and periodically crediting the earnings of the investments to the account. In order to relieve the administrative load and related expenses, many plans have a clause that allows a mandatory distribution of balances if the account balance is below a selected amount, e.g.,

$3,500. The handling of QDROs with defined contribution plans is particularly aggravating and burdensome for the administrator because the individual account balance that the courts are dividing will gain or lose value each period due to investment results. After the QDRO is complete, the account balances can be maintained separately. The problems arise with the calculations required to retroactively split up an account balance.

In a manner similar to health plans, the administration office is responsible to process all pension appeals and present them to the board of trustees for resolution.

The administration office is required to issue 1099 forms to all pensioners each year. The office may also make automatic deposits of pensioners' checks each month. Some plans authorize an automatic deduction if requested by the pensioner for any contribution required for health benefits. It is critically important that pension checks be issued on time each month. If checks are issued late, the administration office and the trustees will receive many calls.

Administration Costs

The determination of the appropriate administration cost for your trust is a function of many factors including:
- ▶ The size of your plans—number of participants
- ▶ The number of employers, i.e., a few large or many small ones
- ▶ The turnover rate among participants
- ▶ The number of self-pay or self-contribution options available
- ▶ The size of your board of trustees
- ▶ The frequency of your board meetings
- ▶ The number and types of benefits provided by your various plans
- ▶ The method of calculating contributions, i.e., per hour, per gig, per shift, flat monthly, percentage of earnings, etc.
- ▶ Geographic area covered and location of administration office
- ▶ Complexity of the eligibility rules
- ▶ The range of services required from the administrator
- ▶ Government rules and regulations
- ▶ Frequency and details of reports required.

Summary

In summary, your administration office is the nerve center of your trust. It is the center of participant communications. Your administrator is the repository of all the official trust records including minutes, trust documents, financial records and all participant records. Your administrator is the first line to ensure that you and your trust stay with the guidelines of the thousands of regulations impacting upon benefit plans with particular attention to ERISA and the many court decisions for jointly administered labor-management plans sanctioned by the Department of Labor and the IRS.

You will want to be sure that your administration office staff obtains continuing education to keep them up on the constantly changing regulations impacting benefit plans. Special attention should be paid to annual audit reports by the independent plan auditor. The management letters that may accompany these audits often contain important information for the trustees to use in monitoring and improving administration services.

The board of trustees as the true plan administrator is responsible for choosing well qualified and competent professionals to provide the best possible administration of the plan within reasonable cost guidelines and for monitoring the performance of all plan providers.

Suggested Checklist for Request for Proposal (RFP)

1. Who will actually work on our account? Provide references and backgrounds for these specific people.

2. How long has your firm been handling Taft-Hartley trusts?

3. How do you handle eligibility problems caused by late submittal of hours and funds from other local union jurisdictions where your members are working under reciprocity agreements?

4. How do you monitor for delinquent employers?

5. How do you monitor specific health claims to know when they have reached either the notification point or the attachment point under the trust's stop-loss policy? How quickly do you submit reimbursement requests?

6. Do you use hospital bill audits? How do you determine which bills have the potential for cost reduction from an audit?

7. How do you handle irate or abusive callers?

8. Describe the computer system used for pension service and benefit calculation and recordkeeping.

9. Is your firm capable of handling direct deposit of pension checks?

10. What are your procedures for handling QDROs?

11. Does your firm have the capability to test pensions for Section 415 limits? If so, describe how you do this.

About the Authors

Jack T. Hayes
President
Printing Industries of Wisconsin
Milwaukee, Wisconsin

As chief executive officer of a 110-year-old state trade association dedicated to promoting the interests of commercial printers in Wisconsin, Mr. Hayes is involved in employee benefits programs. He presently serves as management trustee for two health and welfare and one education fund, and is a founding trustee of a national pension fund in the graphic arts. Mr. Hayes served nine years on the International Foundation's Board of Directors, has served on a number of Foundation committees, and has been a speaker at Foundation meetings since 1977.

Robert J. Cardinal, CEBS
President and
 Chief Executive Officer
Benefit Administration
 Corporation (BAC)
Fresno, California

Mr. Cardinal is president and owner of Benefit Administration Corporation (BAC), which has been a third party administrator of health and welfare and pension plans for Taft-Hartley trusts, public employee trusts and single employers for 43 years. Before purchasing BAC in 1989, Mr. Cardinal served as president of two of the oldest and largest TPAs in the country. He has contributed to International Foundation publications and has been a speaker for Foundation programs since 1979. He also has served on a variety of Foundation committees. Mr. Cardinal currently serves as a Voting Director for the International Foundation and on its Administrators Committee.

Chapter 6

Investment Consulting

by Terrence S. Moloznik

Trustee's Perspective

by Irving W. Cheskin

As Terrence Moloznik clearly demonstrates in the opening remarks in this chapter, a trustee of a pension fund is charged, among others, with the fiduciary responsibility for the prudent investment of all the monies contributed by employers and/or employees into the pension funds to provide the maximum amount of pension benefits.

Yet, standing alone, as important as this function is, we are also responsible for establishment of a pension plan, for approval of all pensions; for review of the work of the administrator, the attorneys, the accountants, the actuaries, the requests of members of the plan for improvements; and for redress of grievances—all of these subject to prudent standards of ERISA.

With the increasing complexity of pension plan operations and administration, we, as trustees, must continually rely on professional information and advice. And, therefore, we turn for such guidance to the professional consultant—particularly in the complicated maze of investment programs for pension funds.

Originally, trustees utilized brokers to handle investments under the fund's direction. As the value of the funds increased and financial markets become more complicated, and alternative investments began to emerge with new investment instruments, trustees needed expert advice, so we turned to investment managers to advise us as to which areas of investment will provide us as prudent investors with the optimum returns and to then execute such investments. Over an extended period of time, more monies became available for investment and more alternative investment programs became available in different emerging markets.

As trustees, we are faced with diversification of our funds and with determination of areas of new investment. Different investment management styles have been developed by various investment managers, producing varying results in growth, income and risk. Value style managers, growth managers, contrarian managers, sector analysis managers, index managers—all developed competing investment programs.

From all of the above, how best can a trustee utilize or select that which will prudently produce the best results for the fund? It is no longer sufficient to simply compare the results of one investment manager to another over time. It now requires the expertise and knowledge of an organization that can compare and evaluate and provide for trustees all the answers to the question of meeting the needs of the trustees in the area of optimum investments. They must provide answers to alternative investments, allocation of assets, appropriate guidelines, and risk evaluation, among others.

Over the last decade, to meet this essential need, the new phenomenon of the investment consultant was developed; and, in this forthcoming chapter on investment counseling, Terry Moloznik outlines the role an investment consultant can play to assist a trustee in fulfilling his responsibility.

The investment consultant can educate the trustees and guide them through the successful development of a complete investment program best suited to their requirements. This can provide considerable reassurance to a trustee who, although a layperson in the area of investments, has the responsibility as a fiduciary to make wise and responsible choices.

INVESTMENT CONSULTING

ACCORDING TO THE FEDERAL RESERVE SYSTEM, TOTAL PENSION ASSETS IN THE UNITED States in 1977 were just above $500 billion. By the end of 1995, they will probably have exceeded $4.5 trillion and represent the largest source of capital in the country. Someone is responsible for these assets and that someone is you, the trustee. To succeed in your role as trustee, you must manage your limited time wisely in order to perform your primary investment functions, which include setting policy, defining objectives, delegating duties and monitoring the resources of your plan.

Many of you are faced with the time demands of working full time and fulfilling your responsibilities as a trustee on a part-time basis. Unfortunately, unlike many directors of corporate boards, you are not compensated for your efforts; yet, you face the legal consequences for imprudent decisions made regarding your plan. Sometimes these legal consequences can have an impact on your personal livelihood. This is particularly true for trustees of Taft-Hartley funds or other funds subject to ERISA.

Since the passage of ERISA in 1974, many of the court and regulatory decisions interpreted trustees' decisions according to a prudent expert standard. So, even though you may perform your role as trustee on a part-time basis, you are expected to act as an expert in areas of investment matters. In addition to the tough regulatory standards facing you, you must be able to maneuver and evaluate your way through the complex financial system that constantly develops new products and services. Because of these legal risks and huge demands, most experienced trustees wisely choose to delegate many of the tasks and responsibilities to investment professionals who become part of the management team. One of these key players should be the investment consultant.

What to Look for in a Consultant

Once a board of trustees decides to hire or replace an investment consultant, it is important for those trustees to identify the specific areas in which a consultant can best assist them. Most of the time, trustees are looking to hire a generalist, that is, an investment consultant that can counsel the trustees on an ongoing basis regarding the entire investment program. Other times, trustees may be seeking only a specialist who can focus on a particular aspect of the investment program or on a special project. Therefore, the needs of the trustees will dictate where to begin the search and what qualities to seek in a consultant.

There are many types of consultants and consulting firms. Some are very large and provide a full range of consulting services to a long list of diversified clients. Other consulting firms choose to remain small and specialize in certain products or clients, or operate in specific geographic regions. Some consultants are independent and owned by the principal officers and employees of the firm while others are wholly or partially owned by other firms. Consultants that are subsidiaries of other financial service firms can sometimes raise conflict-of-interest questions when multiple services are offered to a plan. For example, in recent years some consulting firms have diversified into the investment management business, which has become more profitable than consulting. Although some trustees might want to avoid any perception of conflict, these conflict-of-interest concerns usually can be eliminated with a clearer understanding of the organization's structure, which should be fully disclosed to the trustees at the beginning of the search process.

Regardless of the size or affiliation of the consulting firm, certain qualities are desirable and should be sought in a consultant. Among the more important qualities are:

- *Experience*—There really is no substitute for experience. A thorough working knowledge of the investment industry, knowledge of benefit plans and the regulatory environment, and the maturity gained from living through market cycles should be one of the first qualities to look for in a consultant.
- *Trust*—The integrity, objectivity, reputation and creditability of the consultant is extremely important. Confidence that the consultant is providing counsel that is objective and in the best interest of the beneficiaries of the plan is important for your peace of mind and the ultimate success of achieving your stated objectives.
- *Resources*—In order to adequately assist the trustees in their ongoing monitoring functions, necessary studies, special projects and general reporting capabilities, the consultant should have the necessary resources available to perform the functions expected in a professional, accurate and timely manner. This would normally include access to current and historical manager performance, computer capability, experienced staffing and research availability.
- *Communication Skills*—The ability of the consultant to explain and simplify complex issues and educate the trustees about the more technical aspects of the investment business is also important qualities to seek in a consultant.

Key Functions Performed by the General Investment Consultant

As the named fiduciary, the trustee is ultimately accountable for the activities of the plan. Given the huge demands of the trustees, it would be virtually impossible for the trustees to manage all the activities of the plan. Therefore, in order to effectively direct and control the activities of the plan, the trustees' most important duties begin with setting the overall policy for the plan, delegating responsibilities and duties to the appropriate staff and/or service providers and monitoring the results compared to the stated policy. However, the trustees can obtain counsel in many of the important areas relating to the investment program by delegating certain responsibilities to the consultant. A skilled consultant can provide technical assistance on formulating investment policy and guidelines, recommending realistic and appropriate objectives, asset allocation analysis, and performing the many due diligence requirements associated with investment manager searches, reports and terminations. There are many other services that can be provided by a consultant but the following functions are the most important for most plans.[1]

Investment Policy Design

The foundation of any pension plan investment program is the investment policy statement. This is a document that should clearly express in writing the plan's purpose, trustee objectives, allowable strategies and risk tolerances. The investment consultant can be extremely helpful in assisting the trustees to carefully draw up a well-defined investment policy that coordinates the demographic characteristics of the plan with the trustees' concerns and desires along with the appropriate investment considerations. At a minimum, the investment consultant should be able to assist the trustees in reviewing actuarial data and workforce demographics and analyze accounting data to determine cash flows and potential liquidity needs.

All these factors can help define the risk tolerance of the plan that is so important to understand before finalizing the investment policy statement. Furthermore, the investment consultant should have the technical skills and experience necessary to help trustees quantify their investment objectives at acceptable risk levels and determine the proper investment horizon.

There are at least four critical elements in the design of an investment policy. The first element of the investment policy statement should describe the trustees or committee structure, the investment authority and the purpose of the plan, in order to give the reader a general understanding of the plan profile. An example of this section might read as follows:

> This benefit plan was established in 19___. It covers the full-time employees of the organization. The plan is governed by an eight-member board of trustees. The current members are _____
> _____.
> Contributions to the plan are made on a monthly basis and the con-

tribution rates are collectively bargained, usually over a three-year term. Assets are held in a segregated trust fund out of which benefit payments are made. Growth in the fund results from a combination of contributions and the return achieved from investing the accumulated reserves in the total fund.

The purposes of this statement of investment policy are to:

1. Articulate the trustees' views of the plan's investment objectives and tolerance for risk.

2. Formulate policies to assist the trustees with, first, developing a suitable asset allocation; second, selecting appropriate investment managers or commingled funds within the framework of that asset allocation; and third, prudently monitoring and evaluating the performance of such managers or commingled funds.

The second element of the investment policy should state clearly the objectives of this plan. These objectives can be qualitative in nature, but there should also be some specific quantitative goals defined. For example, a statement of objectives could be expressed as follows:

The plan shall seek to achieve the following long-term investment objectives:

1. A long-term rate of return in excess of the annualized inflation rate, defined as the average annualized compound rate of the CPI calculated on a five-year moving average

2. A long-term rate of return that meets or exceeds the assumed actuarial rate as stated in the plan's actuarial report

3. A long-term competitive rate of return on investments, net of expenses, that is equal to or exceeds various benchmark rates on a moving three-year average

4. Maintenance of sufficient income and liquidity to pay monthly retirement.

A third part of the policy statement should set forth the trustees' allowable investment strategies and risk tolerances. This section of the policy statement should have at least enough detail to provide the reader with a general understanding of the overall investment program. An example of some language describing the kinds of factors to include in this section are:

Consistent with the above, the trustees will determine from time to time a suitable asset allocation that seeks to control risk through portfolio diversification and takes into account, among possible other factors, the above-stated objectives, in conjunction with current funding levels and economic and industry trends.

The trustees will select various investment managers and/or commingled funds and allocate the assets of the plan to seek to achieve the stated investment objectives and to control risk. The assets subject to each such investment manager or commingled fund shall constitute an "investment account."

The trustees will establish reasonable guidelines for each asset class and investment account, specifying (as applicable) acceptable and/or prohibited investments, limits on asset and asset class exposures, risk constraints and investment return objectives. To the extent plan assets are placed in commingled funds, the practices of such funds as identified in the fund prospectus shall be materially consistent with this statement.

The consultant and plan staff will monitor the activity and performance of each investment account and the plan as a whole and report to the trustees on a periodic basis.

Asset Allocation

Asset allocation is the fourth element that should be included in the policy statement and is probably the most important factor affecting investment performance. Once the key factors such as plan liabilities, rate-of-return objectives, risk tolerances and cash flow needs have been determined by the investment team, a skilled investment consultant can analyze the infinite ways to structure the investment portfolio in order to produce an "efficient" portfolio. Simply put, an efficient portfolio is the blend of stocks, bonds, real estate, etc., that provides the best returns for an acceptable risk level. Such a portfolio could reassure the trustees that over their investment horizon, the recommended asset allocation would have a high probability of meeting the stated objectives within the stated risk tolerances of the trustees.

In a study published in 1986 entitled *Determinants of Portfolio Performance*, Gary Brinson, L. Randolf Hood and Gilbert L. Beebower found that the asset allocation set by the policy statement had far more impact on the performance of a plan than market timing or what individual stocks or bonds were selected for the portfolio. This study confirmed the importance for trustees to concentrate more of their time and effort on this strategic asset allocation decision. Therefore, trustees should periodically request a review of the asset allocation to ensure that the plan portfolio is structured efficiently to meet the stated objectives and liability concerns over the plan's investment horizon.

Furthermore, on an ongoing basis, the consultant should provide counsel to the trustees on the need to rebalance the portfolio in order to maintain the proper asset weightings as stated in the investment policy statement. There has been some confusion that rebalancing the asset allocation is a form of market timing. This is not true when it is designed to maintain the portfolio at the approved policy level. For example, if after considering all the vital factors, the trustee and consultant determine that an allocation of 60% stocks, 35% bonds and 5% real estate is an appropriate mix for the plan, then maintaining the portfolio at this level may require periodic rebalancing. This periodic rebalancing, which can be performed quarterly or even monthly depending on market conditions and plan cash flows, will call for some shifting of assets; but it is all geared toward maintaining the asset allocation at the policy level established by the trustees.

Sometimes the trustees will set strategic target ranges such as stocks 60% plus or minus 5% to allow for some flexibility in the plan operation. This is often called weighting or tilting. For example, at 65% stocks you would be overweighted or tilted toward stocks but still be within the approved strategic asset allocation set by the investment policy. However, the wider the allowable range becomes, the more market timing decisions begin to creep into the plan's investment program. There are some plans and managers that use market timing as a tactical way to try to add value. In an extreme case, for example, an investment manager may move to 100% cash, 0% stocks or vice versa. However, it is debatable that these tactical asset allocation methods successfully add value to the plan over any significant time frame.

The asset allocation process is one of the most important steps in the long-term success of the investment program and requires resources and technical experience in order to arrive at an asset allocation that is efficient and appropriate for the plan. A skilled consultant should be able to provide the necessary counsel to the trustees for this task.

Manager Search and Selection

After the important asset allocation work has been completed and the trustees have agreed on a strategic mix of assets, the trustees may want to hire a new manager(s) for the plan. The due diligence required for a manager search is very time-consuming, and trustees will usually look to the consultant for assistance. The standards and guidelines used by professional consultants in the due diligence process for the collection and analysis of data, performance evaluation and manager comparisons are very detailed. In recent years performance standards have been adopted by the AIMR, which require investment firms to calculate and report their investment performance to prospective clients in accordance with these rigorous standards. Additionally, the IMCA has also set forth a detailed list of requirements and standards for manager search and analysis.[2] Some of the more important standards you should expect consultants to follow when conducting a manager search are listed below.

Collection and Analysis of Data

▶ The consultant should obtain information from an investment manager

and confirm the accuracy of this data for as many separate performance composites that represent investment styles that can be potentially used by the client to meet their investment goals and objectives.
- ▶ The consultant should obtain performance composite data on a gross (before fee) basis, as permitted by the SEC in "one-on-one" presentations. Whenever possible, performance composite data should also be obtained on a net (after fee) basis.
- ▶ The consultant should obtain a current copy of the manager's appropriate fee schedule(s) to be presented with the investment manager's results to the client.
- ▶ Cash and equivalents should be handled in a manner consistent with the management of the portfolio.
- ▶ Switching between accounting methods for reasons other than a change in the source of data is discouraged.
- ▶ Sources of data and definitions relating to that data should be disclosed to the client.

Performance Evaluation Factors

- ▶ A time-weighted total rate of return calculation including reinvestment of income that minimizes the impact of contributions and withdrawals is mandatory.
- ▶ Performance composite time-weighted rates of return should be provided on a quarterly frequency at a minimum.
- ▶ The preferred method for calculation of quarterly rates of return is to link monthly returns; but, as a minimum, the quarterly returns may be calculated using quarterly market values and monthly cash flows.
- ▶ The preferred data for calculation of monthly returns are at least monthly market values and daily cash flows.
- ▶ When a cash flow in excess of 10% of a portfolio or segment occurs, and the interim market value is available or can be obtained or estimated, interim time-weighted calculations should be performed for that month.
- ▶ The preferred method of calculating portfolio returns is on a trade data and accrual basis. Interest income must be calculated on an accrual basis as opposed to a cash basis. For dividends and retroactive compliance, it is strongly recommended that income also be calculated on an accrual basis. If calculated on an accrual basis, dividends should be accrued as income from their ex-dividend date. Reasonably accurate estimations of accrued income are permissible.
- ▶ The preferred time period for reporting rate-of-return data from investment managers is either monthly or calendar quarter time-weighted

rates of return for each performance composite from inception of the firm, inception of the investment product or the latest ten years, whichever period is shorter. Rate of return data for periods longer than ten years is acceptable but not required.

▶ All discretionary, fee-paying portfolios must be included in at least one performance composite.

▶ Each performance composite should include all fee-paying, discretionary client portfolios of a similar investment product, both past and present, for whatever time period such portfolios are under management. Portfolios should not be included in a performance composite for only portions of the measurement period, either monthly or quarterly, during which the portfolio is under management.

▶ Performance composite returns should be calculated by equally weighting the performance of the individual portfolios. Performance composite returns weighted by portfolio size may also be obtained if desired.

▶ Balanced portfolio performance composites should include only those portfolios over which the investment manager has discretion with respect to asset allocation.

▶ Information on any exclusions from or changes in a performance composite should be obtained from the investment manager and provided to the client.

▶ Performance composite results should not be altered to reflect personnel or other organizational changes. Any significant changes within the firm should be fully disclosed to the client.

▶ Performance of any client portfolios that are no longer under management should always remain in the historical performance composite.

▶ The consultant may consider using simulated performance results to analyze an investment product and process, provided that a full disclosure is made to the client.

▶ Simulated returns should not be linked with actual results to provide an analysis of long-term investment performance unless specifically requested by the client.

▶ The consultant should obtain confirmation from the investment manager that all information used to construct the simulated returns is readily available upon request.

▶ Past investment performance belongs to the investment firm that achieved those results, not to any single individual.

▶ Performance results achieved by key investment personnel while employed with another investment firm may be used if the consultant determines those professionals are implementing the same investment process at the new firm. If continuity of key investment personnel and

clients exists, and the track record can be traced back for those clients, then transferability should be allowed. Also, if an investment firm is sold, but the investment personnel remain unchanged with the same investment philosophy, then transferability should be allowed. However, that prior historical record may not be linked with results achieved at the new firm to provide a long-term investment record; and disclosure of these circumstances to the client is crucial.
- Any significant changes in personnel or structure which, in the consultant's opinion, may affect future performance should be disclosed.

Investment Manager Comparisons

- Annual and cumulative returns for each performance composite should be presented by the consultant to clients in the format that facilitates the objective comparison of one manager with another. At a minimum, each calendar year should be included in the report. Returns for client-requested time periods, market cycles or other time periods should be obtained and presented when needed.
- Rates of return for longer than one year should be presented in compound annualized form. Returns for periods less than one year should never be annualized.
- Whenever possible, the consultant should present the performance composite investment data to clients on both a gross (before fee) basis for comparative purposes and a net (after fee) basis. A schedule of all applicable fees should always be provided to the client. If only gross return information is supplied to the client, additional information should be provided to enable the client to determine the approximate impact of the manager's fee.
- Any presentations of gross investment results must be in compliance with the Securities and Exchange Commission's (SEC) position on advertising of investment performance.

Benchmarks and Universe Comparisons

- Comparisons should be made for any time periods for which performance composite results are being shown. At a minimum, comparison of annual calendar year returns should be made. The inclusion of other time periods (i.e., quarterly and annual periods, market cycles, cumulative periods) is encouraged.
- Benchmark comparisons should also include the presentation of appropriate measures of risk over time that might include (but not be limited to) standard deviations of returns, beta coefficients and ranges of results.
- If a peer group of investment managers is used for comparative pur-

poses, each of the managers should be represented by similar investment products.
- The consultant should disclose to the client the composition of any investment product universe used.

As you can see, these standards are numerous and complex, so a professional consultant is best suited to assist in the search so the trustee can be assured of a fair, objective and accurate comparison of prospective managers. In addition, the general consultant will have access to large databases of managers containing volumes of data concerning the staffing, qualifications and detailed information on the investment process. The objective is to have the consultant comb through all this information in order to find a handful of qualified candidates fitting your specifications so the trustees can further evaluate their candidates in greater detail.

Once this list of investment firms is cut to a manageable size, the trustees can begin interviews with prospective candidates. A good consultant should orchestrate the interviews, seeking to focus on the investment process and ask the critical questions that probe in greater detail the experience, resources and servicing ability of an investment manager. Finally, the consultant can counsel the trustees concerning the reasonableness of fees and the logistics involved with funding the new manager. Ultimately, the trustee will select the manager that offers the best combination of skill, experience, integrity and trust.

Investment Manager Guidelines

Once the decision has been made to hire a particular manager, it is sound practice to issue specific investment manager guidelines to the manager. Many plans make the manager guidelines part of the investment agreement. The purpose of these investment manager guidelines is to formally convey to each manager what role he plays, what is expected from him, what restrictions he has on the portfolio composition and how he will be evaluated, as well as other matters relating to specific investment practices in his tenure as investment manager for the plan. The consultant is usually best suited to draft these guidelines on behalf of the trustee because of its knowledge of the industry, knowledge of managers and the needs of the plan. In developing these guidelines the consultant should take into consideration the specific role that this particular manager plays within the larger scope of the investment program and any specific concerns or restrictions that the trustees want to impose on the manager.

Monitoring of Managers

Monitoring of the managers is the one function most often performed by investment consultants for the trustees. Evaluating the performance of the plan and the investment managers on a consistent and periodic basis (usually quarterly) keeps the trustees informed on the plan's actual performance compared to the established objectives set forth in the investment policy statement and manager guidelines. By consistently monitoring the plan and each of the managers, the trustees receive the feedback they need to take corrective action or make improvements to the investment program.

Although the reporting format used by consultants to monitor investment managers may differ from one consultant to the next, the professional consultant will generally follow specific standards and guidelines recommended by Investment Management Consultants Association (IMCA) on the collection and analysis of data, performance evaluation benchmark and universe comparisons. Some of the recommended standards you should expect the consultant to follow are:

- ▶ The portfolio accounting data should be obtained on at least a quarterly basis, i.e., quarter-end asset values and all transaction information for each month during the quarter.
- ▶ The preferred source of data is custodial statements from bank trust departments, brokerage firms, insurance companies or others providing independent custodial services. The client should be informed regarding the source of data used.
- ▶ Rates of return should be calculated on a quarterly basis at a minimum using quarterly asset values and monthly cash flows.
- ▶ Cash and equivalents balances should be handled in a manner consistent with the management of the portfolio.
- ▶ A time-weighted total rate of return, including reinvestment of income, which minimizes the impact of contributions and withdrawals is required.
- ▶ On an ongoing basis, interest income must be calculated on an accrual basis as opposed to a cash basis. Reasonably accurate estimations of accrued income are permissible.
- ▶ Comparative indices should be constructed on a total return basis on at least a quarterly basis.
- ▶ The preferred method for calculating rates of return is on a trade date and accrual basis.
- ▶ For dividends and retroactive compliance, it is strongly recommended that income be calculated on an accrual basis. If calculated on an accrual basis, dividends should be accrued as income from their ex-dividend date. Reasonably accurate estimations of accrued income are permissible.
- ▶ When a cash flow in excess of 10% of the portfolio or segment occurs, and the interim market value is available or can be obtained, interim time-weighted calculations should be performed.

- An absolute measure of risk should be provided by an annualized standard deviation calculated from at least quarterly returns.
- Balanced indices weighted in a manner that reflects the portfolio's asset mix policy should be constructed when possible for comparison of total portfolio performance.

Monitoring of managers generally involves more than just evaluating performance. The monitoring process should also review the compliance of the manager to the investment guidelines. Specifically, risk levels, portfolio characteristics, diversification requirements, commission and related costs of execution and possibly proxy monitoring should all be performed by the consultant on a periodic basis and reported to the trustees.

Special Services

The full-service consultant can usually provide all the above functions. Some plans, however, may determine that they do not need a full-service consultant. Instead, they may rely on in-house staff to provide assistance on monitoring the investment program and hire consultants only for one or more specialized tasks such as manager performance reviews or assistance in a manager search. Other times trustees might want the consultant to perform special projects relating to a specific part of the investment program or periodically hire an independent consultant that specializes in a broader in-depth and independent review of the overall investment program to make sure the plan's investment program is operating in a prudent manner. This particular type of large scale review has been growing in demand recently due to the many changes that are occurring on the boards of funds and because of special investment problems that have occurred as exemplified in Orange County, California in 1994.

Conducting a Consultant Search

The common practice followed today when shopping for a consultant is to issue a formal request for proposal (RFP) to two or more prospective consultants. Although the RFP is not mandatory, when drafted thoughtfully, it is an efficient and practical first step for the trustees to control and obtain vital information in order to evaluate the prospective consultants equally on a number of different factors.

The key items that should be requested and focused on in a RFP for a consultant are:
- Description of the firm, including the legal structure, ownership, affiliation, number of years in the business and any particular disclosures
- Biographies of key professional staff beginning with those individuals who will be assigned to this account

- Description of the proposed products, services, resources and summary of process expected to be utilized for this account
- List of current clients, including references
- Specific regulatory issues affecting key employees or the firm relating to convictions, fines or litigation
- Some assurance of the financial stability of the firm including audited financial statements and description of insurance coverage
- Proposed fee structure in a manner that allows for a reasonable comparison to other fee proposals
- Any other specific factor that is particularly important to the trustees.

Cost of Consulting

The cost of consulting services depends on the nature, scope and complexity of the assignment required by the plan. Those costs can run from several thousand dollars for simple projects to several hundred thousand dollars for some of the more complicated assignments. Generally, pension plans pay for these consulting fees in one of two ways. Using industry terminology, the two methods are referred to as *hard dollar fees* and *soft dollar fees*. When the plan writes a check each month or quarter for the cost of consulting services, the plan is paying hard dollars. When a plan arranges for a third party to pay for the consulting service, usually a broker, it is paying with soft dollars. However, this does not mean the plan is getting free services. In order to arrange for the broker to pay for such services, the plan will have to direct a certain amount of commissions to the broker. For example, the broker might require $2 in commissions before the plan earns the equivalent of one soft dollar. In this case, the ratio is 2:1. This ratio is negotiable, generally between 2:1 to 3:1.

The advantage of using soft dollars is that the plan can use some of its commission expenses that it would normally have anyway to pay for the consulting service. The disadvantage is that the commission might be directed to a specific broker that may not be able to trade as effectively as the other brokers normally used by the plan's investment managers. Remember, the investment managers are competing to buy and sell securities for your plan at the best price, and if you force them to use a certain broker the manager might not get the best price. Trading costs due to poor execution may not be apparent at first but will eventually manifest into lower plan performance because the poor execution is reflected in the price of the security being traded. If the trustees require an investment manager to direct commissions to a certain broker that has consistently poor execution, the added trading costs could easily outrun the cost of just paying hard dollars for the desired services. Additionally, directed commissions create the need to be especially diligent in monitoring trading costs, especially with the directed commission broker. If trustees are thinking about using soft dollars to pay for consulting services, they should review the 1986 DOL technical bulletin on this subject and should also discuss the matter with the plan's investment managers.

Trends in Consulting

The consulting industry is undergoing change but then so is the pension industry. According to the Employee Benefit Research Institute (EBRI), from 1975 to 1994 defined benefit plans (also endowments and foundations) grew at a compound annual rate of about 11.6%. However, this annual rate of growth has slowed to 5.7% over the last five years. During the 1950s-1980s, defined benefit plans were the retirement plan of choice and experienced huge growth from a combination of contribution income and investment earnings. The investment consulting industry developed to serve the needs of those defined benefit plans, and asset management was the main focus. As those defined benefit plans grew in size, many of them also reached maturity (particularly the union-sponsored plans); and many are now paying out more in benefits than they are receiving in new contributions. This should not be a problem if the investment program was designed properly to meet its long-term objectives and achieve its performance objectives. Nevertheless, liability concerns are now emerging as a higher priority than ever before.

Therefore, one of the trends beginning to evolve due to the maturity of defined benefit plans is the greater emphasis on liability management compared to asset management. In other words, trustees are beginning to ask consultants to develop investment programs that are focusing on the large benefit payment stream contrasted to previous periods when asset growth was the primary focus. This has caused consultants to begin altering the way they approach their asset allocation work and the way some defined benefit portfolios should be structured during the later stages of a plan's life.

Another trend that has emerged is due to the huge growth of defined contribution plans and 401(k) and 403(b) programs. EBRI estimated that the annual growth rate for defined contribution plans and 401(k) programs over the last five years was about 8.9% and 16.2%, respectively. Naturally, with the slowing growth of defined benefit plans and the higher growth of defined contribution plans and 401(k) programs, the consultants are undergoing a change by developing new products and offering new services geared to these higher growth areas. Some consultants have decided to develop strategic alliances with other consultants in order to achieve certain synergies by combining the specific expertise of each consulting firm.

The increased use of various passive management strategies is another trend affecting the consulting industry. Many trustees have criticized active managers for underperforming the indexes such as the S&P 500 index. This is not just a recent concern. In fact, several past studies confirm this. For example, in 1960, Edward F. Renshaw and Paul J. Feldstein published in the *Financial Analysts Journal*, the first evidence that unmanaged (passive) portfolios performed better than actively managed portfolios.

Fifteen years later, in 1975, Charles D. Ellis published his work in the *Financial Analysts Journal* citing that in the ten years prior to 1975, most active managers underperformed the S&P 500 index. Most recently, the Brookings Institution published a paper that analyzed seven years of pension returns from 1983 to 1989 and found that the average active investment manager underperformed the S&P 500 by 130 basis points before fees.

Finally, Lipper Analytical Services, Inc. showed that for the ten years ending September 30, 1992, the average, general, actively managed equity fund underperformed the Wilshire 5000 Index by 250 basis points after reducing the index by 0.3% for estimated costs and that in eight out of ten of those years the index beat the average general equity fund.

Therefore, in each of the last four decades, formal studies have shown the difficulty that active managers have had in trying to outperform passive strategies. Indexing a portion of the core portfolio is now fairly commonplace. And now with the creation of more style-specific indices such as growth or value indexes or small capitalization, midcapitalization or large capitalization indexes, trustees will begin seeing more passive management products. This will lead to passively managed portfolios constructed with those style indexes that can be weighted based on the recommendations of their consultants in order to capture the expected outperformance of various styles that inevitably occurs over cycles.

As indicated in the first part of this chapter, the time demands, investment complexities and regulatory demands requiring prudent expert standards have created a growing market for outsourcing. Adding to this demand is corporate downsizing by many corporations that have decided to focus their resources on their primary business rather than managing a pension fund.

Additionally, Taft-Hartley funds have also been successfully using outsourcing programs, sometimes called named fiduciary assignments, to manage their investment programs and/or administrative functions. As a matter of fact, the first large fund to successfully use outsourcing for its investment programs was the Teamsters Central States Southeast and Southwest Areas Pension Fund.

Historically there have been only a few consultants experienced in named fiduciary services. However, because of demand for these outsourcing services, more pension consultants as well as some large investment firms are beginning to offer full services or one-stop shopping to pension funds. These services would include establishing investment guidelines, plan design, asset allocation, manager selection, performance measurement, trust and custody services and even administration. With this approach, busy trustees or corporate officials have to deal with only one primary contact for most pension fund matters.

Who Is Watching the Consultants?

If trustees are depending on the advice of consultants and other service providers, how can they verify that this advice is sound? One successful method used by some plans has been to periodically hire a third party consultant that specializes in performing reviews of benefit plan investment programs, operations and organization structure. This kind of review is particularly useful when benefit plans go through changes such as a turnover on the board of trustees or in senior management and the new decision makers have some questions or concerns about past investment practices but do not want to jump to any conclusions without a thorough review of the program.

Suggested Checklist for Request for Proposal (RFP)

Below are examples of questions to include in a request for proposal for investment consulting services. These questions should be refined according to the specific needs of the plan.

Questions

1. Overview of the firm: Describe the legal structure of the firm (corporation, partnership, etc.), its ownership, affiliated companies, principal place of business, lines of business other than investment consulting and the length of time the firm has been in the investment consulting business.

2. Consulting experience: Provide information regarding the number of investment consulting clients of the firm over the last three years and the approximate value of the assets according to the following categories:

    a. Multiemployer pension

    b. Multiemployer welfare

    c. Public

    d. Single employer pension

    e. Single employer welfare

    f. Other investment consulting assignments.

3. Representative list of clients and references: Identify any private pension or welfare plan clients whom you wish to offer as a reference including the name, title, address and telephone number of the person to contact.

4. Identify the name of any clients that have terminated your services over the last year and your explanation for why the termination occurred.

5. Qualifications of consultants and professional staff: Identify each of the consultants employed by the firm who you believe are qualified to serve this account, including names, education, training and experience. Identify that person or persons whom you would propose to have primary responsibility for this account. Has there been any staff turnover in the last year?

6. Proposed services: Provide a description of your approach to each of the following tasks:

    a. Identify the fund's investment needs and recommend overall investment policy.

    b. Recommend an appropriate asset allocation plan.

    c. Assess current investment managers and recommend whether any should be terminated or hired.

    d. Assist in search and selection of new managers.

    e. Establish specific investment guidelines and benchmarks for each manager hired.

    f. Monitor investment managers and custodians.

7. Other services and relationships: Does your firm offer investment management, investment advisory or brokerage services? Does your firm provide any other services to investment managers, investment advisors or registered investment companies? (This question includes the receipt of fees from investment managers in connection with the inclusion of the investment manager in any database maintained by your firm or in connection with any information provided by your firm to investment managers regarding your clients.) If your answer to either of these questions is yes, please describe the services rendered and to whom they are rendered.

8. Regulatory issues: Has the firm or any member or professional employee ever been convicted of any crime described in Section 411(A) of ERISA, fined, suspended or censored by the Securities and Exchange Commission

Investment Consulting

or any securities self-regulatory organization or named as defendant in any litigation involving charges of violation of ERISA?

9. Financial responsibility: Provide the most recent audited financial statement for the firm as well as a description of any professional liability or other insurance or resources available to satisfy any claims for losses resulting to clients.

10. Fee arrangements: Please describe your fee proposal.

Endnotes

1. For a more detailed discussion of each of these functions see *Investment Policy Guidebook for Trustees* by Eugene B. Burroughs published by the International Foundation of Employee Benefit Plans.

2. For a complete and detailed list of the standards, see *IMCA Performance Presentation Standards* prepared by the bodies Task Force, November 30, 1992.

About the Authors

Irving W. Cheskin
Director of Pension
 and Welfare Affairs
League of American Theatres
 and Producers, Inc.
Croton on Hudson, New York

Mr. Cheskin is director of pension and welfare affairs of the League of American Theatres and Producers, Inc. He is a trustee of 14 different pension and welfare funds, ranging in size from $30 million to over $1 billion in assets. Mr. Cheskin is an arbitrator affiliated with the American Arbitration Association. He has been a speaker at International Foundation educational programs, has served on various committees and is a former member of the International Foundation's Board of Directors.

Terrence S. Moloznik
Vice President
Bear Stearns Fiduciary
 Services, Inc.
Washington, D.C.

Mr. Moloznik's primary responsibilities pertain to the development, implementation and monitoring of portfolio strategies for client funds. He is also involved in operational reviews and portfolio restructuring services for defined benefit funds of all sizes. Mr. Moloznik has been a speaker at International Foundation educational programs.

Chapter 7

Investment Management

by James H. Scott and John Van Belle

Trustee's Perspective

by Michael Haffner

On the following pages, James Scott and John Van Belle are going to give you an excellent idea of what an investment manager's responsibilities are together with trustees' responsibilities and duties pertaining to investment managers.

As trustees, the final responsibility of the management of the fund is ours. We must make sure we are making the best decisions to ensure the fund's assets are being invested in a prudent manner. I firmly believe the only manner in which assets should be invested is through an investment manager, no matter what the size of the fund.

As far as investments are concerned, we, the trustees of pension plans, make the decisions regarding the amount of risk we want to incur. The investment people we have hired need to be provided with a set of guidelines to follow. Trustees should be aware that sometimes an ultraconservative approach to investing may be deemed as not being prudent, just as the high-risk approach can also be determined to be nonprudent.

After the guidelines are set, the investment manager should attend almost all the trustee meetings and should always keep the trustees fully informed as to how the investments for the plan are faring. The managers in our plan supply us with the progress of the in-

vestments both in the long and short term and also give reports on the ongoing strategy of the investment plan.

By receiving these reports, the trustees can monitor the fund and ask any questions of the manager as to the status of the investments.

Trustees should not mandate any drastic changes in the short-term interim. Even if a trustee doesn't agree with the performance at the time, the trustees have placed their trust in this manager to invest the way they see fit, provided they are within the guidelines outlined by the trustees. If after a reasonable amount of time, the investment manager is not performing satisfactorily, the trustees will then have to make a decision to determine the best solution to the problem, including the possibility of finding a new manager.

The trustees of a fund should have complete confidence and respect for the investment manager. If the investment manager and the trustees do not have mutual respect and confidence, the manager may never satisfy the trustees regardless of what he or she achieves. This may possibly be something as insignificant as conflicting personalities, or even a dislike of a particular style in which a manager performs transactions.

If the trustees conclude they should make a change in investment managers or hire additional managers, a committee should be formed to search for the new manager. All the trustees would set the guidelines for the search, and the committee can then conduct the interviews and make a recommendation to the trustees. Again, I stress that everyone (the trustees and the investment managers) must have a certain rapport, or I wouldn't advise the trustees to hire a manager even if he or she had great performance records.

In closing, I believe that after you have read through this chapter, you will possess a very good insight of your duties as a trustee pertaining to the investment manager together with the basics of hiring, monitoring and if need be, changing investment managers.

INTRODUCTION

THIS CHAPTER PROVIDES BASIC INFORMATION ABOUT INVESTMENT MANAGEMENT AND answers questions that trustees and plan sponsors have asked us over the past years. The answers should help trustees develop a framework for discharging their investment management duties.

A few questions immediately jump out. Who manages the plan's assets? Do the trustees make investment management decisions? Can or should the trustees hire professional investment managers? What services do these investment professionals provide? Why are these services important? How do you identify and hire a quality investment manager? How do you get the most out of your relationship with an investment manager? Our goal, with this chapter, is to provide insights and answers to these questions.

Who Is Responsible for Managing the Assets?

The trustees are responsible for managing the fund's assets. While they can manage the assets themselves, most boards delegate these duties, either to experts who are full-time employees of the fund or, more frequently, to outside investment professionals.

External Versus Internal Management

Some plan sponsors rely on their own employees to manage all or part of the plan's assets. Most pension plans, however, hire external investment professionals to manage the bulk of their plan assets. A recent study found that about three-quarters of all corporate, public and endowment funds use only external management.

Larger plans can often justify the cost of an internal investment staff and tend to use more internal management. About half the plans over $1 billion (see Table I) manage some of their assets internally. Moreover, the portion of large plans internally managing more than half their assets is about 13%, nearly three times the rate for smaller plans.

There are several reasons why most pension funds use external managers.
1. *Specialized skills:* Like other occupations, investment management requires specialized knowledge and skills. Managers decide which asset class to buy (stocks, bonds or, say, real estate) and which particular securities to buy within each class. Professional investment managers base their strategies on economics, politics and finance, as well as the special characteristics of the markets in which they invest. Professionals also know how to set up, manage and monitor the costs of the special accounts required for pension fund investing.

Table I

INTERNALLY MANAGED ASSETS
% OF FUNDS MANAGING ASSETS INTERNALLY

Size of Plan Assets	% of Assets Managed Internally				
	None	0.1 to 20%	20.1 to 50%	50.1 to 90%	90.1 to 100%
Over $1 billion	55%	16%	14%	6%	7%
$501 to $1,000 million	74	18	4	1	1
$251 to $500 million	74	17	6	2	2
$100 to $250 million	80	12	4	0	2
Under $100 million	82	7	6	1	4
Total	74%	14%	7%	2%	3%

Source: Greenwich Associates.

2. *Legal liability:* Although trustees bear the ultimate legal responsibility for managing the assets, trustees can reduce their own legal burdens by hiring and properly monitoring professional investment managers. Depending on the state they live or work in, investment managers may have to register with the appropriate authority and, in any case, must be adequately prepared to accept responsibility for managing pension assets.
3. *Higher returns:* Talented managers can lower the cost of providing retirement benefits by increasing assets faster than they might otherwise have grown.
4. *Ease of using subcontractors:* By using external managers, trustees gain access to a wide variety of managers and styles. In addition, it is often easier to change external managers than internal ones.

Trustees meet their legal and investment obligations either by managing the assets internally or by hiring outside organizations to fulfill the investment requirements. In either case, the trustees must monitor and oversee these investment activities.

Professional Investment Management Organizations

Financial service firms as well as specialized investment firms provide investment management for institutions. These firms generally fall in the following four categories:

1. *Insurance companies:* In the early days of pension investing, plans were very conservatively managed. Insurance contracts guaranteed

most assets. As plans diversified into riskier and potentially more rewarding asset classes, insurance companies responded with a broad array of investment vehicles.
2. *Banks and other financial institutions:* Banks have a long history of managing personal and corporate trust accounts. As pension funds grew, banks too met the growing demand by offering a wide range of investment services. Some banks provide custody and record-keeping services as well as investment management.
3. *Mutual fund organizations:* Mutual funds' biggest market has traditionally been the individual investor; more recently, however, they too have significantly expanded their offerings for institutional investors, such as pension plans.
4. *Investment management firms:* These vary from large institutions that specialize in several asset classes and employ many managers to small investment boutiques that may rely on the investment expertise of a single individual.

Where Do Your Investment Managers Fit Into the Overall Task of Managing a Pension Plan?

Investment Dilemma

The fundamental investment dilemma facing the trustees of a pension plan is the same as that facing any investor. Safe investments, such as U.S. Treasury bills or certificates of deposit, generate low returns, while investments that can potentially provide high returns, such as stocks or long-term bonds, are risky. Over long periods of time, the riskier assets generally produce higher returns than the safe investments.

However, there is always the potential for the risk to come home to roost and leave the risky asset with even lower returns than the safe asset. A sensible investment strategy prudently balances expected return and risk to best meet the investor's (trustee's) objectives.

Risk Versus Return

While no one can accurately predict future investment returns, investment professionals routinely project the expected returns and risk of different asset categories. What we mean by asset category or asset class is a widely recognized diversified portfolio of investments of the same type. For example, the category *stocks* generally means a broad portfolio as represented by the Standard and Poor's 500 or Wilshire 5000 stock indexes.

The return and risk estimates rely, in part, on the actual history of asset class returns. We use the longest available actual period of returns for each asset cat-

Table II

Asset Class	Expected Return
International Stocks	11.0%
Domestic Stocks	10.5
Real Estate	9.5
Domestic Bonds	6.5
International Bonds	6.5
Money Market	4.0

egory to determine the extreme possibilities as well as the average returns. Minor adjustments to this basic data, so that it conforms more closely to economic and financial theories about how markets function, adds to our confidence that the data provides a good representation of potential risks and returns.

Table II shows projected returns for asset categories commonly used in pension plans. Table III shows projected ranges for the asset returns. The ranges represent the returns you could earn in that asset category within a 95% confidence band. Another way of looking at these ranges is that over the next century, you would expect the returns (in this case, the ten-year annualized returns) for each asset category to fall within its range in about 95 of the 100 years.

Experts disagree about the precise numbers that should appear in exhibits like Tables II and III. Notice that the asset categories with greater risk have higher expected rates of return.

However, higher risk does not always mean higher return. Investors can and should diversify to reduce risk because financial markets only reward risk that cannot be eliminated through diversification.

Diversification

A single stock will have roughly the same expected return as the overall stock category shown in Table II. However, investing in a single stock is risky. The range of possible returns for the average stock is much wider, say from 240% to 50%, than the risk of the stock asset class. Investors reduce risk by holding a large portfolio of stocks. Done properly, diversification across a wide number of stocks provides a "free lunch." You can reduce risk without hurting return. Most sophisticated observers believe diversification is the only "free lunch" in finance.

Systematic Risk

Even if you diversify across all sensible alternatives, the resulting portfolio will still be risky. The risk that remains in a diversified portfolio is called

Table III

TEN-YEAR PROJECTED RANGES FOR ASSET CLASS RETURNS

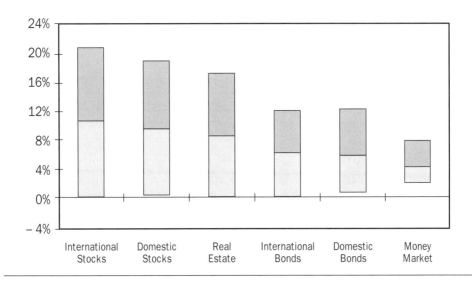

systematic risk, and it is that risk that is rewarded in financial markets. Specifically, portfolios with higher systematic risk have higher expected returns than portfolios with less systematic risk.

Many finance textbooks discuss systematic risk. (The beta of a common stock is a simple and early measure of systematic risk.) Suffice it to say that a good consultant or investment manager can help structure portfolios with enough diversification to eliminate most of the risks that do not bring higher returns.

In fact, most institutional portfolios are reasonably structured in this sense. Table IV shows some portfolios that are well diversified across asset classes. In addition, within each asset class, or category, the portfolio should be well diversified. On the other hand, a portfolio with its money equally split among three stocks, two real estate deals and some U.S. Treasury bills, would not be well diversified. The trustees should reduce risk by moving the asset mix toward a portfolio that looks more like those in Table IV.

Pension Plan Objectives

In addition to assets, a pension plan has (1) liabilities (the pension payments to retired participants), (2) rules to create more liabilities and (3) potential new contributions to the plan. The reality of these circumstances creates multiple objectives for most trustees and complicates the search for the

Table IV

	Mix A	Mix B	Mix C	Mix D
International Stocks	20%	15%	10%	5%
Domestic Stocks	50	40	35	30
Real Estate	15	10	5	0
Domestic Bonds	15	30	30	25
International Bonds	0	5	10	10
Money Market	0	0	10	30

More Aggressive ← → More Conservative

investment strategy that best balances risk and expected return. The fact that these assets will be used to provide important income to retirees tilts the objectives toward safe investments with an emphasis on the preservation of capital. However, since the size of the pool of assets depends only on contributions and investment earnings, getting higher investment returns becomes an important objective. This is especially true if the trustee wants to generate surplus value within the plan so there is room for improving the retirement benefits.

Adding to the pressure for high return objectives is pressure from employers in the multiemployer plans and taxpayers in the public employee plans to limit the cost of the pension plans. This pressure to restrain the cost of the pension benefit shifts the burden for increasing plan assets from contributions to investment earnings and points toward a riskier, more aggressive investment strategy. See Table V.

Investment strategy is complicated by the fact that investors have multiple objectives and the priority of these objectives changes over time. The caricature of this is the investor who wants to get both the highest return possible (100% of the portfolio in very risky assets) without any risk (100% of the portfolio in safe assets). When fear dominates this investor, such as during a period of sharply falling stock prices, he wants safety. However, when the stock market is persistently hitting new all-time highs and greed dominates, he wants the high returns. It takes dramatically different investment strategies to achieve these extreme objectives. Most investors are more moderate, but would still shift between objectives that imply less extreme but still significant shifts in investment strategy.

During periods when fear dominates, common objectives are: (a) to avoid losses or (b) to earn a set nominal return such as the actuarial assumed rate of return for the plan assets. When fear subsides and the striving for upside potential dominates, a common objective is to earn a set real return so that the real

Table V

PRESSURES AFFECTING TRUSTEES' INVESTMENT OBJECTIVES

Stress Low Risk	*Focus on High Returns*
(Conservative)	**(Aggressive)**
1. Need to preserve assets so that plan can meet benefit obligations to retirees.	1. Need to generate surplus assets so benefits can be improved to keep up with cost of living.
2. Avoid any surprise increase in annual contributions.	2. Lower the overall level of contributions required to provide the pension benefit.
3. Legal responsibility to manage prudently (especially when returns are low on risky assets).	3. Legal responsibility to manage prudently (especially when risky assets have shown consistently good returns).
4. Actual return falls below actuarial assumed interest rate.	4. Other similar plans generate higher returns.
5. Workers express concern about the security of pension benefits.	5. Employers or taxpayers complain about high cost of pension benefit.
6. News of bankrupt corporation with an underfunded pension plan.	6. Employers express desire to withdraw from multiemployer plan.

purchasing power for the assets grows by a set amount. Another is to earn more than the average of all pension plans. For those striving to get very high returns, the goal may be to earn more than 75% or 90% of all pension plans. Investment strategies to achieve these aggressive goals necessarily involve significant risk.

In a nutshell, the task facing any investor (trustee or investment manager) is to determine an investment strategy that balances risk and expected return in the way that can best achieve the objectives for the assets, and to recognize that if your long-run objectives change, the investment strategy should be modified accordingly.

An ironic aspect of risk in most real-world situations is that it cannot be eliminated, just managed. The more you work to eliminate risk in one area of your business, the more likely you are to increase the risk in another area. This is also true for pension plans. If trustees reduce the risk associated with pension investments by following an ultraconservative, very safe, low-risk investment strategy, they most likely will raise the risk associated with two other aspects of the pension plan. First, the purpose of the pension plan is to support the standard of living of the retirees. If returns are low and benefits do not increase, then there is a higher risk that the retiree's check will not keep up with cost-of-living increases.

A second risk is that the costs of providing the pension may rise. If costs rise too high, there is a risk of backlash from employers or taxpayers that could hurt the viability of the pension plan. With high costs, employers could pull out of multiemployer plans, and taxpayers could rebel and vote to cut the extent of coverage of public funds. Therefore, a trustee must examine the specifics of his pension plan and oversee an investment strategy that best balances risk and expected return in order to achieve the multiple objectives of the plan.

What Do You Want Your Investment Managers to Do?

The whimsical yet all too frequent answer to that question is that you want your investment manager to generate phenomenally high returns every quarter without taking any risk. This is similar to wanting the vendor of your lottery ticket to make sure he gives you the winning ticket. Such wishes may always be in the back of your mind, but they should not dominate your investment decisions.

The relationship between the trustees and your investment managers is important and can affect the returns for plan assets. In establishing this relationship, we recommend that trustees foster a collaborative rather than an adversarial relationship. The trustees, the plan administrator, and possibly even consultants to the plan have devoted a good deal of time and effort to hiring your investment managers. To get the most out of the relationship, you can expect your investment managers to do the following:

- ▶ Manage the plan's assets within the confines of the long-run guidelines in such a way that they generate a value added over and above a passive benchmark return for your guidelines.
- ▶ Contribute their insights and experience to the establishment or modification of the pension plan's long-run investment guidelines.
- ▶ Communicate how their investment management works, as well as any changes in organization or investment philosophy.
- ▶ React to changing financial opportunities or changing conditions within your pension plan to recommend modifications of the investment guidelines.

In this section, we will address each of these four aspects of your investment managers' activities.

Long-Run Guidelines

The single most important investment decision for a pension plan's assets is the establishment of the plan's long-term investment policy guidelines. The guidelines specify the plan's normal allocations to different asset classes and show how much actual allocations are allowed to differ from normal allocations.

Long-run investment guidelines for managing pension assets vary from pension plan to pension plan. These guidelines should be determined by such long-term considerations as the pension plan's liability structure, the potential for new contributions, and the underlying expected return and risk associated with the various potential investments, as well as the trustees' perceptions of the risks involved. Short-term developments, such as the recent performance of the stock and bond markets, should not be an important factor in determining the long-run guidelines for investing the plan assets.

Many investment managers can provide useful insights about the expected returns and risks associated with the various investment options. In addition, through their existing client base, they have direct experience with how a number of other pension plans have resolved this balancing act of shooting for high returns without taking on too much risk.

Asset/Liability Considerations

A good way to establish the long-run guidelines for a pension plan is to carry out an asset liability study. This study provides rough estimates of what is likely to happen to the plan in the future. You can vary the assumptions about the future and you can change the asset mixes or investment guidelines and see how those changes affect the estimates for assets, liabilities and pension costs in the future.

The first step in such a study uses the plan's actuarial report to determine its current liability and estimates of its future liabilities. The second step uses estimates of the potential returns and risks in the various investment markets, such as those in Tables II and III. With these as inputs, the third step uses computer simulations to estimate what is likely to happen to future liabilities, assets and the costs of the pension plan. These developments can be studied for the whole spectrum of possible asset allocations, from 0% to 100% on stocks and from 100% to 0% for bonds.

The studies do not just look at the most likely scenarios. Rather they show a range of possibilities and the impacts on liabilities, assets and contributions. In the end, a careful examination of the array of possibilities provides useful insights into which long-term asset allocations appear too risky for the specific liability structure of your plan and your current pool of assets. You should also be able to identify asset allocations that should be avoided as too conservative for your plan. This normally results in a reasonably wide range of asset allocations that could meet the objectives of the plan and fall within the trustees' risk tolerances. The trustees should then select a normal asset allocation as well as set maximum and minimum bounds for each asset class so that all possible asset allocation options fall within this reasonable range.

For large pension plans, this type of comprehensive asset liability study

Table VI

AVERAGE ASSET ALLOCATION—PUBLIC FUNDS

Asset Class	Proportion of Portfolio
Stocks	50%
Fixed Income	40
Real Estate	4
Short Term/Cash	3
Other	3

can be spearheaded by in-house staff, the plan's actuary or an investment consultant specializing in such studies. In this event, your investment managers would play a minor role in establishing the long-run guidelines but they should be consulted about how the guidelines may impact their ability to achieve the plan's objectives.

Small pension plans may view the cost of a detailed asset liability study as excessive. They may try to get a close approximation by determining how similar pension plans typically have resolved these issues and then customize their own guidelines based on any significant specific issues of the trustees. For these plans, investment managers can help by providing estimates of the expected returns and risk of various investments and the resulting guidelines developed by similar clients.

Average Guidelines and Characteristics of Pension Plans

Telling trustees that an appropriate set of long-run guidelines for your investment strategy depends on the specifics of your pension plan may be a fundamental truth, but it provides you with little useful information. It will be much more practical to provide you with the "typical" or average pension plan's investment strategy and then provide some broad average characteristics of pension plans. In this way, you can quickly get a rough idea of whether or not your plan is close to average in its characteristics and/or its investment strategy. Studies by Greenwich Associates as well as our experience with our clients provide the basis for the following details about typical investment strategies and plan characteristics.

We should begin this look at the average plan by considering the **asset mix**. The average investment profile for **public funds** is shown in Table VI.

A portion of the stock category in Table VI is allocated to foreign stocks, and this portion tends to increase as the size of the plan assets increase. For the larger public funds, the average exposure to foreign stocks is about 10%.

Another characteristic of the typical or average public fund is that the proportion of the U.S. stock portfolio that is passively managed (or indexed) rises along with the size of the plan assets. The larger plans, on average, index about a third of their U.S. stock portfolio.

Taft-Hartley plans tend to be a bit more conservative than the public plans. Their willingness to invest in U.S. stocks may approach the level of public plans, but historically the Taft-Hartley plans have not invested in foreign stocks, and on average this kept their total stock investments lower than public funds, with closer to 40% than 50% in stocks. Recently, however, we have noticed a developing willingness among Taft-Hartley plans to both begin buying foreign stocks and to raise their overall stock allocation toward the levels of public funds.

Corporate plans tend to be a bit more aggressive and on average have about 60% in stocks with 30% in fixed income. The rest of the asset mix profile closely parallels the public plans, including the pattern of investing in foreign stocks and indexing for U.S. stocks.

Plan Characteristics

Some of the elements that go into determining the liability structure of a pension plan are (a) the actuarial interest rate to discount future liabilities, (b) the net cash flow, (c) the average age and (d) the average length of service for plan participants. The actual value chosen for the actuarial interest rate significantly affects the measure of the present value of the plan's liabilities. Raising the rate will lower the measure of liabilities while lowering the rate raises the measure of liabilities. See Table VII.

Conservative plans tend to use lower actuarial interest rates. The average actuarial interest rate for public plans has been relatively stable for a few years at about the 8% level. Among the public funds, about 35% use rates lower than 8%, while about 40% use rates between 8% and 8¼%. Only about 1% to 2% of public funds are so aggressive as to use rates 10% or higher. In contrast to the relative stability of actuarial discount rates for public funds, there is a clear downward trend for the rates used by corporate funds. Historically, corporate plans were more aggressive and on average used higher rates to discount their plan liabilities.

However, over the last few years, under pressure to use market-related rates as the actuarial discount rate, corporate plans have reduced their rates. Actuarial discount rates are now marginally lower for corporate plans than for public funds. Nearly 70% of corporate plans use rates below 8%; about 20% use rates between 8% and 8¼%; and we are not aware of any corporate plans that use rates above 9% to discount their liabilities.

The net cash flow for pension plans is measured by subtracting withdrawals from the plan (benefit payments) from new contributions to the plan.

Table VII

ACTUARIAL DISCOUNT RATES

Year	Average Rates	
	Public Funds	Corporate Funds
1991	—	8.7%
1992	8.1%	8.4
1993	8.0	8.2
1994	8.1	7.8

Source: Greenwich Associates.

Table VIII

AVERAGE AGE OF PLAN PARTICIPANTS

Year	Public Funds	Corporate Funds
1991	41.1	40.5
1992	41.2	40.7
1993	41.1	41.0
1994	41.6	41.3

Source: Greenwich Associates.

Plans with large net cash inflows tend to be able to be more aggressive than plans with net cash outflows. The actual experience varies significantly between pension plans. It is interesting to note, however, that on average there has been a net outflow of funds from pension plans, for the past few years, of about 1% of plan assets.

The average age of workers covered by pension plans is about 41 to 41½ years old. With a young workforce, plan liabilities tend to be farther in the future and this would tend to support a more aggressive investment strategy. Conversely, an old workforce would foster a conservative investment strategy. Only about 15% of plans have an average age below 39; while about 30% have an average age of 43 or above. See Table VIII.

The average length of service for workers covered by a pension plan is also an important determinant of liabilities. For corporate plans, this has been stable for a few years at 12 years of service. Public funds tend to have workers

Table IX

AVERAGE YEARS OF SERVICE

Year	Public Funds	Corporate Funds
1991	11.2	11.8
1992	11.0	12.0
1993	10.9	11.9
1994	11.5	12.0

Source: Greenwich Associates.

with slightly less service, but recently the average length of service for public funds has risen from 11 to 11½ years. In general, about 25% of pension plans have an average length of service below ten years, and only about 15% have an average higher than 15 years. See Table IX.

Two factors that can affect the trustees' formulation of an investment strategy are the level of pension costs and the possible need to improve benefits. The past few years, the cost of funding corporate plans has been rising from just under 2½% of payroll to nearly 3½%. Only about 15% of these plans have costs that are 7% of payroll or higher. With regard to raising pension benefits, there is a distinctly different pattern for public funds than for other pension plans.

For corporate and Taft-Hartley plans, benefit increases tend to be an infrequent occurrence. A survey of benefit increases for retirees in corporate plans reveals that many of these plans (about one-quarter of them) have had virtually no benefit increases. For most of the others, a significant benefit increase appears to be an event that occurs about once in a decade.

In contrast, most public funds have relatively frequent benefit increases for retirees. This appears to be either an explicit or implicit form of adjusting benefits to keep up with inflation. It appears as if about 85% of public funds raised retiree benefits within the past two years. See Table X.

You are now armed with some insights as to what the average asset mix is for pension plans, as well as insights into some average characteristics of these plans. This should provide useful perspective for developing your plan's own investment guidelines and strategy. Your investment managers' experience can augment these observations.

Invest the Plan's Assets

The primary reason for hiring a professional investment manager is to invest the plan's assets, buying and selling securities, and to generate good re-

Table X

YEAR IN WHICH BENEFITS WERE LAST INCREASED FOR CURRENT RETIREES

	(% of Plans)	
Year	Public Funds	Corporate Funds
1994	67%	9%
1993	19	8
1992	4	8
1991	2	6
1990	1	5
1989	2	5
1988	1	5
Before 1988	5	25
Never	2	30

Source: Greenwich Associates.

turns. Ideally, the investment manager should produce returns that exceed your passive benchmark. This will not happen every quarter or every year, but should over longer intervals. This passive benchmark is the return that your assets would generate if they were passively invested in the market indexes of the asset categories (say S&P 500 for stocks and Lehman Aggregate for bonds) in the proportions set by your long-run guidelines. Accordingly, if your guidelines were 50% stocks and 50% bonds, then you should expect your investment manager to produce returns higher than one-half the S&P 500 returns plus one-half the Lehman Aggregate returns. This return over and above the passive guideline benchmark return can be viewed as your manager's value added.

In hiring investment professionals, the trustees have the option of hiring balanced managers or specialist managers. Balanced managers invest the plan assets in conjunction with the overall investment guidelines for the plan. Balanced managers generally invest in stocks, bonds and money market instruments. They can also invest in other asset classes, such as foreign stocks, foreign bonds and real estate. Specialist managers, on the other hand, restrict themselves to a single asset class (say stocks) or a particular segment of an asset class (such as growth stocks or small capitalization stocks). If the trustees hire an array of specialist managers as opposed to a balanced manager, then the trustees will retain the responsibility for the fund's asset allocation strategy. They will directly control the overall asset allocation strategy for the plan assets through their allocation of funds to the various specialist managers.

There are essentially three ways investment managers can generate value added over and above their benchmark. They are (a) effective security selection within the benchmark universe, (b) effective security selection by investing in securities outside the benchmark universe that generally have higher risk and expected returns than the universe, and (c) effective asset allocation strategies.

An example of security selection within the universe would be a portfolio of 50 of the stocks within the S&P 500 Index (the universe). Security selection outside the universe would occur if the portfolio manager added 20 small capitalization stocks and ten foreign stocks that are not in the universe. For a bond portfolio, security selection outside the universe could be the selection of lower rated, higher yielding bonds, possibly even including junk bonds. Asset allocation is generally viewed as an aspect of balanced management. Balanced managers can generate value added by tilting the plan's assets in favor of the asset class that generates the best returns in a given period. For example, if the plan's guidelines are 50% stocks and 50% bonds, and the manager invests 60% of the assets in stocks, this will generate value added if the stocks do better than bonds.

Specialist stock and bond managers can also add value through asset allocation by raising cash during periods when their market is in decline. Accordingly, all investment managers can add value both through security selection and through asset allocation. In addition, it should be noted that with both security selection and asset allocation, investment managers can generate value added over a benchmark both through skill or through exposing the portfolio to more risk than the benchmark.

Communications

In addition to their ongoing management of the plan's assets, investment managers need to communicate regularly with the trustees. The main focus of these regular (say semiannual) meetings should be an investment report that focuses on the what? how? why? and results! of the investment manager's activities. This enables the trustees to do their due diligence in monitoring and evaluating the investment manager.

The managers should also notify the trustees of any significant changes in the investment manager's ownership, organizational structure, personnel or investment philosophy. With this information, the trustees are able not only to consider the stark numbers of investment performance, but can also form judgments as to whether the returns were generated in line with the trustees' expectations when they hired the investment manager. This review of the manager's activity and review of any significant organizational changes should give confidence to the trustees that the investment managers are performing in line with the trustees' expectations and can be expected to continue to deliver this performance in the future.

An important side effect of regular meetings with in-depth discussions is that the investment managers and trustees better understand each other. With close communication, the investment manager can often detect and clarify fundamental changes in the objectives of the trustees. This can enable the investment manager to modify his strategy and possibly the plan's long-run guidelines in conformity with the changing needs of the plan. Without this communication, investment managers may persist in strategies that are no longer appropriate for the plan and no longer desired by the trustees. Over the long run, this discrepancy can create an adversarial relationship that is detrimental to all parties involved.

Insights

As the investment manager's knowledge of the trustees' objectives and plan characteristics increases, he may have insights that lead to a more effective means of achieving the plan's objectives. In a collaborative environment, the investment managers will recommend changes in the investment guidelines or strategy that could prove valuable to the plan. These recommendations could be based on changing plan characteristics that cause the trustees to shift their objectives; significant developments in the risk or expected return of an asset class; or the development of new investment alternatives that may be appropriate for the plan assets. Trustees should solicit the investment manager's insights and recommendations, but the ultimate decision still rests with the trustees.

How Do You Manage Your Investment Managers After You Hire Them?

Just as it is very important for the investment managers to communicate with the trustees, it is very important for the trustees to communicate with the investment manager. This is the crucial element in managing your managers to get the most out of them. The first step in managing your managers is to clearly communicate your long-run guidelines for the plan's assets.

The second step is to develop reasonable expectations about performance. Investment management is a highly competitive business, and it is very difficult to consistently produce above-average results. Moreover, while the scope for superior performance in a single year may be significant, as the time period increases even moderately, "value added" on the order of 1% per year can place you among the top 25% of *balanced managers*. (See Table XI.)

For *stock managers*, it has recently been difficult to beat the S&P 500. The

Table XI

PERFORMANCE OF BALANCED MANAGERS

	Periods Ending 12/31/95					
	One Year	Two Years	Three Years	Four Years	Five Years	Ten Years
Top Quartile: SEI	29.2%	13.2%	12.5%	11.4%	14.1%	12.8%
Median: SEI	26.7	12.0	11.1	10.4	12.8	12.3
50% S&P 500/ 50% Lehman Aggregate	28.0	12.7	11.7	10.6	13.0	12.2
Top Quartile—Median	2.5	1.2	1.4	1.0	1.3	0.5
Top Quartile—50/50	1.2	0.5	0.8	0.8	1.1	0.6

Source: SEI.

Table XII

PERFORMANCE OF STOCK MANAGERS

	Periods Ending 12/31/95					
	One Year	Two Years	Three Years	Four Years	Five Years	Ten Years
Top Quartile: SEI	38.0%	17.9%	15.9%	14.3%	18.3%	15.5%
Median: SEI	33.5	15.5	14.4	12.4	16.5	14.0
S&P 500	37.6	18.1	15.3	13.4	16.6	14.8
Top Quartile—Median	4.5	2.4	1.5	1.9	1.8	1.5%
Top Quartile—S&P 500	0.4	−0.2	0.6	0.9	1.7	0.7%

Source: SEI.

S&P 500 did better than the median manager for virtually all periods ending December 31, 1995, and for most of these periods it took less than a 1% per year value added over and above the S&P 500 to get into the top 25% of stock managers. (See Table XII.)

Bond managers have done a bit better than stock managers when compared to their benchmark, but still value added on the order of 1% above the

Table XIII

PERFORMANCE OF BOND MANAGERS

	Periods Ending 12/31/95					
	One Year	Two Years	Three Years	Four Years	Five Years	Ten Years
Top Quartile: SEI	19.4%	7.5%	9.2%	9.0%	10.4%	10.2%
Median: SEI	17.8	6.9	8.5	8.4	10.0	9.7
Lehman Aggregate:	18.5	7.3	8.1	7.9	9.5	9.6
Top Quartile—Median	1.6	0.6	0.7	0.6	0.4	0.5
Top Quartile—Lehman	0.9	0.2	1.1	1.1	0.9	0.6

Source: SEI.

Lehman Aggregate would put a bond manager among the top 25% of his peers. (See Table XIII.)

The third step in managing your investment manager is to develop a clear understanding of the manager's modus operandi. This generally should occur during the interview process before you hire the manager, but clear communications over time can enhance this understanding. In addition to the particulars of the manager's track record, you should have a thorough understanding of the manager's investment philosophy and investment process. This helps you understand how the track record was generated and provides the basis for your expectations with regard to how and how much value added will be earned by the manager. You should know whether it is done primarily through asset allocation or security selection and whether it is done through extraordinary skill or selectively taking on more risk than the benchmark.

Once you have established a clear understanding of how your investment manager operates and develop an understanding of what to expect from the markets, then you are prepared to monitor the investment managers and provide the critically important feedback to them. For investment managers, how they generated their value added in any given period is just as important and sometimes even more important than the size of the value added. This is because investment managers have particular skills and styles that have significantly different levels of success (or failure), depending upon the prevailing investment environment. In monitoring his activity and performance, you should determine not only how he compares to the median manager or the best (top quartile) managers, but you should also determine how he compares to other "similar" managers. You should monitor how the manager is operating and make sure he is still adhering to his investment philosophy and discipline because that is where the manager's skill lies.

A period in which your manager does well for his particular investment style but still underperforms the average manager could set the stage for damaging communications and recommendations. What should you tell your manager in an investment environment that is temporarily hostile to his style? A common knee-jerk reaction would be to express displeasure and tell him he better turn things around and do better by the next meeting. But, what can the manager do better? He can try to get better results by abandoning his style (say growth stocks) if it is temporarily out of favor, and quickly adopt a new style that is currently in favor (such as value stocks or cyclicals). Aside from generating a lot of transactions costs, the manager has shifted from operating in an area where he has special knowledge and skills to an area where he is at a competitive disadvantage.

A second option for a beleaguered manager is to maintain his style, but significantly increase the risk of the portfolio in the hopes that this will generate enough returns to satisfy you. You should recognize that "cracking the whip," or taking your manager out to the tool shed for a talk will often result in changing the manager's investment activity in ways that may be detrimental to the plan.

Whenever you decide to exert pressure on your investment manager to produce better results, you need to communicate clearly not only how good you want the results to be, but also how you expect the manager to achieve those results.

What Do You Do When You Are Unhappy With Your Investment Manager?

Any attempt to answer this question places us in grave danger of appearing to be craven, self-serving investment managers. Nevertheless, we have suppressed our cowardly impulses and boldly recommend that you avoid frivolously or precipitously firing investment managers.

There are several good reasons for these words of caution. First, our experience has taught us that in many instances, the trustees' unhappiness with their investment manager is misplaced and would exist no matter who was managing the assets. A few examples of inappropriate disappointment with your investment manager would be if the manager's returns were good in comparison to his performance benchmarks but were still insufficient to (a) eliminate the plan's underfunded status, (b) reduce the required contributions to the plan to zero, (c) generate enough surplus in the fund to raise benefits substantially, (d) place the manager among the top 1% of all pension plans, or (e) beat the returns for pension plans that have much more aggressive guidelines. In such situations, clear and frank discussions about reasonable expectations for investment performance should resolve the difficulty.

Even in instances where your investment manager's performance falls short of reasonable expectations and is appropriately disappointing, there are reasons for caution in changing managers. An important reason is the difficulty of determining whether the poor performance is temporary or permanent. This is related to the difficulty in distinguishing whether the manager's performance was due to skill (lack of it), luck, or the level of risk in the portfolio. Presumably, when you hired the manager, you felt that he had superior skill. This skill could very easily be concealed for a year or two by the bad luck of an economic environment that penalizes his style or skills.

Another very important factor is the high costs of firing and replacing a manager. In addition to the costs of searching for a replacement, there are transactions costs associated with liquidating the current manager's portfolio and establishing the new manager's portfolio. Normally, such a transition results in all or part of the portfolio being uninvested or held in money market instruments for a short time. This adds to the cost, with the risk of being out of the market when it rises. The total cost of changing managers could easily be 5% to 10%. Over the long run, the superiority of a good manager (top quartile) over an average or median manager may only be about 1% per year. Accordingly, even if you pick a better manager, it may take many years to recoup the transactions costs.

Finally, it is extremely difficult to identify which managers are going to be good (top quartile) over the next five to ten years. It is probably just as hard or harder for the trustees to pick the best managers as it is for the investment managers to pick the best stocks or bonds. Studies have shown that picking from among the current crop of top quartile investment managers only gives you about a 50/50 chance of selecting an above-average manager over the next five years, let alone choosing one that will remain in the top quartile.

These factors suggest that even if your current manager disappoints you by falling short of your expectations, (1) you can't be sure he is an incompetent that will underperform in the future; (2) it is costly to replace him with another manager; (3) it is difficult to find a replacement that has a high probability of being good (top quartile) over the next five years; and (4) even if you get lucky and do replace him with a good manager, the superiority of this good manager still may not be sufficient to overcome the costs of changing managers.

Does this mean that once you hire a manager you are stuck with them forever? The quick answer to that question is obviously no, but we should elaborate with two analogies. You should be very careful in selecting a manager.

Get to know them very well before you hire them, just as you get to know your prospective spouse well before marriage. In both cases, separation is always possible but not without pain.

The second analogy suggests that you should treat your investment manager like your new car. Before buying the car, you looked at several makes and models, checked out their specs and selected the one that best met your needs and objectives. But what do you do if after a while you become unhappy with the car? Perhaps the gas mileage or acceleration isn't quite as good as you expected. Or, perhaps your car performs fine but a friend tells you about a model that does even better. Do you immediately junk or sell your car in the hopes of getting a better one? From our perspective, it would be better to hold onto your car until you would normally replace it and then go after the hopefully better model. To carry this over to your investment manager, I would recommend switching from a disappointing manager with your normal cash flow. We would take all withdrawals from that manager and give all net contributions to the new manager or other existing managers.

On the other hand, if we return to the car analogy and you discover that your new car is a lemon, how long would you keep it? We recommend quickly dumping a lemon and replacing it with your new dream car. The problem with this part of the analogy is how to determine if your manager is a lemon. We believe it is difficult to find a lemon by looking only at returns. To find a lemon, you have to look under the hood and see if the manager's investment philosophy, process, or people are still functioning as they did in the showroom. If any of these three elements are malfunctioning, then you should quickly trade in your investment manager.

Suggested Checklist for Request for Proposal (RFP)

The Firm: Questions designed to determine the nature of the firm and ensure appropriate legal status

1. Describe the firm's ownership, founding, corporate structure and major affiliations.

2. Is the firm a registered investment advisor?

3. Does the firm carry fiduciary liability and/or errors and omissions insurance?

4. How much is the coverage?

5. Has the firm or any of its personnel been subject to any litigation over the last five years?

The Investment Professionals: Is there a stable, well-motivated group of investment professionals?

1. How many senior investment professionals work for your firm? How many have joined or left in the last five years?

2. How are investment professionals compensated?

3. Which investment professionals will have primary responsibility for the proposed account?

The Investment Process: Describe the investment process and philosophy for the proposed account. (Read the following questions first since they cover more detailed aspects of the process.)

1. Performance: What benchmark or benchmarks are appropriate in assessing your performance?

2. How does your process provide returns above the stated benchmark?

3. Please provide returns and assets under management over the last five years.

4. Portfolio characteristics: Describe basic portfolio characteristics, e.g., number of securities, industry or sector concentration, beta, duration.

5. Compliance: Describe review procedures that ensure that portfolios comply with client and/or firmwide guidelines.

6. Describe other parts of the investment process designed to control risk.

Client Relations:

1. Describe client communications.

2. Provide a fee schedule.

About the Authors

Michael Haffner

Vice President and Business Representative
Teamsters Local Union No. 301
Waukegan, Illinois

James H. Scott, Ph.D.

Chief Executive Officer
PDI Strategies
Chairman
PTC Services
Short Hills, New Jersey

John Van Belle, Ph.D.

Managing Director of International Asset Allocation
PDI Strategies
Short Hills, New Jersey

Mr. Haffner is also a labor trustee for Teamsters Local Union 301 Health and Welfare and Pension Funds, treasurer for the McHenry County Building Trades Council and the McHenry County Building Trades Council Political Action Committee. He is a teamster representative for the National Heavy and Highway Committee for Illinois. Mr. Haffner also serves on the Co-Policy Committee of the Central Region Teamsters Construction Division.

Prior to joining PDI in 1987, Dr. Scott was professor and divisional coordinator for finance at the Columbia University Graduate School of Business. He graduated from Rice University and holds a master's and Ph.D. in economics from Carnegie-Mellon University and is a director of the Institute for Quantitative Research in Finance. Dr. Scott has been a speaker at International Foundation educational programs.

Dr. Van Belle is responsible for PDI's foreign-based full-service clients. He manages PDI's Global Balanced Portfolios and PDI's Equity Allocation Fund. He taught economics and finance at the University of Virginia and the Rutgers Graduate School of Management and has published numerous articles in the fields of economics and finance.

Chapter 8

Custody: Not Simply a Vault

by Gerard M. Arnone

Trustee's Perspective

by John A. Viniello

Webster defines "custodian" as . . . "one that guards and protects or maintains; one entrusted with guarding and keeping property of records. . . ." For the trustee, this definition, although simply stated, defines the role of the custodian, which is a critically important component to ensure the smooth functioning of the trust fund that you represent.

Trustees rely on a number of professionals to provide a wide range of services while exercising their fiduciary responsibilities. Investment, legal, actuarial, performance evaluation and administration professionals are all necessary ingredients that assist the fund in a multitude of ways in conducting its day-to-day business.

While all of these functions serve a very real and specific purpose, the role of the custodian in maintaining custody over transactions that affect the very heart of investment decision making is probably the most critical.

As trustees, we should think of the custodian as the depository for security transactions made by your investment managers. In effect, the custodian acts as a caretaker and is responsible for processing all financial transactions on instructions from the various money managers. With the complexity of financial instruments now available in the marketplace, it is the custodian's responsibility for recording trades and *providing the investment professionals with financial information such as daily cash balances and securities information. As with most large multiemployer funds, the speed and accuracy of the numerous transactions taking place in the course of a business day are essential to leveraging the best return on investment for the various securities being traded. The custodian is a team player. He must develop points of contact and cultivate excellent working relationships with each of the investment managers, which can only benefit the funds that they mutually represent.*

In my view, every trustee should think of the custodian as one would think of the hub of a multispoked financial wheel. This hub is truly the engine that drives all financial transactions performed by your investment managers and fund administrator.

The following chapter describes in some detail the various aspects of how a custodian functions. It will serve as an excellent primer for experienced trustees and absolutely essential reading for those newly elected to the position.

BACKGROUND

SAY THE WORD "CUSTODY" TO MOST PEOPLE AND THEIR EYES GLAZE OVER WITH VISIONS of a huge vault door closing slowly on a room lined with metal shelves piled with stock certificates and a few loose dollar bills. An elderly security guard is sitting beside the door and might be coughing from the dust raised. It is not a very exciting picture.

But that's the way it was. Wall Street (the securities industry) was nothing but paper, paper and more paper that moved from brokerage house to brokerage house to banks by messengers carrying both securities and checks. The lines of these messengers at the various vault "cage" areas were as long as lottery lines when it hasn't been hit for weeks. And all of those certificates and checks were being watched over by that elderly security guard who probably had no idea that the unbelievable conglomeration of paper represented billions and billions of dollars in value.

It was all that paper and the signing of ERISA into law on September 2, 1974, that brings us to where we are today. Figure 1 shows the pre- and post-ERISA progression.

The fact is that the custody business has become an extremely dynamic piece of the exploding worldwide securities industry. An argument can be made that of all the talented team members that the trustees have put together for the benefit of better plan performance (both investment and administrative/operational), the custodian is one of the most important, because it is the custodian that must successfully implement and execute the strategies of the others.

Figure 1 illustrates how far we've come from the static image of warehousing stock and bond certificates. The custodian is the trustees' representative at the hub of a large number of complex activities needed to implement

Figure 1

Pre-ERISA	Post-ERISA
— Single investment managers (usually bank trust departments or insurance companies)	— Multiple investment managers
	— Multiple plans
	— More volatile financial markets
— Simple asset classes	— Greater asset diversification
— Assets held by trust departments or insurance companies as part of the investment management process	— Governmental disclosure requirements
	— Assets still held by bank trust departments but under more demanding accounting and reporting structures

the investment strategy devised by trustees' consultants and investment managers. Because of the diversity of investment programs, custodians do not just physically safekeep securities, but rather they keep track of their clients' securities at various central depositories[1] and subcustodians. Other daily interfaces are with clients, investment managers and transfer agents; pricing vendors' input daily to assist custodians in valuing their clients' assets, which is no small task. Large custodians have tens of thousands of domestic issues to price, and when managers move to broad global investment for diversification purposes, the number of securities needed to be priced is increased manyfold. Combining all the above with greatly enhanced reporting capabilities, including online, real-time data center hookups, it's easy to see why the custodian is no longer just a warehouse for assets, but rather a very modern information processor.

What Are the Duties of Your Custodian?

There are seven primary duties and a number of ancillary functions that your custodian can perform.

The primary functions are discussed below:
- Trade settlement
- Safekeeping
- Income collection
- Cash management/sweep
- Corporate action/reorganization
- Accounting
- Reporting.

} Assets

Trade Settlement

Everything begins with a security transaction made on behalf of the trustees. Trustees hire investment professionals to manage the assets and custodian banks to implement the whole process. As such, the custodian is responsible for acting on the trade instructions from the investment managers and for providing them with important information like daily cash balances and corporate actions like stock splits and dividends. Custodian banks have become very good at working with investment management firms to service their mutual client.

Safekeeping

Remember the elderly guard? He's been moved to another job. Through technology and the establishment of various central depositories, custodians now can settle trades, move portfolios or entire funds with the relative ease of pressing a button. This is one of those cases where the good old days aren't

Figure 2

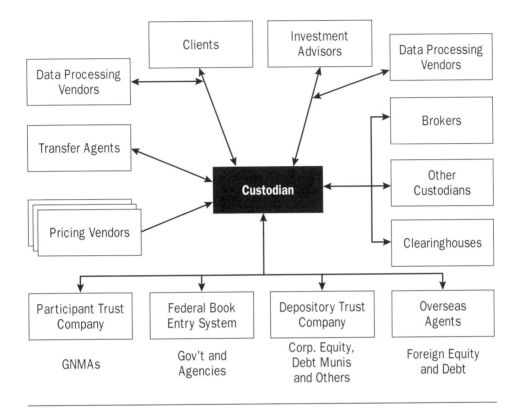

so good. Depositories have been a wonderful and very necessary addition to the custody business—in no way could the current daily trading volume of 400+ million shares be handled without central depositories. However, there are still some securities that are retained in the vault since they are not depository-eligible, i.e., individual mortgage contracts held by a fund.

Figure 2 reflects the use of three major depositories:
- Participant Trust Company (PTC)—used for mortgage-backed securities for the Government National Mortgage Association (Ginnie Mae) and the Federal National Mortgage Association (Fannie Mae)
- Federal Book Entry System (FBE)—used for all Treasury securities
- The Depository Trust Company (DTC)—the world's largest, used for domestic stocks and corporate bonds.

Income Collection

In this function, income due the fund is collected from the security's paying agent. Differences from late trades, taxes and security reconciliation items are resolved by sending "claims" to the paying agent. Income can be credited on either "payable" date or upon actual receipt. Obviously, the preferred method is payment on payable date in "Fed Funds," which is equivalent to investible cash. (See Cash Management section below.)

Cash Management/Sweep

Cash management, which involves both balance management and income collection, is a very important subject. While it may appear to be a fairly simple function that is easily performed, it can be quite complex. Because of the total assets involved and the daily cash flows in the modern day employee benefit fund, there are significant additional earnings to be gained with an intensive cash management program.

The cash balance is simply the amount of uninvested cash in the portfolio at the end of the business day; but good cash management must also consider the income collection process, which can be done on an actual receipt basis (which is usually many days after the normal payable date), on the normal payable date in all cases or some combination of the two. The methods that custodians use reflect their operational capabilities and their approach to crediting income.

A first rate custodian must be able to provide an effective balance management service for an employee benefit plan. The vehicle that is used most frequently is a commingled or pooled portfolio of cash equivalent investments called a short-term investment fund (STIF). Virtually every custodian bank has such a commingled vehicle. In fact, most large custodians have a number of these STIF vehicles that range from minimal to high risk. Depending upon the guidelines the trustees have in place, investment managers can choose the sweep vehicle of choice. Those custodians that do not have STIF funds make use of master notes and other instruments of demand and commercial paper. Other banks use pools of government or agency securities, and sometimes government bills or notes directly. While the capital safety of government-backed securities is unquestionable, the rate of return is lacking versus a well-managed STIF. The advantages of the short-term investment fund are those of a typical commingled fund, i.e., diversification, cash flow advantages, negotiated brokerage advantages, etc.

Corporate Action/Reorganization

A first tier custodial bank will have a strong "reorg" unit that enables custodians to notify investment managers of recently announced corporate actions. It is paramount that a custodian communicate accurate information on a timely basis to ensure that investment managers have the information they need when a change with a security is pending.

As an example, to monitor whether a bond is being "called" prior to maturity, a reorg unit will scour the following as a daily source for pending or announced corporate action:

Domestic
1. DTC & Financial Information Incorporation (PC-based system)
2. Standard & Poor's
3. NYSE letters
4. Wall Street Journal
5. Company correspondence
6. Telestat (for stock splits and dividends)

Foreign
1. Extel
2. IDSI
3. The WM Company (over 80 sources)
4. Valorinform
5. Subcustodians
6. Reuters
7. Telekurs
8. Bloomberg.

Accounting

While accounting and reporting are considered the same by many, in actuality they are quite different. This section describes the accounting process within the bank, otherwise known as "posting to records."

There are three basic accounting systems (procedures) that custodians utilize to maintain their own records:
1. Delivery date (cash) accounting
2. Settlement date (contractual) accounting
3. Trade date (accrual) accounting.

The history of the trust industry includes the evolution from delivery to settlement and now to trade date accounting. Most people can easily understand accounting on a cash basis and in fact it is still used today. "Give me my security and I'll give you your money" is the guiding principle. The custodian's records reflect only the actual movement of cash and securities so the so-called accounting is really just a snapshot of the trust's physical holdings on a given day. Looking at it from another angle, it's a picture of the security movement industry in general. It's not very accurate as an accounting (report), but it does fill the custodian's need to keep the trust "whole" at any given point in time, because you either have securities or cash.

But obviously, delivery date accounting is very lacking in the true accounting sense, and to a certain extent hampers the investment programs of money managers. The accountings aren't accurate since they do not reflect the true position of a trust at a given point in time. Investment managers may have made commitments to either buy or sell securities, but that is not yet identified on the custodian's books. In addition, the managers themselves keep a supplementary set of records (typically as of trade date) so that they are aware of the commitments they have made. Also, the investment managers are affected by the "fail" situation in the security movement industry. Under a delivery date system, the manager might sell a security today for settlement in three business days while also wishing to make a purchase with the proceeds from the sale. However, since there is always a danger that the buy transaction will settle before the sell transaction (creating an overdraft), the manager must wait until the sale proceeds are received before making the purchase; if the security to be purchased has increased in price in the interim, the trust has not realized that gain in value (lost opportunity).

A third major deficiency of delivery date accounting is that it makes the income collection process much more difficult to track. Since the transfer agent frequently doesn't know who owns a given security on the date when dividends are credited, the buying and selling custodians must clear this up in a costly manual process called "claiming."

Settlement date, or contractual accounting, is a major improvement over delivery date accounting. A settlement date process means the custodian will record the purchase or sale of a security on the records of the trust on the contractual settlement date (usually the third business day after trade) regardless of the physical location of that security. As long as the custodian knows about the trade and considers it a good trade, the trust records will be credited. This is an enormous improvement because of the discipline that it applies to both the accounting and investment procedure. On the accounting side, the custodian is showing a much more disciplined and logical position of a trust's assets on a given day. As far as the investment process is concerned, settlement date accounting allows the investment manager to make a sale and a purchase on the same day, knowing in full confidence that in three business days the sale will produce proceeds which in turn will be used to settle the purchase, eliminating the possibility of overdraft and therefore eliminating the need to keep excessive cash balances available. Also, the discipline of settlement date accounting simplifies somewhat the procedure for tracking of income; and there is less possibility that a dividend will not be collected.

Trade date, or full accrual accounting, is the next logical step. Trade date accounting, which reflects ownership of a security on the date actually traded, has been used by mutual funds for many years; and investment managers keep their own records as of trade date. It was inevitable that trade date would become the goal in the securities industry, and it has become the most commonly accepted accounting methodology being practiced today.

Reporting

After the custodian has accounted for all the purchases and sales, reorganization issues, income collection and cash management earnings, it must be reported to the trustees and their professionals.

While actual and delivery date reporting is still widely utilized, most major custodian banks have adopted at least some form of trade date reporting package. Some have done it on an annual basis, some on a quarterly basis and others are rendering monthly security reports on a trade date basis. Where an online real-time link with the custodian's data center is available, trustees can create daily trade date positions.

Trustees should not fail to appreciate the complexity and difficulty to produce a trade date report. It requires the custodian to maintain duplicate and sometimes triplicate records. The "factory" of the custodian, the security clearance area, must be maintained on a cash basis. Obviously, no custodian is going to pay cash to a broker until the broker shows up with the security. On the other hand, the assumed discipline of a security clearance area is a contractual settlement date basis, because that is the way the securities industry strives to operate. As a custodian is made aware of a trade, various "pending" records have to be maintained, anticipating the settlement on a given day. Finally, the three sets of records are melded to create the actual trade date report for the plan trustees and investment managers.

There are two primary ways which this information can be distributed: hard copy and online. A third method is the use of CD ROM technology.

Reports are typically issued monthly, quarterly and annually. In special situations, interim reports are also available. Following is a list of what a custodian can supply:

Daily:

    Daily Statement
        Opening and closing balances
        Complete purchase and sale information
        Redemptions and maturities
        Interest and dividends
        Cash receipts and disbursements
        Corporate actions (stock splits, tender offers, etc.)
        Other transactions

Monthly, Quarterly and Annual:

Transaction Statement
Opening balances
Cash inflows and outflows by transaction types in summary and detail
All interest and dividend transactions
Noncash transactions
Closing balances
Detailed elements of the trades

Statement of Changes in Net Assets
Inflows in summary
Outflows in summary
Administrative expense in summary
Total net inflow/outflow
Net gain/loss on sales
Change in unrealized appreciation/depreciation
Net assets at beginning and end of period

Analysis of Earnings
Income collected and accrued for current and previous periods
Earnings by category (e.g., interest, dividends)

Statement of Assets and Liabilities (Schedule A)
Overview of total book and market values for all categories of assets and liabilities
Net assets
Percentages each category represents of net asset amount

Diversification of Assets (Schedule B)
Total book and market values by industry classification within security type
Percentage each industry classification represents of total book and total market and value of its security type
Accrued income

Statement of Assets (Schedule C)
Securities within industry classification
Total book and market values for each security based on fully committed positions
Unit book and current price
Percentage each security represents of total book, total market and market value of its security type
Accrued income

Statement of Liabilities
    Call options written
    Percentage each option represents of total options outstanding
    Aggregates liabilities into major "payable" categories

Security Transaction Report
    Acquisition/disposition by security
    Book value, unit costs, unit proceeds, aggregate proceeds
    Gain/loss on sales
    Investment activity
    Capital changes
    Payments/maturities
    Free receipts and deliveries

Brokerage Commission Report
    List of brokers
    Total commission by broker
    Percentage of total commission by broker
    Total commissionable trades by broker
    Percentage total commissionable trades by broker
    Annual broker commission information

5500 Reporting Package (Annual Only)

Ancillary Services

Five other custodial services are available as options to the primary custodian package:
- Securities lending
- Online services
- Benefit payments
- Performance measurement
- Investment management.

Securities Lending

Although securities lending is not considered a true primary deliverable by a custodian bank, it has become the number-one option utilized.

Securities lending is a way for institutional investors to gain incremental income from their portfolios by lending securities to counterparties. The counterparties need to borrow securities because:
1. Institutional investors have sold a security short and need to deliver it.
2. Short selling is required to hedge positions related to a derivative instrument.

Figure 3

HOW IT WORKS

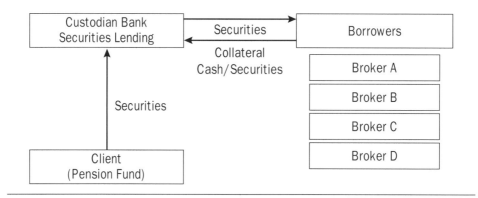

3. Brokers are having problems delivering securities for settlement and they want to avoid a "fail."
4. Government securities are needed as collateral for other types of investments such as repurchase agreements (repos).

In the majority of cases, institutional investors borrow securities through a broker. The broker contacts a custodian bank that acts as a lending agent for either institutions with large portfolios or an institutional investor that lends directly. From the lender's point of view, the broker is the borrower, and the actual counterparty remains unknown. Brokers may also borrow for their own account. Figure 3 shows the process.

Securities may be lent either for a specific period of time (a *term* loan) or for an undefined period of time (an *open* loan). In any case, the lender may demand the return of the securities at any time.

Whenever securities are lent, the borrower is required to provide collateral to the lender that has a value of 102% of the borrowed securities (105% for international securities). This collateral is marked to market daily to maintain the required level. Generally, acceptable collateral includes cash, U.S. government securities and irrevocable letters of credit.

Cash collateral is placed in a high-quality, short-term investment fund (STIF) or money market mutual fund. Under certain circumstances, customized investment funds can be created with the goal of exceeding the standard money market rate. The lender's profit is the interest earned on the collateral reduced by two items, a rebate given back to the borrower (a common industry practice) and a fee earned by the custodian for implementing and monitoring the transaction.

Online Service

The ability to access information directly from a custodian's data center is becoming increasingly important to trustees and their fund office. With today's personal computers and the custodian's technological support, the possibilities are virtually limitless. Fund offices can view daily asset listings, pending trades, income projections and other data, and often prepare customized board reports that can reduce consulting expenses.

Benefit Payments

A custodian can prepare and distribute monthly retiree checks and lump-sum payments, including all the tax filings.

Performance Measurement

The custodian's technological capabilities make performance measurement calculations simple. By servicing literally thousands of accounts, the compilation of complete and unique indices is a natural byproduct.

Investment Management

In addition to cash management services noted earlier, most, if not all, custodian banks offer comprehensive investment management services, from total passive products to very specialized investment vehicles.

Looking for a Master Custodian

While we have made the case for a dramatic change of the role of the custodian in the increasingly complex securities industry, it is still banks and limited purpose trust companies that provide the service. Indeed, the banks may have been the only institutions that possessed both the technical/data processing knowledge and the financial resources to participate in the metamorphasis of the custodian. Their technical knowledge was enhanced by the experience of implementing modern retail banking systems; the financial resources were committed to protect and hopefully grow their market share in the securities industry. And, let's face it, "custody," "trust" and "fiduciary responsibility" go hand in hand; the banks are good at it and want to protect their franchise.

There are over a thousand banks in the country that have some form of custodial service. They range from a simple warehousing capability for your stock certificates only to a truly global capability to settle a transaction on your behalf virtually anywhere in the world, and then safekeep, collect income and report almost instantaneously. While multinational corporations are the primary user of this premier service, all professionally managed funds are quickly moving in that direction.

It is incumbent on trustees to very carefully consider the qualifications of custodians before committing plan assets to their care, so a significant part of this chapter is devoted to the selection of a custodian.

Conducting a Search

Use of Consultants

The consultant industry has grown almost as fast as the custody industry. For many years, the role of a consultant was primarily that of a benefits advisor. The major actuarial firms employed a staff of consultants to assist the plan trustee in determining what benefits should be implemented and how best to do it. But with the advent of performance investing in the '60s, the need to help determine how to achieve that performance arose. Some major firms were formed at that time, and their early work consisted primarily of performance measurement and evaluation.

Consultants became a clearinghouse for the performance data generated by the major investment managers in our industry. As multiple investment managers became commonplace, the problems associated with the administration and operation of multiple portfolios grew significantly. Therefore, it was a very logical step for the consultants to expand their expertise into the area of custodian banks.

The decision to use a consultant is typically made on the basis of the other responsibilities of the trustees, their sophistication in employee benefit services and whether or not the trustees want some type of a "buffer" between them and the selection process.

Consultants can perform a valuable service and can be a powerful tool. Because of their position as an impartial third party, and because of their implied power in directing business, managers and custodians make a considerable effort to influence them. Consultants who are forthright and capable are recognized as such, and many enjoy an open communications channel with the major custodians in our industry. Custodians are comfortable being candid in these situations and therefore the information gathered by these consultants is the best available. The expertise and the sophistication of the consultant should be used to ferret out information from those custodians who are not so open and candid.

Doing It Yourself

Many trustees have chosen to go it alone in selecting a custodian. This is not only a viable alternative but can actually be rewarding if the trustees have time to devote to the project. Doing it properly and thoroughly will not only increase their confidence in the final decision, but can also save a few dollars in a budget that may be tight.

Identifying the industry leaders in the custodian field is easy. A periodic reading of the trade publications will keep trustees right up to date on not only who is receiving the majority of the new business but, more importantly, who is doing the best thinking in our industry. In doing this, however, one has to be careful not to be unduly influenced by the ad campaigns that are being mounted. Ads are good at determining who is aggressively seeking the business, but they are the shallowest documents at determining the capability of properly servicing the business.

If time is not of the essence, trustees have the option to just wait until they are contacted by custodians in their normal marketing efforts. The value of these initial presentations can be significant in terms of "education" when the custodian sends out a knowledgeable marketing/sales representative. Unfortunately, sometimes the meaningful education process has to wait until the trustees ask to see some of the administrative personnel back at the bank.

After sitting through some initial presentations and feeling ready to expand the scope of the study, trustees can then contact the remaining prospective custodians they would consider. These meetings should be spaced over a number of days since daily pressures can cause trustees to be distracted in some presentations and miss important points. The general experience of these presentations is that new insights will be gained with each meeting. People express thoughts differently, and what may not have been appreciated in the previous meeting will suddenly become clear. More importantly each new presentation will, of course, stress that particular firm's strong points. To the extent that these strong points are appealing, trustees should not hesitate to go back to custodians who have already made a presentation in order to clarify a certain item. In fact, there is much to be gained in finding an excuse to get back to the earlier applicants even if you feel you have a good understanding of what they have to offer. Calling up someone unexpectedly and putting him on the spot for quick information, especially information which he did not volunteer during the initial interview, is a very good way of testing the experience and responsiveness of the firm. After all, the custodian is seeking a long-term service relationship and responsiveness is the name of that game.

But your emphasis should be at the contact level. One of the advantages of a responsive organization is that particular questions can be answered at the contact level, i.e., with a single phone inquiry. The administrative officer who is the contact point for the plan trustee should be a decision maker, i.e., he should be able to commit the custodian for certain actions. If he or she cannot commit the custodian, then the trustees are destined to be given the runaround every time a nonstandard question is asked. This can happen at both small and large banks and is not symptomatic of size. Indecision or non-action is merely symptomatic of a custodian organization that is inexperienced and incapable of functioning on its own. The department head should be there for guidance only and not be necessary for day-to-day operations.

Questionnaires

The use of a request for proposal (RFP) in the custodian search has become commonplace, and it does have value. If the trustees have a significant number of banks to be considered, the RFP can be extremely useful in the initial weeding-out process. The RFP should be used as an information-gathering device, indicative of the bank's overall capabilities in the securities processing area and its capabilities of expressing itself in a coherent manner.

RFPs generally reflect the style of those who construct them. Whether it's a consulting firm or the trustees, a typical format is as follows:

1. General statistics
2. Organization
3. Operations
    a. Securities processing
    b. Data processing
    c. Securities lending
    d. Global custody
    e. Performance measurement/evaluation
4. Administration
5. Training
6. Reports
7. Investments (including STIF)
8. Benefit payments
9. Fee schedule
10. References

Under the general statistics category, the trustees should be looking for not only total current statistics (trust department, employee benefit department, custody business specifically) but should also be looking for trends (first major custodial appointment and what the growth pattern has been). A range of the size of custodial accounts handled is also useful since it's an indication of their ability to be responsive to customers of various sizes. In looking at the general organization of a custodian, look closely at its independence and contribution to the bank's profitability. Does the bank look at custodial services as a separate business? This is important because without the status of being a separate, profit contributing business, it's doubtful whether sufficient capital will be allocated when that business needs resources.

Looking further into the organization, ask some specific questions on how the administrative account load is established. What will your account do to the existing organization and if your account is sizable, how will the bank cope with it? The bank that is extremely aggressive in seeking new business very often takes liberties with the quality of service that it delivers to existing customers. Look at that particular bank's plans for handling new business as well as maintaining and upgrading the quality of staff. Don't accept a general answer here, but pin the bank down to specific courses of action.

Evaluating reporting capabilities can be tricky. Because custodians call the same reports by different names and because custodians typically have, in total, the same amount of information spread out or allocated differently among different reports, it's extremely difficult to compare reporting packages without a personal interview. What you can and do want to get committed to writing is the timing of various reports. No matter what a custodian calls its reports, as long as they are rendered within a reasonable amount of time, trustees will have the information they need.

Significant questions should be devoted to ancillary investments offered by custodians, the most important of which is the short-term investment fund. This is a major area of leverage, and the performance aspect should not be overlooked even though the primary purpose of these funds is short-term liquidity. This area of the RFP is also the appropriate spot for asking questions about a custodian's index fund capabilities, fixed income capabilities, etc.

Pension payments is an area of great concern to the administratively oriented trustee. In this section questions should be asked not only on the volume of payments handled now, but more specifically on the input required by the fund office to set that procedure in motion, turnaround time for special requests, information, etc.

The section on fee schedules should include much more than the actual fee schedule. Trustees should supply adequate statistics and ask for a specific fee quote for their particular situation. Insist that the worksheets be included. This is important when dealing with custodians that have unbundled fee schedules and who therefore must make estimates in terms of activity, etc.

References are, of course, a very important part of the process. Ask for a spectrum of references going from large to small customers, from old to new customers, and specifically for the size account you represent.

Organization of the data center is important, especially if you are considering a custodian that does not control its own data center (i.e., must share it with the commercial side of the bank). In fact, a shared data center is true more often than not because of the huge expense of running a modern installation. A custodian that maintains its own facilities has a very decided advantage over the competition. The operating configuration of the data center is less important but no less interesting. It's *not* a safe assumption that most major custodians are equipped to handle the volume of business that they are seeking. Staffing statistics in the data center are as important as they are in the administrative area, especially in terms of programming capabilities.

Key elements of the securities settlement process are important. A potential weak link in any custodian's operation is the manner in which information is gathered from the outside investment managers and brought into the custodian's shop for processing. The leading banks in this field are those that have put considerable time and effort into automating the process, the interaction with investment managers, with central depositories and sometimes trustees.

There's a temptation to try to make the RFP as easy as possible for the custodian to answer and for the trustees to compare responses. Obviously, this would be done by asking closed-ended questions (yes or no). This is the biggest mistake that a trustee can make when using an RFP. While there is a place for yes or no questions, the trustees should go out of the way to ask open-ended questions, questions that require thoughtful, complete answers. When asking such questions, a trustee has a unique opportunity to separate the men from the boys, or should we say the salesman from the technicians. If an RFP has asked the proper open-ended questions, a trustee has a better chance of getting back a response that reflects the thoughts and abilities of the administrative people who will be handling the account.

Examples of how questions should be asked are listed below:

WRONG	RIGHT
1. When are interest and dividends credited?	1. Explain your system for crediting interest and dividends.
2. Do you give credit for fail float?	2. What is your system for fail float?
3. Do you have a quality control system?	3. Describe your quality control system.
4. Do you offer automated cash management?	4. Describe your system for automated cash management, including all advantages and disadvantages.

See the sample questions for request for proposal on pages 172 and 173.

Interviews

The initial interview for a custodian should be in the trustees' office. First of all, the initial interview should cover a good number of custodians and it's simply more efficient to have the custodians do the traveling. Secondly, the initial interviews should be spread over a period of time so as not to interrupt daily work flow and, equally as important, to keep your mind fresh and open for each presentation. Third, final interviews are best held in the custodian's offices, as explained below.

After initial interviews and evaluating responses to the RFP, finalists can be narrowed down to between three and five. Onsite visits are made for primarily two reasons:

1. You want to bring experts with you, possibly including a data center expert, to inspect physical facilities. Meet not only your main administrative contact, but also his or her backups. The environment in which these people work will give you an idea of what status they really have within the entire bank, questionnaire responses aside.
2. Visit the bank to meet some senior management of the custodian department. Typically, these people do not, and should not, have the time to travel around the country making final presentations. Their job is management, and a well-run trust department needs specialists in this area, not general managers. Trustees should meet with some of these senior people in order to get a better sense of their knowledge and commitment to the custody product.

Trustees should "load" the meeting. This should be done in terms of both the number and quality of personnel that come to the meeting, Obviously, the higher the ranking of a plan trustee that comes to the bank, the higher the ranking officer the bank will supply from custodian department management. This makes for a better meeting to begin with and also provides another test for the bank personnel with whom you will be working on a day-to-day basis, i.e., you want to see how they operate in a highly charged atmosphere of senior people.

A tour of the facilities is mandatory and should include both the securities settlement operating area and the data center. Lastly, be sure to leave plenty of time for these interviews. Frequently, operating and administrative areas are geographically separated.

Post-Interview

Each interview is a learning process. Even if you had two interviews with a prospective custodian and have evaluated an RFP response closely, it is almost inevitable that additional questions will come up. This is partially true because each custodian will, of course, emphasize its strong points and these particular items may not have been covered at all with the other finalists. Therefore, don't hesitate to go back with any questions. This can be done over the phone very conveniently and rarely is an additional meeting necessary. The custodians involved will not mind at all. In fact, the most capable ones will very much appreciate the diligence with which you are exploring the situation.

Fees

Fees are generally quoted in one of three ways or some combination thereof:
- Transactional
- Flat fee
- Percentage of market value.

Transactional

The fee is calculated by applying a unit cost against different variables, i.e., number of portfolios, number of holdings, etc.

Flat Fee

A flat fee for all the services a custodian has agreed to provide, based on estimates provided by the trustees.

Percentage of Market Value

In market value fees, a basis point[2] charge is applied against the market value of an individual portfolio or the total market value of the fund.

All three of these methods are used throughout the industry. Which one trustees might use is a matter of preference since most custodians will quote fees on different bases when asked. No matter which method is used, a top tier custodian will provide the same quality service that the trustees expect.

Current Trends

The metamorphasis of the custodial industry is very much a good news–bad news situation. In fact, each trend has a good news–bad news element.

Consolidation

Since custodians are banks, they cannot escape the pain of the current wave of consolidations in the banking industry. Even where the bank is remaining independent, some custodial/trust departments are selling their book of business rather than commit the many millions of dollars necessary to compete in the large trustee market. The bad news is that trustees will have a shrinking number of options from which to choose. The good news is that the remaining vendors are stronger and more likely to survive future threats to their businesses.

Extreme Price Competition

Some large custodians have adopted an aggressive market share philosophy. Since they believe that a very high market share is one of the keys to success, they have submitted low bids for some very large pieces of business, setting off a price war for "mega" accounts and causing other pricing to remain static if not decline slightly. The bad news is that some vendors of quality services are leaving the marketplace rather than compete on price. The good news is that trustees should have no problem in finding good services at fair prices.

Global Custody

As the world's economies become more interdependent, so does professional investing. Very few investment programs are domestic only. So when plan trustees decide that global investing has become appropriate for their plan, literally a whole new world is opened with regard to the custodianship of those assets, and having a custodian with global capabilities is becoming necessary and commonplace. The basic options are to allow each global manager to work with a custodian of his choosing (the common practice in the UK), appoint custodians in each country, appoint a single international custodian (for assets outside the United States) or appoint a single global custodian (the widely preferred choice). But asking your domestic custodian to accept global responsibilities is not without risk. The diligence which trustees exercise in evaluating domestic capabilities must be doubled and tripled when considering global investing.

The custodian must make arrangements for local (onsite in the foreign country) trade clearance and settlement, currency exchange, local safekeeping, income collection, tax reclaiming services, corporate actions, communications flows between the local market and themselves and multicurrency accounting/reporting.

Since even the largest global banks/custodians do not have securities processing facilities in every country where investments are made, a custodian's network capabilities are paramount. Even where a global custodian is using its own branch facilities, networking is important because that branch, while having the parent's name on the door, is really a foreign entity.

Therefore, the most important elements to consider when selecting a global custodian are commitment to the business, experience of staff, data center/communications capabilities and the multicurrency accounting system utilized. Without these tools, a custodian's ability to provide a superior service to its clients in a reasonable time frame is severely hampered.

The good news is that the custodian community is meeting the challenge. The bad news is that the global custodian's fixed cost base is growing in order to satisfy demands for capabilities in all the world's markets. This will eventually set some prices too high for investors not utilizing the "emerging" markets.

Wholesale Outsourcing

Because no custodian does it all itself anymore (see Figure 2 on page 155), it has become competitively acceptable to outsource part or all of the securities operation. There are high-quality systems and/or domestic operations vendors available, and many of the larger global custodians lease or outsource part or all of their global network to competitors. The net result is good news for both the small investor and small custodian—even a regional custodian can supply global services to local investors, thereby protecting its market.

Suggested Questions for Request for Proposal (RFP)

1. What is the procedure to monitor, advise and follow up on DKs and other fails? What is your policy for reimbursing clients for lost interest due to fails?

2. Is there anything special or distinctive about your safekeeping abilities that the board of trustees should know? If yes, please describe.

3. Do you credit all regularly scheduled dividend and interest payments on payable date, regardless of whether these monies have been received? If no, please explain your process. If yes, include discussion of errors and omissions and procedures used.

4. Describe the infrastructure you have built for providing investment accounting services. Be sure to include a description of your computer hardware configuration, a separate description of your software applications and a discussion of the staff dedicated to the accounting function.

5. Please provide a sample copy of all standard and optional accounting reports and custody statements for global accounts. Please indicate on the cover sheet of each report which are for standard services covered by the basic fee, and which reports are optional and available only for additional fees. The actual fees for the optional reports should be provided in the fee proposal.

6. Describe your procedures for sweeping uninvested cash balances from investment accounting into your short-term investment funds (STIF). How many types of collateral STIF funds (commingled, separate or customized) do you offer in the program? Provide investment guidelines for each. Provide a description of each as enumerated below.

    a. Investment policy

b. Objectives and guidelines

   c. Quarterly investment performance gross of fees

   d. Indicate the fee (bp) for each type of STIF or collateral reinvestment fund. Please specify if fees are deducted before or after stock splits.

7. Describe your securities lending program. Do you offer "indemnification"? Describe your policies for accepting collateral and describe your required collateral margin.

8. Describe your proxy administration policies. What alternatives (such as endorsing and sending back to clients or investment managers, or voting with management) do you offer?

9. Describe your system of controls to assure the accuracy of the processing and reporting of the master custody division. Include a copy of your documented policies and procedures.

10. Describe your firm's commitment to service quality and customer service. Does your organization have a total quality management program? If yes, please describe. Do you survey your clients? If yes, provide the results for the last three years.

Endnotes

1. A central depository is a custodian's custodian. Financial institutions like banks, broker-dealers, investment companies, etc., have formed and/or joined depositories to transfer securities among themselves with just a bookkeeping entry. This is often referred to as security immobilization.

2. A basis point is $1/100$ of one percent.

About the Authors

John A. Viniello
President
National Fire Sprinkler
 Association
Patterson, New York

Mr. Viniello has served as president of the National Fire Sprinkler Association since 1984. He has been a trustee of the National Automatic Sprinkler Industry Pension and Welfare Funds since 1974. As a member of the funds' investment subcommittee, Mr. Viniello works with fund evaluators reviewing investment performance and making recommendations to the full trust board on a variety of issues, including asset allocation. He also serves as a trustee for the Apprentice Fund of New York.

Gerard M. Arnone
Vice President
National Director–
 Jointly Trusteed Funds
Global Assets–Retirement
 Services
Bankers Trust Company
New York, New York

Mr. Arnone is the Taft-Hartley market segment head for Bankers Trust Master Custody services. He has overall responsibility for sales and client relations. Mr. Arnone has over 25 years of experience working with jointly administered funds. He has been a speaker at International Foundation educational programs.

Chapter 9

Accountants and Auditors

by Thomas E. Seay

Trustee's Perspective

by Chris Silvera

When I was elected as the principal officer of a local union, I was not expecting the enormous responsibilities I immediately faced as trustee of the local union's welfare and pension fund. Like most union officers who also serve as trustees, I suppose, I had to focus on the duties of serving the membership as a salaried officer and serving the plan participants as an uncompensated trustee. Admittedly, I wondered at that time whether or not the challenges before me would be worth the risks and responsibilities. Today, however, I can look back and say that it has been worth it. Our members and their families are enjoying wonderful benefits and our welfare and pension funds are stronger than ever before.

Our boards of trustees carefully assembled a team of specialists to assist us in managing our funds: a strong administrator with strong employees, a strong ERISA attorney, a strong actuary, strong investment advisors and a strong independent accountant. Each plays important roles, and as trustees we need to rely on them all, especially the independent accountant.

The trustees can't possibly manage the funds on a daily basis; however, we're the ones with the ultimate responsibilities for seeing that the funds are run properly. In order to have the confidence that our established policies and procedures are properly being car-

ried out, the trustees look to the independent accountant as our monitor and watchdog as well as our reporter.

We expect more from our funds' accountant than annual audit opinions on the financial reports; we want our accountant to regularly review our operations and transactions and report to us his findings and opinions about our funds' compliance with our policies, plan documents and regulatory matters. We expect our accountant to keep us apprised of changes in Internal Revenue Service and Department of Labor regulations affecting our funds and our participants. We count on our accountants' presence at trustees meeting and we value their opinions and suggestions.

As chairman of the board of trustees of our funds, I'm pleased to introduce the chapter on accountants and auditors for employee benefit plans. Our experiences in our funds with accountants and auditors have evidenced the need for and the results of selecting the right professionals who specialize in employee benefits. They can help you build the confidence needed to understand and accept your fiduciary responsibilities.

TRUSTEES NEED RELIABLE INFORMATION AND ASSURANCE ABOUT THEIR PLAN'S OPERATIONS

LIKE DIRECTORS OF CORPORATIONS OR OFFICERS OF UNIONS, TRUSTEES OF EMPLOYEE benefit plans need timely and accurate information to properly manage their plans and to make sound decisions affecting their plans. Because trustees typically do not actively participate in the day-to-day operations of their plans, they must look to others to administer their policies and decisions and to provide them information about all aspects of the plan's design and operations. Although these administrative functions are delegated to others, trustees are ultimately responsible for the management of their plans; and they need assurance and confidence that the information they rely on is accurate.

Also, like businesses and unions, controls must be established and monitored to ensure safeguarding of plan assets, adherence to policies, procedures and plan provisions, and to ensure accountability. All aspects of trust funds require controls: contribution determination and collection, participant data and eligibility records, benefit processing and payments, banking, investing, paying plan administrative expenses, communicating with participants and regulatory compliances—all require controls. Without adequate controls, the risk of errors, fraud or other abuses increases; and the level of confidence in the accuracy of information provided to trustees decreases.

Trustees are responsible for establishing and monitoring plan policies and procedures that include controls, such as requiring more than one signature on trust fund checks, assuring accuracies and timeliness of contributions, paying correct benefits to or for participants, separating duties among administrative personnel and maintaining proper records to assure accountability. Trustees often look to their fund administrator to formulate suggestions for these policies, procedures and controls; but trustees should formally approve and adopt these, together with policies for monitoring their results and effectiveness.

The most common means of monitoring plan policies and their effectiveness is a regular audit performed by a certified public accountant (CPA). Most plans with 100 or more participants are required by the Employee Retirement Income Security Act (ERISA) to have audits performed on the plan's annual financial statements attached to the plan's annual report (Form 5500) filed with the Internal Revenue Service and the United States Department of Labor (and the Pension Benefit Guaranty Corporation for Pension Plans). Additionally, plan documents such as the trust document or trust agreement usually contain specific language requiring annual audits.

Independent Audits of Plan's Financial Statements

Currently, ERISA requires audits to be performed by an independent qualified public accountant (IQPA). Although certain states may license non-certified practitioners to practice as public accountants (PAs), most accountants in public practice have been required to pass state-administered Uniform Certified Public Accountancy examinations; and they must meet other licensing requirements in order to practice as certified public accountants. Whether the annual audit is performed by a CPA or by a PA depends on the language of the trust documents and, of course, the preferences of the plan trustees. In either case, the auditor must be *independent* and *qualified* in order to perform the audit.

An *independent* auditor means he or she has no conflict of interest with the plan or its fiduciaries. There should be no financial interest between the plan and the auditor other than the fee arrangement, and auditor fees should never be contingent upon the outcome of an audit or a particular event. The auditor should not maintain plan records because an *independent* auditor should not audit his or her own work. There should be no direct or indirect relationships between the plan's fiduciaries and the auditor or the auditing firm that might create an appearance that the auditor is not independent. Trustees should carefully review the issue of independence before engaging an auditor and readdress this issue at least annually.

The term *qualified* means more than the initials following an auditor's name: Whether the auditor is a CPA or a PA is not as important as the question of whether or not a plan's auditor possesses the skills, expertise and resources to properly conduct an audit of an employee benefit plan. Employee benefit plans, especially multiemployer plans, require specialized accounting and auditing skills different from the typical business-driven disciplines taught to accountants in colleges and universities. To be *qualified* as an auditor of an employee benefit plan, an auditor must be very familiar with ERISA and its regulations as well as other labor and tax laws affecting employee benefit plans. Additionally, a *qualified* auditor should know and understand the generally accepted accounting principles and generally accepted auditing standards unique to employee benefit plans.

In addition to issuing a report on the audit of a plan's annual financial statements to the plan's trustees, ERISA requires the auditor to issue an opinion on the fairness of the presentation of the required supplemental schedules accompanying the plan's annual Form 5500. These supplemental schedules include a Schedule of Assets Held for Investment Purposes, a Schedule of Investments Which Were Both Acquired and Disposed of Within the Plan Year, a Schedule of Loans or Fixed Income Obligations, a Schedule of Leases in Default or Classified as Uncollectible, a Schedule of Reportable (5%) Transactions, and a Schedule of Nonexempt Transactions.

At the conclusion of each annual audit, the auditor should report the following to the plan's trustees:

1. The auditor's report on the plan's financial statements
2. The auditor's report on the supplemental schedules accompanying the annual Form 5500
3. Matters coming to the attention of the auditor during the course of the audit concerning any deficiencies in the design or operation of the plan's internal control structure (which could adversely affect the plan's ability to record, process, summarize and report financial data consistent with the assertions of the plan's management)
4. Other matters relative to the audit including:
   - The level of the auditor's and the plan's responsibility for the fairness of the presentation of the financial statements (and for any other information accompanying the financial statements)
   - Significant accounting policies adopted by the plan
   - Significant accounting estimates used in the preparation of the plan's financial statements
   - Any significant audit adjustments to the plan's financial statements proposed during the audit
   - Any disagreements between the auditor and the plan administrator (and whether or not satisfactorily resolved)
   - The auditor's views about significant matters that may have been discussed between the plan administrator and other accountants
   - Major issues, such as the application of accounting principles and auditing standards, that were discussed with the plan administrator prior to retaining the auditor
   - Any serious difficulties the auditor encountered in dealing with the plan administrator related to the performance of the audit.

Plan trustees should be sure they understand the auditor's reports, and questions should be asked if any parts of the reports are unclear. These reports are more than the plan's financial statements: The auditor's communications to the trustees should be considered as "report cards" on the effectiveness of the administrator's recordkeeping and adherence to plan policies and controls. After the auditor's reports are presented to the trustees, the trustees' meeting minutes should reflect actions taken to either accept or reject the reports.

Internal Auditing Versus Independent Auditing

Some of the larger employee benefit plans may employ in-house or internal auditors to perform auditing functions in many areas such as audits of employer payroll records (to assure the accuracies of employer contributions and participant eligibilities), audits of claims paid and processed, and audits of administrative expense allocations among plans (where more than one plan is administered by the same board of trustees). Use of internal auditors often results in cost savings for plans because their salaries and their related payroll costs are usually less than the fees that an independent auditor might charge for the same services.

If plan trustees decide to hire internal auditors, lines of authority should be clearly defined. Internal auditors, like independent auditors, should report directly to the trustees instead of the plan administrator because many of the internal audit functions involve auditing the work of the administrator. (If the administrator controls the internal auditors' paychecks, it may be unlikely that the trustees would receive reports unfavorable to the administrator.)

Trustees may engage independent auditors to perform audits of employer payroll records, audits of claims paid and processed, audits of expense allocations among plans and for other services. (Depending on the language of the trust documents or the collective bargaining agreements, trustees may be required to use independent auditors instead of internal auditors for some or all of these additional services.) The annual audit of the plan's financial statements and the audit of the supplemental schedules accompanying the annual Form 5500 cannot be performed by an internal auditor. These may only be performed by an independent auditor as required by ERISA.

Many plan administrators prepare their own annual Forms 5500 for their plans and attach the independent auditor's reports on the audits of the plan's financial statements and on the required supplemental schedules to the Form 5500. Additionally, many plan administrators prepare their own Forms 990 (for welfare plans) instead of engaging independent auditors to prepare these forms. The decision to engage an independent auditor to prepare these forms or to look to the plan administrator to prepare them is a matter that plan trustees should consider. Because inaccurate, incomplete or untimely filings of these forms may result in penalties assessed against the trustees, the trustees should pay special attention to the quality and due care exercised in the preparation of these required government filings.

Governmental Monitoring of Plan's Reporting and Auditing

The U.S. Department of Labor's Pension and Welfare Benefits Administration (PWBA) office is the government agency most responsible for overseeing employee benefit plans' compliance with ERISA. Working together with the Internal Revenue Service and the Pension Benefit Guaranty Corporation, the PWBA closely monitors the quality of plans' filings of annual Forms 5500 through computer-assisted editing procedures as well as "desk reviews" and field audits by government auditors. Series of letters are mailed to plan administrators if Form 5500 filing deficiencies are noted, and corrective actions are usually required. If corrections are not made to the satisfaction of the PWBA, statutory penalties assessed against the plan's trustees (and not the plan) are often the result.

As fiduciaries, plan trustees should be very aware of their responsibilities for their plan's compliance with ERISA and of the PWBA's enforcement authority. At the risk of facing civil (or perhaps criminal) penalties, trustees should be very careful in the selection, monitoring and evaluation of the quality of their independent auditor and his or her reports. Why? Because the PWBA looks to plan auditors for more than just reporting on the fairness of the presentation of the plan's financial statements: The plan auditor is expected to search for errors, irregularities and possible illegal acts that may have occurred in the operation of the plan; and his or her report should disclose certain violations if detected. The PWBA also looks to plan auditors to report any restrictions (or scope limitations) imposed by trustees or administrators that might have prevented an auditor from performing the audit in accordance with generally accepted auditing standards.

ERISA's requirement that an annual audit be performed by an independent auditor and included with the plan's filings with the government shifted the privacy of plan auditor's reports from trustee meeting rooms to the public eye. Plan participants have ERISA-protected rights that include examining their plan's annual reports and auditor's reports. As Congress' watchdog, the PWBA actively reviews the quality of these reports and the quality of the independent audits as a means of protecting participants' rights. Given such governmental oversight, trustees should look to their independent auditors as their plan's watchdogs; and they should insist on the same professional qualities expected by the PWBA.

Conducting a Search for an Independent Auditor

Trustees searching for independent auditors should investigate a prospective auditor's qualifications, resources, experience and abilities to successfully perform the required audit for their plan. Each of these attributes is equally important in selecting an auditor, and trustees should carefully consider these in their decisions.

Qualifications

To be *qualified*, a prospective auditor should have successfully completed all educational and professional licensing requisites of the state having jurisdiction over the situs of the plan's trust. Preferably, the auditor should be a certified public accountant. He or she should be thoroughly familiar with all financial and reporting requirements of ERISA regulations and the American Institute of Certified Public Accountants (AICPA) prescribed applications of generally accepted auditing standards to audits of financial statements of employee benefit plans. The prospective auditor should have a thorough knowledge of the AICPA's financial accounting and reporting principles and practices for employee benefit plans, and he or she should have in-depth knowledge of the tax and labor laws affecting the plan (such as the Taft-Hartley Act, the Multiemployer Pension Act and the 1986 Internal Revenue Code as it affects employee benefit plans).

A prospective auditor must be independent. There should be no conflict or any appearance of a conflict between the plan (or its fiduciaries or employees) and the auditor. Both the trustees and the prospective auditor should carefully review all relationships to be certain no direct or indirect conflict of interest exists.

Resources

A prospective auditor of an employee benefit plan should demonstrate to plan trustees that he or she has sufficient resources available for research of issues unique to employee benefit plans and for possible consultation for necessary matters. Trustees should look at depths of professional talents employed by the auditor, not only for assurance that the engagement can be timely performed with competent assistants, but also to assure the trustees that there is sufficient professional support in case the primary auditor should become ill or otherwise be unable to personally complete the engagement.

It is now a rarity for sole practitioners in public accounting to perform independent audits of employee benefit plans. The laws governing plans and the auditing, reporting and compliance requirements are so complex that most auditors need the resources of diverse professional talents to support them: Tax specialists, labor specialists, computer specialists, up-to-date libraries and teams of qualified assistants are necessary to properly service employee benefit plans.

Experience

Most trustees prefer not to allow their plans to serve as training grounds for their auditors. Like scrutinizing a resumé of a prospective employee, trustees should look for experience in the resumé of a prospective auditor that relates to *their* plan. Commercial auditing is not the same as employee benefit plan auditing. Single employer plan auditing is not the same as multiemployer plan auditing. Defined contribution pension plan auditing is not the same as defined benefit pension plan auditing, and insured welfare plan auditing is not the same as self-insured welfare plan auditing, etc.

References should be checked, and questions about a prospective auditor should be posed to existing (and perhaps former) clients: Does the auditor provide quality, timely and efficient service? Does the auditor charge fair fees? Has an audit by the Department of Labor or Internal Revenue Service resulted in findings of deficient reporting relative to the auditor's reports? Has there been any disagreement between the client and the auditor?

Ability to Perform

An auditor's qualifications, resources and experience may look good on the proposal and resumé, but trustees must be able to assess a prospective auditor's abilities to serve them and their plan. The most qualified, experienced and resourceful auditor must be able to demonstrate that he or she will commit the necessary time, energy and resources to properly serve the plan and its trustees in a timely and efficient manner. If these cannot be demonstrated, then the trustees should look for another auditor.

Auditor Fees

Trustees must weigh many variables in making decisions about purchasing goods and services for their plans. They are often reminded of their fiduciary responsibilities to incur expenses "only necessary for the operations of their plans" and are pressured to seek auditing services for the lowest possible fee. The pressures on the trustees are enormous in this area: Quality audits by qualified independent auditors are necessary, but they do cost money.

Over the past several years, many plans' boards of trustees have solicited competitive bids from prospective independent auditors. Very often trustees award engagements to the lowest bidder while attempting to satisfy their responsibility to preserve plan assets. However, as the U.S. Department of Labor recently reported after reviewing a sample of 267 plan audits, many "low bidder" auditors have performed audits that are "woefully deficient." The Department added that "low bidders often are reluctant to report irregularities or illegal acts to their clients, let alone the government." This is not to say that quality audits can't be performed for low fees. They can be. Caution should be exercised, however, to be certain that trustees know what they're paying for.

The best ways to minimize plan auditing fees are maintaining quality records and maintaining strong controls. Any weakness in these areas requires additional auditor time. Simply put, the better the records and controls, the higher degree of reliability can be assessed by the auditor and auditing tests may be limited. On the other hand, unreliable and poorly controlled records cause auditors to spend many more hours in order to draw their conclusions about the audit results.

Traditionally, auditing fees have been based on hourly rates. Depending on the expertise within the team levels of auditors assigned to the engagements, hourly rates typically range from approximately $60 for the lower levels of experienced auditors to $180 or more for the most experienced auditors. Many plans and their auditors have moved away from fees charged based on hourly rates; instead, auditing fees are often negotiated at "fixed fee" levels. Trustees seem to prefer fixed fee arrangements because they know in advance what the fees will be, and they don't always need to be concerned about the volume of hours it takes the auditors to perform the work.

Contracts With Independent Auditors

Like all arrangements between service providers and employee benefit plans, there should be a written contract entered into between the plan trustees and the independent auditor. Often called an *engagement letter* signed by both parties, it should spell out the terms of the engagement and clearly define the services to be provided and responsibilities the auditor has to the plan and its trustees.

The contract (or engagement letter) should also address the payment(s) of fees, the timing of the performance of services and the delivery of reports, the expected document preparation to be readied in advance by the plan administrator prior to the audit, whether or not the auditor is to attend trustee meetings and provisions for terminating the engagement. It is also suggested that the contract should include language about steps to be taken in the event unusual difficulties are encountered that may require expansion of auditing procedures.

Monitoring and Reevaluating the Plan's Independent Auditor

Perhaps jokingly, plan trustees sometimes ask, "Who audits the auditor?" While it certainly isn't practical to hire another auditor to audit the plan auditor, it is practical (and prudent) for plan trustees to regularly address the quality, timeliness and overall performance of their plan's independent auditor. This should be accomplished at least annually, perhaps after the plan's independent auditor presents the annual report and discusses the results of the audit with the board of trustees.

Trustees should discuss among themselves their level of satisfaction with their plan's independent auditor as well as making inquiries to the plan administrator and perhaps other plan professionals. Trustees should always be alert for possible warning signals that the auditor may not be performing up to professional standards, such as not staying current with changes promulgated by the AICPA or by government authorities, or by adverse findings in an IRS or Department of Labor examination.

As an additional monitoring tool, plan trustees should ask their independent auditor about the results of any "peer review" conducted on the auditor's practice as may be required by licensing authorities or professional membership associations. Caution should be exercised if a peer review resulted in unfavorable findings about the quality of an auditor's practice. This may be a warning signal that the plan's audit is not being conducted in accordance with professional standards.

Summary

Plan trustees should carefully select, monitor and reevaluate the performance and quality of their plan's independent auditor as a means of fulfilling their responsibilities to their plan's and their participants. Additionally, plan trustees should consider the roles of the independent auditor to be more than just complying with annual reporting requirements: Trustees should expect and insist that their plan's independent auditor should be their "watchdog" in assuring that the plan is operating in accordance with its policies and in financial compliance with plan documents and government regulations.

The risks of noncompliance with ERISA and tax regulations can be severe, and weak controls over plan assets and transactions may create opportunities for inadequate accounting or financial losses. Trustees should look to their independent auditors to provide them with regular "report cards" on their plan's compliance, controls and results of operations. If the plan's independent auditors don't provide trustees with this service, then the trustees should either begin to demand it from their current auditor or look to other auditors who will provide this service.

Suggested Checklist for Request for Proposal (RFP)

1. Is the auditor and his or her firm independent with respect to the plan?
   - ▶ Does the auditor have any financial interest in the plan?
   - ▶ Are there any direct or indirect relationships between the auditor and the plan that might create an appearance that the auditor is not independent?
2. Is the auditor experienced in audits of multiemployer benefit plans?
3. Is the auditor familiar with all financial and reporting requirements of ERISA?
4. Is the auditor familiar with the Taft-Hartley Act?
5. Does the auditor have sufficient resources available for research into matters affecting the plan?
6. Does the auditor's firm have sufficient depths of professional talent to service the plan?

7. Has the auditor's firm undergone a "peer review" recently? If so, did it receive an "unqualified opinion" on its performances and quality control procedures?

8. Has the auditor or the auditor's firm been sanctioned by authorities or by professional associations for any professional misconduct?

9. Has the auditor or the auditor's firm been replaced by other auditors on any engagements with employee benefit plans in recent years? If so, why?

10. What is the auditor's experience in representing employee benefit plan clients in matters involving the U.S. Department of Labor's Pension and Welfare Benefit Administration and Internal Revenue Service?

About the Authors

Chris Silvera
Chairman, Board of Trustees
Local 808, I.B.T. Welfare
 and Pension Funds
Long Island City, New York

As the principal officer of the International Brotherhood of Teamsters Local 808, Mr. Silvera serves as chairman of the local union's Welfare and Pension Funds for its Building Maintenance and Railroad Maintenance-of-Way members throughout the New York City and Long Island area. Since 1989, Mr. Silvera has implemented benefit plan improvements, benefit cost-containment programs and investment performance policies that have resulted in significant financial growth and benefit enhancements for the funds and their participants.

Thomas E. Seay, CPA
Partner
Bond Beebe
Washington, D.C.

Mr. Seay is a partner with Bond Beebe, an accounting firm specializing in employee benefits and labor organization fields. He has 25 years of experience in accounting, auditing, compliance and litigation support services for multiemployer and single employer health and welfare, pension, annuity, apprenticeship, legal services and other employee benefit funds. Mr. Seay has taught accounting subjects for the International Foundation's Certified Employee Benefit Specialist program and has been a frequent speaker on employee benefits at International Foundation conferences. Mr. Seay is a past chair and current member of the International Foundation's Accountants Committee.

Chapter 10

Arbitration

by Mark E. Brossman and Morton I. Lorge

Trustee's Perspective

by Bruce S. Raynor

I have had the opportunity to participate in numerous arbitrations during my career. I believe that arbitration is the most effective and efficient way of resolving disputes, and it is usually preferable to litigation from the point of view of all parties to the dispute.

As a union official, my early experiences were with labor arbitration. As a trustee of several Taft-Hartley employee benefit plans, I have also participated in a number of employee benefit plan arbitrations. As the chapter notes, while each type of arbitration has different rules and varying legal concerns, all types of arbitration share the virtues of being fast, comparatively inexpensive, and final and binding.

Recently, I participated in an arbitration involving a health plan's claims against a former third party claims administrator. The arbitrator had significant experience in the benefits area and was able to focus on complicated legal and factual issues unique to the relationship between health plans and their service providers. I do not believe that a court would have understood or had sufficient concern about the issues or the interests of the participating employees and employers. The plan prevailed in the arbitration and obtained a significant recovery that allowed it to merge with a larger plan to the benefit of all concerned. An adverse or confusing decision could have wreaked havoc on all parties.

I have also participated in a number of Taft-Hartley impasse arbitrations. While it is preferable to administer a plan without reaching deadlocks, the impasse arbitration process—and the threat of impasse arbitration—has been extremely helpful in resolving contentious disputes among trustees. Each board has its own dynamics, and in many cases having the threat of arbitration allows good decision making in the interests of plan participants.

Some funds are utilizing arbitration rather than litigation to resolve benefits claims brought by participants and beneficiaries. Arbitration in this context raises a number of legal and practical issues and continues to generate a great deal of interest in the benefit plan community. Several of the funds on whose board of trustees I currently serve are considering using arbitration in the benefits claims area.

I am also on the board of trustees of several multiemployer pension plans that have had disputes with contributing employers over withdrawal liability. These disputes are generally subject to arbitration, and hearings tend to be extremely technical and require expert actuarial and legal testimony.

The increasing use of arbitration in each of these areas is a significant development impacting employee benefit plan administration. Many trustees, including myself, are enthusiastic about this development and believe that arbitration in the benefits area can be as productive as labor arbitration. I think you will find the following chapter extremely informative and helpful in addressing some of the key issues relating to arbitration of employee benefit plan disputes.

INTRODUCTION

THIS CHAPTER FOCUSES ON ARBITRATION, AN ASPECT OF EMPLOYEE BENEFIT PLAN ADministration that differs in significant respects from the services described in the other chapters in this book. *Arbitration* cannot be categorized neatly as a "professional service" in the way that investment management, accounting, custodial, legal and other pure services might. *Arbitration* is more accurately described as a process by which employee benefit plans can resolve disputes. *Arbitration* is a form of alternative dispute resolution (ADR) that allows parties to submit disputes for resolution to an impartial individual or individuals, rather than to a court. Thus, while the other chapters in this book focus on different types of professional services available to employee benefit plans, and on trustees' roles in selecting and monitoring professional service providers, this chapter will attempt to familiarize trustees with the concept of arbitration and its use in the employee benefit plan setting.

This chapter will describe arbitration in a variety of contexts and will address legal and practical issues relating to each type of arbitration. The first section provides an overview of arbitration and the arbitration process. This is followed by a section on the advantages and disadvantages of arbitration compared to litigation. Trustees should become familiar with these general principles to make informed decisions about whether a plan should attempt to arbitrate disputes. A section on current legal issues relating to arbitrating benefits and other claims brought by participants against a plan follows. The chapter also discusses some of the legal and practical issues concerning legally mandated impasse and withdrawal liability arbitration.

Arbitration Overview

Types of Disputes That Are Arbitrated

For Taft-Hartley plans, arbitration is generally used to resolve either internal disputes or "deadlocks" among plan trustees, or disputes between plans and other entities, such as participants, contributing employers, or service providers. Single employer plans, that do not reach trustee "deadlocks," may utilize arbitration to resolve disputes among the plan and its participants, contributing employers and service providers.

Certain types of disputes, such as trustee deadlocks and withdrawal liability disputes with contributing employers, must be arbitrated by law. Other disputes, such as disputes with plan participants or service providers, *may* be arbitrated *if* the parties enter into an agreement to arbitrate. For these types of disputes, there is no legal requirement for plans to arbitrate. *Arbitration* in this context may be referred to as "voluntary" or "contractual" arbitration, as distinguished from legally mandated arbitration.

Voluntary arbitration may result from the inclusion of an arbitration agreement in a contract, such as a summary plan description, trust agreement or service provider agreement. Parties can also agree to arbitrate disputes after a dispute arises, even if a contract does not contain an arbitration provision.

Selecting an Arbitrator

There is no special licensing requirement for arbitrators. Indeed, virtually anyone can be an arbitrator. Generally, however, employee benefit plan arbitrators are lawyers, professors or business people familiar with the types of disputes that arise in the employment and employee benefit area. The American Arbitration Association (AAA), which is probably the most widely used service for employee benefit plan arbitration, has special arbitration panels for arbitrating disputes over benefit entitlements, withdrawal liability issues and impasses among the trustees of Taft-Hartley plans. The arbitrators on these panels are experienced in adjudicating these types of disputes.

Sometimes arbitrators are designated in advance by the parties. For example, an employee benefit plan document or contract may identify a particular individual or individuals who will act as arbitrator for all disputes. More often, however, arbitrators are chosen from lists of individuals maintained by a private arbitration association, such as the AAA, or a federal service, such as the Federal Mediation and Conciliation Service (FMCS). The parties review the lists of potential arbitrators provided to them at the beginning of a case and cross off the names of unacceptable arbitrators, if any. The remaining arbitrators are then listed by each party in order of preference. Thus, if a list is provided that contains ten names, a party can deem all the potential arbitrators as unacceptable. If any or all of the prospective arbitrators are acceptable to a party, that party may designate its preference by listing the arbitrators in the order preferred, e.g., 1-10. If both parties select the same arbitrator or arbitrators, the arbitrator with the highest ranking by both sides will be designated. This process may be repeated several times before a mutually agreeable arbitrator is selected. If the process results with the parties unable to agree on an arbitrator, the agency will typically make an administrative appointment of someone not on the lists provided to the parties.

Selecting the arbitrator is one of the most important strategic aspects of arbitration. Indeed, selecting an arbitrator is akin to selecting a juror in a trial. It is extremely important for parties to review carefully potential arbitrators before making a selection.

There are a number of ways to obtain information about a potential arbitrator. The AAA, for example, typically sends the parties a short biography on each of the approximately ten arbitrators on a list. These biographies are useful starting points since they provide important background information on the arbitrator, including the nature of an arbitrator's work, his or her experience, education and professional affiliations. These biographies also indicate the per day or "per diem" fee that the arbitrator charges.

After reviewing a potential arbitrator's background, it is important to review cases in which the individual served as an arbitrator, if possible. The arbitrator's decisions may provide insight as to how the arbitrator would approach a particular type of case.

Several services publish arbitration awards or contain information about arbitrators. For example, the Bureau of National Affairs (BNA) publishes a volume called *Employee Benefit Cases (EBC)*, which contains employee benefit plan arbitration awards. The EBCs are indexed according to topic. Several other BNA publications contain arbitration awards or information about arbitrators, including the *BNA Labor Arbitration Reports, the BNA Pension and Benefits Reporter,* and the *BNA Labor Relations Reporter: Directory of Arbitrators*. A number of these, and other publications are available online through WESTLAW® and Lexis.

It is also helpful to contact colleagues and practitioners that have appeared before or have knowledge about an arbitrator. This information can be helpful in understanding the way an individual approaches a case and the type of hearing he or she conducts (i.e., formal or informal).

Finally, it is important to try to match the arbitrator's background and skills to the case at hand. For example, in a withdrawal liability arbitration the parties may seek someone familiar with actuarial principles. In a contract interpretation case, on the other hand, an experienced attorney may be preferable.

Advantages and Disadvantages

Advantages of Arbitration

Informality of Process

Arbitration is less formal than traditional court litigation. There are no formal rules of evidence or procedure to be followed, unless the parties have agreed to such rules beforehand. Because arbitration is more informal, it tends to proceed faster than court litigation since less time is spent on technical matters. The reputation of the arbitration process for informality, however, will depend on the arbitrator since some arbitrators may be as formalistic and technical as the most formal judge.

Speed and Economy

Arbitration should be a quicker and less expensive process than court litigation. Arbitration generally provides for limited discovery, if any, which may reduce significantly the time to resolve a case. There is considerably less "pretrial" activity in arbitration, such as filing motions. Moreover, parties usually schedule hearing dates within a few weeks or months from the commencement of arbitration proceedings. In contrast, parties may have to wait years before trying a court case.

Furthermore, because arbitrators are generally more sophisticated triers of fact than juries and may be more knowledgeable about employee benefit plan issues than the average judge, less time is spent "educating" an arbitrator; and, as a result, parties may save considerable time and money. This can be particularly useful in complicated disputes between a plan and a third party service provider or a participant.

Several factors may slow down an arbitration proceeding, reducing or even eliminating its advantages over having a case heard in court. For example, parties may dispute whether a particular claim is subject to arbitration, which could result in a separate court proceeding to determine the "arbitrability" of a dispute. In arbitrations involving more than one arbitrator, accommodating each arbitrator's schedule may result in scheduling problems extending the arbitration longer than a court case. The same results may occur when the parties use one arbitrator whose schedule is very busy. Most arbitrators are unable to schedule consecutive days for hearings without significant advance notice.

Finally, the cost-effectiveness of arbitration can sometimes be undercut by an arbitrator's fees, which are generally paid by the parties, and by an arbitrator's reluctance to dispose of a case by motion.

Despite these considerations, practitioners agree that, in most cases, arbitration is a speedy and cost-effective alternative to the court system.

Avoidance of Unpredictable Jury System

Arbitration can be advantageous to employee benefit plans in certain instances because it avoids the unpredictability of the jury system and the large awards a jury can impose. In a benefits case, for example, a jury may be more sympathetic than an arbitrator to an individual's claims and may be inclined to disregard the pertinent facts and relevant law because, in the jurors' minds, the plan is in a better financial position to pay a claim than an individual. Indeed, a jury trial in a benefits case raises similar concerns that a jury trial would raise for an employer in a lawsuit brought by an employee.

In other situations, however, a plan may want to be in front of a jury. For example, suppose a plan retains an investment manager and the manager imprudently manages the plan's assets, resulting in a significant loss. In addition, suppose the manager engages in "foul play" or engages in a prohibited transaction to the benefit itself and its affiliates at the expense of the plan. In this situation, the plan may prefer to try the case in front of a jury, which might be more inclined to grant a higher damage award to the plan. This example illustrates how important it is for trustees to consider the types of disputes that might arise before agreeing to arbitration.

Confidentiality

The arbitration process is not an open public proceeding as is a court trial. There is no public record of arbitration proceedings and often the arbitrator's decision is not published. In certain types of cases, such as benefits cases, trustees may view the privacy of arbitration proceedings as an advantage.

Nature of Representation and Associated Cost Savings

A party in arbitration does not necessarily need to be represented by a lawyer. Thus, employee benefit plans may employ in-house counsel or other technically knowledgeable personnel to represent them in arbitrations. Cost savings may result from the repeated use of the same expert attorneys or other personnel familiar with the arbitration process and with the types of issues disputed in the employee benefit plan setting.

Final and Binding Nature of Arbitration Award

An arbitration award is usually final and binding and, therefore, avoids the lengthy appeals process present in judicial proceedings and the uncertainty that goes along with it. Although this results in an overall faster disposition of a dispute, it leaves only a narrow avenue of review for an unsuccessful party. An arbitration award can be set aside by a court, but only in very limited situations that are specifically outlined in federal law or state arbitration law.

Disadvantages of Arbitration

Increase in Claims

Perhaps the biggest disadvantage of arbitration arises in disputes with participants over benefits. By inserting an arbitration provision into a plan document, a plan provides participants with an easy, inexpensive way to formally pursue a claim against a plan. Indeed, participants may pursue claims against the plan in arbitration that they would not pursue if they had to retain an attorney and file a lawsuit in court. It is unclear, however, whether the cost of defending—and possibly paying out—additional benefits claims is outweighed by the advantages of arbitration over litigation.

Limited Remedies

For certain types of disputes, arbitration may offer a plan fewer remedies than a court proceeding. For example, in delinquent contributions actions, employee benefit plans are granted expanded remedies under ERISA, which are designed to reduce the likelihood that an employer will fail to contribute to a plan. Under ERISA, courts are required to grant plans interest, liquidated damages, costs and attorney fees if a plan prevails in a collections action. If a plan elects to arbitrate these types of claims, however, it could relinquish its right to recover these extra damages. Trustees and plan counsel may avoid this problem by ensuring that any arbitration agreement with a contributing employer requires the arbitrator to award the plan the same remedies as those available under ERISA.

Arbitration Awards Are Not Self-Enforcing

When a plan is attempting to collect money from an entity of uncertain financial condition, e.g., a contributing employer, arbitration may not be the most effective method because the arbitration award is not "self-enforcing." Court judgments provide a legal basis for collecting the amount of the judgment against the defendant's assets. For example, a plaintiff with an unpaid judgment can lawfully "freeze" a creditor's bank account. To execute on an arbitration award, however, the prevailing party must commence a separate lawsuit in court to "confirm" the award. This process has the effect of turning the arbitration award into a court judgment.

Most proceedings to confirm arbitration awards are straightforward and can be concluded in a short time. Therefore, the additional step is not usually a major issue in deciding whether to arbitrate or litigate. However, when more complicated issues are raised in the court proceeding, for example, bias on the part of the arbitrator, the additional step can delay the effectiveness and the speed of arbitration.

Participation by Arbitrators

In arbitration, the arbitrator is free to participate in the hearing to seek out information. While some judges also participate in hearings, arbitrators are more likely to ask questions and take an active role in the hearing. This may benefit an unrepresented individual, such as a participant in a benefits case, at the expense of the plan.

Arbitrators' Tendency to Compromise

Some contend that the goal of arbitration is to reach a solution that preserves or enhances the parties' relationship, rather than to determine who is right and who is wrong. Arbitrators may therefore be more inclined than a judge to issue compromise awards. In view of the improbability of reversing an arbitration decision, a truly meritorious claim or defense can be impaired or destroyed by tendencies of some arbitrators to compromise.

Lack of Motion Practice

The relaxed evidentiary rules in arbitration may result in a party being able to present more evidence than they would have been able to present at trial. In a benefits claim arbitration, this will usually be advantageous to the participant and harmful to the plan.

Arbitrators are also less likely than courts to entertain motions, although that reluctance appears to be waning. Trustees should determine before agreeing to voluntary arbitration if their case can be disposed of by motion. If a case can be disposed of through a motion for summary judgment, for example, on account of a legal defense such as statute of limitations, arbitration may not be the best choice and may very well be more costly than the court system.

Limited Discovery

Critics of arbitration often cite discovery limitations as a major drawback. Generally, unless the parties provide otherwise by agreement, the discovery devices normally available in court proceedings are not available in arbitration. If allowed at all, discovery is usually limited significantly. Because arbitration is informal, the arbitration process itself may be used as a substitute for pre-trial discovery.

Arbitrating Disputes With Participants—Legal Issues

Arbitration in the commercial context generally does not raise significant legal issues. If the parties agree contractually to arbitrate a dispute, a court will typically require the parties to honor their agreement to arbitrate. Therefore, arbitration agreements in commercial contracts between an employee benefit plan and a service provider—such as an investment manager, custodian or third party claims administrator—will generally be enforced.

More complicated legal issues arise when a benefit plan attempts to require arbitration outside of the commercial context, for example, in a dispute with a participant over an entitlement to benefits.

At one time, the enforceability of these types of arbitration provisions depended on the type of claim the participant was asserting. If the claim was strictly a claim for benefits, courts would generally enforce the plan's right to compel arbitration. Statutory ERISA claims, such as a claim for breach of fiduciary duty, were deemed by some courts to be nonarbitrable on public policy grounds.

The distinction between benefits claims and statutory claims has all but evaporated since most courts now enforce arbitration agreements in both contexts. Thus, there appear to be few legal hurdles to requiring participants to arbitrate disputes with employee benefit plans.

One issue that is attracting interest is whether a plan can limit substantive rights granted to participants under ERISA. For example, some plans may attempt to reduce the statute of limitations for participants to file a claim against a plan, or may attempt in arbitration to limit the amount of damages or other remedies available against a plan. Few courts have addressed these issues in the employee benefit plan context. The courts that have addressed these issues in the employment context have taken a case-by-case approach in determining how far an employer can go in curtailing an employee's statutory rights.

The United States Supreme Court's arbitration decisions suggest that, while a plan can require a participant to arbitrate rather than litigate claims, attempts to scale back on substantive, statutory rights in arbitration would be met with judicial resistance. It is therefore important for trustees and plan counsel to consider carefully any limitations that the plan attempts to impose on participants' statutory rights in an arbitration proceeding.

Taft-Hartley Impasse Arbitration

Taft-Hartley employee benefit plans are plans established pursuant to Section 302(c)(5) of the Labor-Management Relations Act (LMRA). Such plans are administered by a board of trustees that has equal representation by union-designated trustees and employer-designated trustees. The LMRA provides that it is illegal for an employer to contribute to a plan unless the plan satisfies certain specific requirements set forth in the LMRA. One of these legal requirements is that the plan contain a provision requiring arbitration of all disputes involving the "administration" of the plan when the trustees have reached a deadlock. Thus, impasse arbitration, unlike voluntary arbitration, is expressly required under law.

Not all impasses are subject to legally mandated arbitration. Indeed, arbitration is required only when an impasse relates to the "administration" of the plan. Thus, trustees generally cannot force arbitration over an issue that does not relate to plan administration. For example, disputes over the proper level of employer contributions to a plan is a collective bargaining issue that is generally not within the control of plan trustees and not subject to arbitration.

When the deadlocked issue relates to the administration of the plan, it is likely to be a contentious issue that pits the interests of labor directly against the interests of management. The arbitrator in such disputes is required to focus on the fiduciary issues at stake, rather than labor relations issues. In essence, the arbitrator sits as an additional trustee to break the deadlock and may be bound by ERISA's fiduciary standards. Because of the arbitrator's potential role as a plan fiduciary, impasse arbitrators usually request that the plan cover the arbitrator under the plan's fiduciary insurance policy. This usually can be accomplished at little or no cost to the plan by obtaining a rider to the plan's fiduciary insurance policy naming the arbitrator as an additional insured.

As a fiduciary, the arbitrator must determine how the respective trustees' positions comport with the plan's governing documents (e.g., the trust agreement), and which position best furthers the interests of the plan's participants and beneficiaries, regardless of the impact of such a decision on labor relations.

Impasse arbitrations typically arise after the trustees reach a tie vote over a particular resolution. For example, suppose the union trustees of a pension plan propose at a trustees meeting that the plan increase the formula for calculating participants' service credit under the plan. After discussion over the merits of the proposal, the union trustees propose a formal resolution to increase service credit. The trustees vote on the proposal and reach a tie—the union trustees voting in favor of the resolution and the employer trustees opposed.

The union trustees declare that a deadlock has occurred and proceed to arbitration. Typically, the plan's trust agreement specifies a particular arbitrator or a method of selecting an arbitrator to resolve deadlocks. Some trust agreements specify the arbitration service to be used or the rules that will govern the conduct of the arbitration. If the trustees are unable to agree on an arbitrator, federal courts are empowered to appoint the arbitrator.

Once an arbitrator is appointed, the process moves forward. Because impasse arbitration is usually a result of a tie over a proposed trustee resolution, the arbitrator will be presented with a very specific issue to resolve. This contrasts with the usual collective bargaining grievance arbitration, in which parties may spend considerable time simply attempting to frame the issue. This also underscores the importance of carefully phrasing any trustee resolution that may lead to deadlock.

After the deadlocked issue is presented to the arbitrator, each side has the opportunity to present its case through witnesses and documents. Like other arbitrators, impasse arbitrators generally conduct hearings that are less formal than court proceedings.

Evidence in an impasse arbitration typically takes two forms—relevant plan document provisions and testimony from witnesses concerning the impact of the proposed resolution on the participants and the plan. Thus, in the example described above, each side can be expected to focus on plan provisions concerning service credit calculation. In addition, each side can be expected to procure the testimony of an actuarial or accounting expert concerning the impact of the proposed amendment on the plan's financial condition. Parties may call other witnesses to explain the impact of the amendment on the plan's participants.

After each side concludes its case, the arbitrator reaches a decision to resolve the deadlock. The decision is usually in writing. The arbitrator's decision is subject to extremely limited review by the courts and is, for all intents and purposes, the final word.

A key practical issue for Taft-Hartley trustees is when to create an impasse over an issue that requires arbitration. Arbitration can be time-consuming and can create an adversarial atmosphere on a board of trustees. Going to impasse arbitration is, in some sense, an admission that the process has failed. Moreover, because impasse arbitrators are generally asked to vote "for" or "against" a particular resolution, there is less room for compromise solutions in impasse arbitration than other proceedings. By forcing an impasse, the trustees relinquish control over the administration of the plan to an individual whose decision is essentially final.

As a result of these practical considerations, impasse arbitration is not the preferred form of reaching decisions over the administration of a plan and tends to be the exception rather than the rule. Nonetheless, in accordance with Taft-Hartley, contentious issues that result in a deadlock are required to be resolved through impasse arbitration.

Withdrawal Liability Arbitration

Under ERISA, when a contributing employer ceases to have an obligation to contribute to an underfunded multiemployer pension plan, the employer may be assessed "withdrawal liability." *Withdrawal liability* is a type of exit fee designed to allocate to a withdrawing employer a proportional share of the plan's unfunded liabilities.

Title IV of ERISA contains detailed provisions regarding the imposition and calculation of withdrawal liability. The statute also provides for the manner in which a pension plan notifies the withdrawing employer of its withdrawal liability and the manner in which an employer may contest the liability.

At the heart of these notice and review provisions is the mandatory arbitration provision set forth in Section 4221 of ERISA. Section 4221(a)(1) of ERISA states, in relevant part, that:

> any dispute between an employer and the plan sponsor of a multiemployer plan concerning a determination made under Sections 4201 through 4219 shall be resolved through arbitration.

Sections 4201 through 4219 contain virtually all the mechanical provisions relating to withdrawal liability, including provisions defining when a withdrawal occurs and the manner in which withdrawal liability is calculated. Thus, most of the issues that arise in connection with a withdrawal liability assessment are subject to mandatory arbitration. Withdrawal liability arbitrations are to be conducted in the same manner as other arbitration proceedings under the Federal Arbitration Act.

The AAA has its own special rules and arbitration panels for withdrawal liability disputes. These arbitrators have experience in adjudicating the unique, complex issues that arise in withdrawal liability arbitration.

Generally, prior to commencing arbitration, an employer will request that the plan sponsor review the withdrawal liability assessment, as provided for in Section 4219(b)(2) of ERISA. For an employer to challenge a pension plan's withdrawal liability determination, the employer must initiate arbitration proceedings against the plan within a 60-day period after the earlier of:
  (a) the date the employer receives notification from the plan sponsor of its decision on review; or
  (b) 120 days after the employer's request for review.

If the employer does not commence arbitration in a timely fashion, the amount demanded by the plan is deemed to be "due and owing." The federal courts have been vigorous in enforcing the mandatory arbitration provision contained in Title IV of ERISA. Employers that fail to initiate arbitration within the statutory period are routinely held to be barred from challenging various aspects of the withdrawal liability assessment, including the amount assessed.

Even if an employer commences arbitration to challenge a withdrawal liability assessment, the employer is required to pay all withdrawal liability installment payments that become due during the pendency of arbitration. Again, the federal courts have been vigorous in enforcing the "pay now, dispute later" statutory mechanism. An exception has been recognized by some circuit courts when requiring the employer to make withdrawal liability installment payments would result in irreparable harm to the employer and when the employer can otherwise demonstrate entitlement to preliminary injunctive relief.

Withdrawal liability arbitrations can be extremely technical and often entail exhaustive review and analysis of financial calculations and plan assumptions relating to the plan's funding levels. Hearings often focus on the methodology and manner in which plans (and their actuaries) calculate withdrawal liability under the various methods permitted by law.

Withdrawal liability arbitrations may also focus on legal issues concerning whether and when the employer actually withdrew from the plan. These issues may require testimony from the collective bargaining parties to establish the parameters of the employer's obligation to contribute to the plan.

Typically, prior to arbitration, the employer (and its actuary) will have had an opportunity to review the actuarial worksheets and plan assumptions used to calculate the employer's withdrawal liability. At the arbitration hearing, each side can be expected to present actuarial expert testimony concerning these calculations and assumptions. The employer bears the burden of demonstrating by a preponderance of the evidence that the plan's calculations are incorrect. Each side may also present testimony concerning the applicability of various provisions in ERISA that provide for the reduction of the withdrawal liability.

Like Taft-Hartley impasse arbitration, a key issue that trustees face is whether to proceed to arbitration at all. ERISA's withdrawal liability provisions encourage the parties to engage in dialogue and disclosure prior to arbitration to identify issues in dispute. Indeed, the employer has the statutory right to request certain information relating to the calculation of its withdrawal liability. As a result of these review provisions, the parties often can determine the precise issues in dispute and may be able to reach an agreement prior to arbitration. Such resolutions may be more likely when factual issues are in dispute, such as the accuracy of the withdrawal liability calculation, then when purely legal issues are at stake, for example, whether the employer has withdrawn from the plan.

Courts are granted more discretion to review arbitration awards in withdrawal liability cases than in other types of arbitration proceedings. In fact, legal determinations made by an arbitrator are reviewed by a district court without any presumption of correctness. The arbitrator's factual conclusions, however, are presumed to be correct.

Conclusion

The increasingly favorable legal environment for alternative dispute resolution suggests that arbitration of employee benefit plan disputes is likely to increase. It is important for trustees to familiarize themselves with arbitration, including the advantages and disadvantages of arbitration, to determine the extent to which arbitration should be utilized in both commercial dealings and in disputes with participants. It is also important for trustees to consider fully the ramifications of proceeding to arbitration in situations where arbitration is the legally mandated dispute resolution mechanism.

About the Authors

Bruce S. Raynor
Executive Vice President and Southern Regional Director
Union of Needletrades, Industrial and Textile Employees (UNITES!)
Union City, Georgia

Mr. Raynor is a trustee of the UNITE! national pension and insurance funds in the Textile, Clothing, Laundry and Cotton Garment Industries and is the national chairman of the AFL-CIO Task Force of Elected Leaders on Organizing, which is composed of regional leaders from 12 different labor unions. He also served as a speaker at the 1994 International Foundation's annual conference.

Mark E. Brossman
Partner
Chadbourne & Parke LLP
New York, New York

Mr. Brossman, partner in the law firm of Chadbourne & Parke, co-authored *Social Investing of Pension Funds: For Love or Money* and has contributed chapters to *Employee Benefits Today: Concepts and Methods* and articles to *Employee Benefits Journal* and other publications. He has taught several courses in the Certified Employee Benefit Specialist program and has served as a speaker for many of the Foundation's educational programs. Mr. Brossman is Chairman of the International Foundation's Arbitration Committee and is a member of the Educational Program Committee.

Morton I. Lorge
Associate
Chadbourne & Parke LLP
New York, New York

Mr. Lorge is an associate in the Employment Law and ERISA Department in the New York office of Chadbourne & Parke. Mr. Lorge has contributed to articles published in International Foundation books and periodicals.

Index

Accountants and auditors, 175-186
    audits-financial statements, 178-179
    internal versus external, 179-180
    monitoring and evaluation, 184-185
    monitoring by government, 180-181
    request for proposal checklist, 185-186
    search for, 181-184
    trustee's perspective, 175-176

Actuarial services, 41-51
    actuarial code of professional conduct, 49-50
    conflict of interest, 49-50
    duties and responsibilities, 44-46
    fees, 49
    request for proposal checklist, 50-51
    selection of actuary, 46-48
    service organizations, 44
    services provided, 43-44
    trustee's perspective, 41-42

Actuary, 14
    see also Actuarial services

Administration services, 87-103
    contracting agreements, 89-91
    costs, 102
    request for proposal checklist, 103
    services
        all funds, 91-95
        health and welfare plans, 95-98
        pension plans, 98-102
    trustee's perspective, 87-88

Administrator, 12
   see also Administration services
Advisory team
   members of, 11-15
Arbitration, 187-200
   advantages/disadvantages, 191-195
   disputes–types of, 189-190
   legal issues, 195-200
   selection of, 190-191
   Taft-Hartley impasse disputes, 196-198
   trustee's perspective, 187-188
   withdrawal liability, 198-200
Auditor, 12
   see also Accountants and auditors

B **Benefit consulting**, 53-63
   consulting firms, 58-59
   health and welfare fund issues, 56-58
   pension fund issues, 55-56
   request for proposal checklist, 61-62
   selection, 60-61
   trustee's perspective, 53-54

C Checklists *see* Request for proposal checklists
Consultant, 14
   see also Benefit consulting
Consulting *see* Benefit consulting
Counsel, 13
   see also Legal counsel
Custodial services, 151-173
   ancillary services, 161-164
   duties, 154-161
   hiring, 163-170
   interviews, 168-170
   questionnaires, 166-168
   request for proposal checklist, 172-173
   services checklist, 159-161
   trustee's perspective, 151-152

D **Department of Labor (DOL) Guidance**
   investment management, 8-9
Duplication of services, 59-60

E **Employee Retirement Income Security Act (ERISA)**
   standards for plan advisors, 1-15, 25-36, 45, 177, 180-181

F **Fiduciary responsibility**
   delegation of, 4-6
Fiduciary standards, 3-4

H **Health care service providers**, 65-85
   administration design, 69-70
   contract negotiations, 76-80
   implementation, 80-82
   monitoring and review, 82-84
   payment, 70
   plan design, 68-69
   provider organizations, 71
   request for information (RFI), 72-73
   request for proposal (RFP), 73-75
   sample provider contract table of exhibits, 85
   selection of, 75-76
   trustee's perspective, 65-66

I

Investment consultant, 15
 see also Investment consulting, Investment management
Investment consulting, 105-124
 cost, 119-120
 functions of, 108-112
 manager search and selection, 112-119
 qualities of, 107-108
 request for proposal checklist, 122-124
 trustee's perspective, 105-106
Investment management, 125-148
 asset management responsibility, 127-128
 candidate selection criteria, 9-11
 diversification, 130
 duties of manager, 134-142
 evaluation of manager, 142-146
 plan management, 129-134
 professional organizations, 128-129
 request for proposal checklist, 147-148
 systematic risk, 130-131
 trustee's perspective, 125-126
Investment manager, 14
 selection criteria for, 9-11
 see also Investment management

L

Legal counsel, 21-40
 authority to hire under ERISA, 25-30
 compensation, 32-34
 documentation, 31-32
 number needed, 30-31
 request for proposal checklist, 37
 responsibilities of, 34-36
 role of, 23-25
 trustee's perspective, 21-22

M

Monitoring procedures, 7-8
 see also Accountants and auditors, Health care service providers, Investment management, Professional advisors, Trustee areas of concern

P

Professional advisors
 effect of using, 4
 evaluation, selection and monitoring of, 1-18

R

Request for proposal checklists
 accountants and auditors, 185-186
 actuarial services, 51
 administration services, 103
 benefit consulting, 61-62
 custodial services, 172-173
 health care service providers, 73-75
 investment consulting, 122-124
 investment management, 147-148
 legal counsel, 37

S

Selection and monitoring process, 6-7

T

Trustee areas of concern, 15-18
 choosing competent people, 16
 compensation, 16-17
 duplication, 15
 monitoring, 17-18